The Last Word

Yusuf K Dawood

an imprint of

Published by **Sasa Sema** Publications
An imprint of Longhorn Publishers

Longhorn Kenya Ltd.,
Funzi Road, Industrial Area,
P.O. Box 18033-00500,
Nairobi, Kenya.

Longhorn Publishers (U) Ltd
Plot 731, Kamwokya Area
Mawanda Road, P.O. Box 24745
Kampala, Uganda.

Longhorn Publishers (Tanzania) Ltd
Kinondoni
Plot No. 4
Block 37B
Kawawa Road
Dar es Salaam, Tanzania.

© Yusuf K Dawood

All rights reserved. No part of this publication may be reproduced, stored in a retrieval system or transmitted in any form or by any means, electronic, mechanical, photocopying, recording or otherwise without the prior written permission of the copyright owner.

First published 2012

Cover Illustration and design by Tuf Mulokwa

ISBN978-9966-36-993-2

Printed by Printpoint Ltd.,
Changamwe Road, Off Enterprise Road, Industrial Area,
P.O. Box 30975 - 00100, Nairobi, Kenya.

Prologue

The 'Surgeons Diary' has been running as a full page column in the *Sunday Nation* for over 33 years and still commands a wide readership. The first volume of the trilogy based on the *Diary* was published in 1985 under the title, *Yesterday,Today* and *Tomorrow*. This happened because readers asked for it arguing that a newspaper column, however popular, is ephemeral and deserves a permanent home in the sanctuary of a book.

The first volume proved a runaway success and so a sequel entitled *Off My Chest* appeared in 1988. After that, there was a lull, but not for long. Once again, my loyal readers asked for more and eventually, in 1995, *Behind the Mask* made its debut on the literary scene. The blurb indicated, quite categorically, that *Behind the Mask* concluded the trilogy. In the prologue, in what was supposed to be the third and final volume, I wrote, "Now comes, perhaps, the final volume in the series" and proceeded to give plausible reasons why it was likely to be so. I even toyed with the idea of entitling it *The Last Word*, but Mrs. Janet Njoroge, the Managing Director of Longhorn, the firm which published the whole trilogy, persuaded me not to use that title. I suppose it was her female intuition which gave her a deeper insight into the future and superseded my logic. She is proven right because we have yet one more volume to make the series a quartet! Just as well, for I can now use the title, *The Last Word*.

This has to be the last word because, contrary to popular belief, surgeons are also mortal. A time must come when both my scalpel and my pen, two essential instruments required to produce the 'Surgeon's Diary', must come to rest. However, unlike surgeons, authors have the potential to become immortal. They sometimes leave behind a legacy of their literary work, by which they may be remembered by generations to come. I am, therefore, glad that an ephemeral newspaper column – however compelling it was – has found a safe sanctuary in a four-volume series which my readers may be able to savour long after the author has departed.

Happy Reading.

Dedication

To all the good people who have featured in this book for, without them, there would be no book.

1
Friend or enema

"Death and disease are dreary subjects," wrote my favourite author, Somerset Maugham. "If I were you, I would have nothing to do with them! "In the case of surgeons, however, death and diseases are part and parcel of their professional life and they meet them almost on a regular basis. In spite of their frequency and regularity, each one of them leaves a mark on a surgeon's coronaries. Happily, these unfortunate moments are counteracted by triumphs under most difficult surgical conditions and also the amusing experiences amongst their patients.

In fact, if surgeons did not share some light moments in the course of their work, they would be driven to early graves by the heartaches and stresses they constantly endure.

As things stand, the commonest cause of death amongst members of my profession is a heart attack. Sadly, many of my colleagues have undergone either a coronary bypass or an angioplasty – an innovative and relatively a non-invasive procedure to unblock the coronary artery and put a stent in to keep it open. It is no wonder then that surgeons always try to capture the few happy moments they come across in their professional lives. They not only remember but also cherish them. In my practice, with a mixture of diverse cultures, ethnicity and race, the varied responses and reactions of my patients never cease to amuse and charm me.

Friend or enema

I remember well what the Irishman said when he brought his wife to see me a few years ago. After examining her, I took the man aside and, to give him an indication of how ill his wife was, whispered in his ear. "I don't like the look of your wife." "Neither do I!" he retorted.

* * *

Then there was my little friend, Kuria, who was born without a back passage. I had to do a temporary colostomy soon after he was born. This meant bringing his large bowel on the surface so that he could pass his motion. Thereafter, the poor mite underwent a few operations on his colon, which had to be preceded by an enema to cleanse his bowel pre-operatively. When he came for the final major operation, he inadvertently received three enemas. Staff on day shift, in an attempt to save the ones on night duty from extra work, gave Kuria an enema before they went off duty. They forgot to enter it in the report and so those on night shift gave him another enema.

In the early hours of the morning, the Sister on night duty wanted to demonstrate to the probationers how to give an enema and found easy prey in Kuria. So, at eight, when the theatre nurse went to collect Kuria and bring him to the operating theatre, she found that he had locked himself inside the toilet. Her entreaties were of no avail and she came to the theatre empty-handed.

I had known Kuria since birth and had treated him for almost ten years. So I thought I would go and explain to him that the operation he was to undergo that day was the final one and was not very different from the others.

On arrival in the ward, I was escorted by the Sister to the toilet. I knocked at the door and shouted from outside. "It's me, Kuria. Please open the door." He, obviously, recognised my voice because, in a little while, I saw him popping his little head out of the little chink he made in the doorway. Holding it at a rakish angle, he asked, "Friend or enema?"

The other day, an obstetrician friend told me a story related to his specialty. He delivered twins and phoned the father, a professor at the local university, who was known for his absent-mindedness. He often came to lecture wearing different coloured socks. When this was brought to his attention by an intrepid student, his stock reply was, "How odd. I have another pair like that at home!" On hearing the news about the twins, he replied, "Excellent news. Just do me a favour. Don't tell my wife because I want to give her a surprise!"

I always remember, fondly, this obese, strictly vegetarian, Hindu lady who consulted me for the removal of her gall bladder, filled with stones. She was grossly overweight and it would have meant digging through eight inches of fat before 'striking gold'. I gave her a diet sheet and asked her to come and see me in a couple of months, hoping that she would lose some weight and make her operation technically less difficult. When she came back, the scales in the clinic showed that, in fact, she had put on more weight. When I asked her, in a reproaching tone, how she had achieved this almost impossible feat, she explained, cowering under the couch, "Blame your diet sheet, not me; I religiously took all the items on it immediately after I finished eating my normal meals!"

* * *

In the case of the Arab lady, it was I who provided the punch line! On the day of her discharge from the hospital, after a successful major operation, she thanked me in her customary manner. "I pray that you have seven sons," she said. It was her way of expressing her gratitude because, in Arab tradition, sons are a bigger blessing by virtue of the fact that they carry the family name, continue the family business and take care of their parents in old age. The Arab lady then noticed the presence of Sister Nyagah who was accompanying me on the ward round and who looked a little left out of the bounties being dished out. So that she could also share the feast of profligate fertility, the old lady turned to her and added, "I will pray that you are also blessed with seven sons."

Birth control measures and family planning were topical subjects in Kenya then and Janet Nyagah was one of our very attractive young nursing sisters. Looking at her pretty face, I could not help quipping, "It would be much more fun, and it would also help our population control programme, if Sister Nyagah and I had the seven sons together!"

* * *

Finally, I must relate my encounter with Mr. Sohan Singh, a Sikh gentleman who had established himself as a renowned bonesetter in Nairobi. He considered himself a part of alternative parallel medicine.

Like faith-healing, witchcraft and homeopathy had flourished in the country at the time and people often went to him with broken bones where he treated them with massages and oily bandages. Many of them came, later, to my Fracture Clinic with disjointed bones and disunited fractures. So when I met him at a Sikh wedding, I took the opportunity to draw his attention to the many patients who came to see me with complications arising out of his treatment. "That's interesting," he replied, "because many of your complications end up with me!"

Friend or enema

* * *

Now, to the main story, about Charles Oloo, which is equally hilarious. He was one of those persons who slowly grew on you. The more I came to know him, the more I was convinced that he was a likeable rogue. Somehow, his prosperity seemed to be connected with the operations I carried out on members of his family. I am not implying that people should undergo surgery by me if they want to prosper materially! However, the coincidence in Oloo's case was uncanny. When I circumcised his firstborn, he was promoted to a senior position in the Ministry of Health. By the time I repaired an umbilical hernia on his daughter, he had launched a grocery business in Pangani. He, however, kept his job following the Ndegwa Commission's Report that allowed government employees to have other sources of income.

"But how can you manage two full time jobs?" I asked.

"Simple," he said, "I have invested in two jackets. One stays on the back of the chair in my office at the ministry and the other stays on my back!"

In the case of his third child, Oloo wanted her ears pierced. That brought luck too because, that year, he opened another branch and resigned from his job. "I realise that we cannot and should not serve two masters," he justified his decision.

By now, he had moved up the ladder. One fine morning, he stood beside me pointing at a car as we stood looking out of the window of my office. "I have come in my wife's 'yellow jalopy'", he informed me, "because my Pajero has gone for servicing."

"So you are now a two-car family?"

"Oh yes," he replied, "but to maintain that lifestyle, I have decided to limit my family."

"I am glad that this family planning campaign is making an impact on you at last."

"Sure," Oloo replied. "By the grace of God and with the help of Liz, my wife, I have produced three children – two girls and a boy. It is time we closed shop." Then, with a wicked smile on his face, he added. "My friends tell me that you doctors have some alchemy whereby the factory can run full blast without any production!"

As I laughed uproariously, I explained to him the two methods of permanent sterilisation. "I can ask a gynaecologist to tie Liz's tubes or I can tie your vasa."

Without the slightest hesitation he opted for the former. "I don't trust a knife anywhere near my vital anatomy," he said, "one slip and I'm *kaput*!"

Much as I tried, I could not shake him off his fear that vasectomy would make him impotent. I, therefore, referred his wife to my gynaecological colleague and all was well for a couple of years until Oloo sat in front of me one day making a strange request. "I would like to undergo a vasectomy," he said.

"But your wife has had her tubes tied, so you don't need to have your vasa ligated," I explained.

"It is better to be doubly sure," Oloo said with an impish look on his face. "Her operation ensures her safety, not mine."

"I didn't know that you want to run other factories full blast without any production and, therefore, need a safety valve of your own!" I teased him.

"Yes," he replied. "Better to have one's own safety catch."

"Last time we discussed the subject, I remember you saying that you were scared to undergo vasectomy because you thought it would affect your potency."

"In my culture, they say one grows wiser with age," replied Oloo without batting an eyelid.

I consulted my surgical colleagues, lawyers, our ethical committee and members of the Medical Board. None of them could see a legal bar against acceding to Oloo's request, however, strange it was. Consequently, I carried out a vasectomy.

Friend or enema

Over the years, I saw Oloo become a very wealthy man. This was most evident in his sartorial outlook and style of dressing. The bottom of his trousers went from broad to narrow and then back to medium broad and no turn-ups. The lapels of his jackets changed in their width and their tapering, and the number of buttons varied from two to three and the style from single-breast to double-breast.

One day, out of the blue, he rang me. "Doc," he said in his warm, friendly tone. "I wonder if you will do me a favour." Before I could reply he continued. "A certain lady will want some medical details about me. Please disclose them to her without any reservations. You have my authority to do so."

"This sounds like a very unusual authorisation," I replied. "What's it all about?"

"Don't ask me Doc," he pleaded. "I'm not asking you to do anything illegal. If you divulge all the details that this lady will demand to know, you will, literally, let me off the hook."

"Okay," I said, "but usually such permissions are put in writing."

"You have got it Doc," Oloo replied. "Trust me. My word is my honour."

Three days later, Alice was sitting in front of me with a prior appointment made by Oloo. My secretary was, naturally, unaware of the background information that I was privy to and had made a file for her. "Yes, what can I do for you Alice?" I asked, knowing, from the mode of referral, that there was no history or physical examination involved.

"I understand, from Mr. Oloo, that you carried out a surgical operation on him." she came straight to the point.

"That's true."

"Could you tell me the nature of that operation?"

"Usually these matters are strictly confidential," I explained, "but in this particular case, Oloo has given me permission to let you have the necessary information." I paused for some reaction but there was none. "He underwent a vasectomy." I dropped what I thought must have been a bombshell for Alice. By now I had guessed the situation.

"What does that mean?"

"It means that the tubes that conduct his sperms from inside his body to the outside are tied and, as a result, he cannot sire a child."

"There cannot be any slip up in surgery?" she asked.

"Not if I have done it." I could not hide my irritation at someone doubting my competence. "We always do a semen analysis three months after surgery," I added. "In Oloo's case it was reported as "No sperms present."

"Good day," Alice said, "you have been very frank."

"Anyway," I asked, "what's it all about?"

"Never mind," Alice replied curtly. "Many thanks all the same."

A week later, Oloo was in my office. He had a way with women and could always get my secretary around to fitting him between patients, even when the appointment list was very tight.

"Thank you for the surgery you carried out on me and also for informing Alice about it," he said with a broad grin on his face.

"Can you please tell me what it is all about?" I said. "I am tired of this hide-and-seek game," I feigned a slight annoyance.

"You know," he said. "Man is a polygamous animal. We in Africa are honest and do it officially. Others are dishonest and do it unofficially. This unofficial bug hit me recently and Alice thought she had me in her clutches and decided to palm me off with her unborn child. So when she tried to place the paternity of that child at my door, I came out clean. I could not be the father because I had undergone a sterilisation operation. She wouldn't believe it so I had to refer her to the maestro who had made it all possible."

"I am sorry you involved me in all this. Alice has all my sympathies," I said.

"Don't be sorry Doc," he comforted me. "This young, flashy, fun-loving lass is a gold digger who saw my thick wallet and decided I will be the father of her child. She thought that I was a good catch but she picked up on the wrong one this time. She didn't reckon that I cannot father a child, thanks to your subtle scalpel." As if to comfort me for my inadvertent role in this drama, he added. "Anyway, she has got a few puppets at the end of her string. If I am sterilised and she is pregnant, the inference is clear; she is obviously double-crossing me and another sucker too. I'm sure some poor beggar will succumb to her vile designs."

He then gripped my hand tight as he got up to go. "Thank you for carrying out that operation and leaving no tell-tale scars behind. Those invisible scars are a big advantage to me and quite deceptive to the other party!"

2

It pays to be naughty - sometimes!

A couple of years ago, while I was flying from Dublin to London, I saw an enticing headline in a newspaper. Before I give away the actual wording, let me whet the appetite of my readers by telling them something about the Association of Surgeons of East Africa – ASEA – on whose behalf I had flown to Dublin.

ASEA in the region was formally inaugurated on the 9th of November 1950, in the Council Chamber of the City Hall in Nairobi. The three constituent countries were Kenya, Uganda and what was then known as Tanganyika. The aim of the association was to promote fellowship amongst surgeons, surgical training and research. By 2008, it had added six more countries to its list: Zambia, Zimbabwe, Malawi, Mozambique, Ethiopia and Rwanda.

In the intervening period, our region underwent cataclysmic changes. In the more than 50 years of its existence, we, the Fellows and Members of ASEA, witnessed and, indeed, suffered from coups and countercoups, border closures, strict visa regulations, radically changing political systems and climates, currency restrictions, devaluations, wars, landmines, gross financial mismanagement, poor governance, entrenched corruption, gross human rights violations and, finally, genocide. We lived through it all and survived. In fact, we did better. While politicians were busy disintegrating the East African Community, which finally collapsed, we surgeons went on adding new territories to our organisation, growing from the initial three to nine, with more countries knocking at our door.

In the year 2000, at the dawn of the new millennium, we decided that ASEA should take on the role of a college. In addition to fellowship, training and research, it could examine suitably trained candidates and produce home-grown surgeons of the highest standard. By doing so, perhaps we could minimise brain drain and also create surgeons who could work within the limited resources available locally. Thus, the College of Surgeons of East, Central and Southern Africa – COSECSA – was born.

Naturally, the fledgling college needed help in financial matters, preparing the syllabus and constitution, structuring special courses for our post-graduate students and conducting examinations. Initially, The Royal College of Surgeons of Edinburgh gave us tremendous help and put us on our feet. In 2007, The Royal College of Surgeons of Ireland came on board and an official collaboration between us, the Irish College and Irish Aid was established. Soon, the need for a project manager to run the partnership became apparent and the post was advertised by the Irish College. Interviews of shortlisted candidates were set up in Dublin and I was asked by the COSECSA Council to represent it on the interviewing committee.

It was while I was flying from London to Dublin to attend the interview that I saw the catchy headline on the inside page of a British daily newspaper handed to me by the Air Lingus stewardess. It read, 'How playful squeeze by a husband saved his wife's life'. Under the caption was the news item which ran as follows: 'A husband saved his wife's life when he playfully touched her breast and felt a lump. The couple was spending a quiet evening on the sofa with a bottle of wine when the husband squeezed his wife's left breast and found a hard lump. The wife was diagnosed with cancer within a week. She had the growth removed soon after and being an early case she was pronounced cured.'

The wife's comment, also mentioned in the paper, was equally interesting. "If my husband hadn't given me that cheeky squeeze, it might have been too late. The cancer could have spread."

As a surgeon who has devoted a large part of his professional life to the female breast, I could see, in this true story, a salutary message for my readers and my patients, and also a useful message to promote the breast cancer awareness campaign, in which I am heavily involved. It would sound something like this: *Please examine your breasts regularly. If you wish to delegate the 'duty' to someone else, it is entirely up to you. The important thing is the examination of your breast. As to who carries it out is immaterial – surgically speaking!*

I had decided that, on the flight, I would peruse the applications of all shortlisted candidates. These had been sent to me in advance. However, the intriguing story in the newspaper, so close to my specialty, pleasantly distracted me. As I sipped the delicious Jamieson Irish Whisky and munched on the news item, I was taken a few years back and was reminded of one of my patients who went one stage further than the lady in the newspaper.

This pleasant experience also started with a flight, this time from Nairobi to Bangkok, where I was invited to attend a surgeon's conference. As I approached the check-in counter at the Jomo Kenyatta International Airport, I saw this bustling old lady, pushing her trolley, and attempting to get ahead of the queue. Somehow, she reminded me of Mrs. Marples, the character made famous by Agatha Christie, the renowned British detective-fiction writer. As she passed me, I had a close view of her. She had a round, unwrinkled cherubic face with short, curly, coppery, grey hair. After she had managed to giggle away her way in front of me, she turned her head, looked at me and stopped. "Doctor ...?" she asked.

"Dawood," I said.

"You might not remember me but you took out my gall bladder 20 years ago." As she noticed the lack of recognition on my face, she added. "I can understand your difficulty in remembering me. I was much younger and more glamorous then. Perhaps if I showed you my scar," she almost unbuttoned her blouse and then stopped. "I better leave it until we get on board. Then I can show it to you in the privacy of the cabin!"

"I believe you," I said, my face flushed with embarrassment, as I noticed people in the queue watching us with gleeful interest.

After I finished my check-in formalities, I walked over to the business class lounge and made myself comfortable with a soft drink and the 'cholesterol free' macadamia nuts. I was still savouring my embarrassing moment with the old lady. Once again, my memory went into a high gear and I remembered an incident when the shoe had been on the other foot. Marie and I had visited Mombasa for Easter and were staying at our usual haunt on the North Coast. One evening, as we took our walk on the beach, I was confronted by a buxom lady wearing a skimpy two-piece bathing costume. "Do you remember me?" she asked, stretching her hand out to shake mine. I was trying to remember who she was and how to respond to this overt challenge appropriately.

I was a bit anxious because Marie was with me and she was watching the encounter with more than a passing interest. Looking at my totally blank face and, presumably, to give me a

It pays to be naughty - sometimes!

clue, the lady added. "Five years ago you removed a very large lump from my breast and told me that you had done so through a tiny keyhole incision which would leave me with a scar almost invisible." Relieved to know that she had no incriminating evidence against me, and elated by her complimentary remark, I replied, "Now madam, if you had shown me the scar first, I would have definitely recognised you!"

Quietly relishing my own repartee, I got up to pick up the *Daily Telegraph* from a stack of British newspapers lying on a low table in the lounge when, lo and behold, I saw Mrs. Marples at the door showing her boarding card to gain entry. She was laden with duty free whisky, cigarettes and chocolates.

"Ah," she beamed as she saw me. "We meet again! I went to pick up my duty free. The bar prices at my hotel in Bangkok are exorbitant." She then looked at me quizzically and changed the topic of her conversation.

"I hope you didn't mind my jumping the queue to the check-in counter. I wasn't being rude. It's just that, as you grow older, you realise that the lease is getting shorter and you must make the most of the limited time at your disposal." I was now convinced that I had come across an interesting character when she added, "Some unkind folks even think that we are sitting in God's waiting room." She then looked around to make sure that, after all, she was not inside the ominous room she had just referred to and walked over to the bar in the far corner. She poured herself a stiff Scotch, added some ice to it and said, "I like it on the rocks. Adding anything else other than ice is sacrilege!"

Soon, the flight was announced and the lady was on her feet again. She quickly gulped her drink, quite unnecessarily I thought, because our seats had already been assigned. But then, she had given me her reasons earlier and her remarks had aroused the writer's interest in me. I was thus pleasantly surprised when the stewardess escorted me to a seat next to her. From our initial interaction, I thought she might turn out to be a character worth writing about. Who knows, she might even give me a story! Once again, I remembered Agatha Christie but, this time, it was a remark her archaeologist husband had made about his aging wife. "In my line of work," he had said, "the older my wife gets, the more interesting she becomes!" So in my line of work too, I reckoned, the more unconventional and Bohemian the character, the more exciting for my readers.

"Well, well, well, we couldn't have organised it better if we had done it ourselves," she said as she clicked her seat belt. "I was so busy reminding you of your handiwork on me that I forgot to introduce myself." Extending her hand, she added, "the name is Jenkins... Mrs. Jenkins."

From then on, it was a non-stop monologue that kept me absorbed during the delicious meal and drinks we were served with each course. "I lost my husband soon after you carried out gall bladder surgery on me," she said. "He worked himself to death and died one morning of a heart attack, bless his soul. He was so busy making money that he forgot to use it!"

"He had no time to even write down what to do with it when he passed away. So here I am, a widow left with more money than I know what to do with."

"You are not complaining, are you?" I laughed.

"Not at all," she replied. "I take two holidays a year, each lasting six months." It took me a little time to figure out her weird arithmetic.

She was now on her third gin and tonic and finished with a large goblet of Courvoisier brandy. Naturally, she slept soundly after that.

I thought I would also get a brief respite but this proved a pipe dream because, with all the good food and alcohol, she began to snore. It was difficult for me to make out if the noise

It pays to be naughty - sometimes!

came from the jet engine or the cute little nostrils and gaping mouth perched on the puckish face parked next to me. As we were descending into Bangkok airport, I asked her, "Where are you staying in Bangkok?"

"At the Oriental," replied Mrs. Jenkins.

Now, I knew that Oriental Hotel to be as famous as it is expensive; it is considered one of the best 100 hotels in the world. For once, I had decided to indulge in unaffordable luxury and had booked myself in the Oriental too. I knew it was going to make a big hole in my budget – after all I did not have the resources of a rich widow! I had made a reservation there because I knew that my favourite and famous authors, like Somerset Maugham, Morris West and Graham Greene, had stayed there. In fact, the hotel has an author's lounge where autographed works of these writers adorn the bookshelves.

Though I did not belong to that category of writers, I thought it would be nice to sit in that lounge and enjoy their posthumous company.

"I'm booked there too," I said.

"This is really uncanny," Mrs. Jenkins said. "If you haven't arranged an airport transfer, I could give you a lift in the taxi I ordered from home."

"That's very kind of you," I said.

As soon as we emerged out of Arrivals, we saw a uniformed taxi driver waving a placard with her name written on it. He quickly relieved Mrs. Jenkins of her luggage trolley and led us to the parking area. I should have known; the taxi which had come to collect Mrs. Jenkins was a Mercedes limousine. The driver opened the rear door for her and as he was walking on the other side to do the same for me, I walked the other way indicating my desire to sit with him in the front. I have got this boyish desire to sit in the front seat to catch a good view of where we are driving to. Little did I know that the taxi driver was

The last word

equally delighted with my decision. After starting the engine, he casually dropped a folder in my lap. Inside were glossy photographs and phone numbers of 'hostesses' available to give 'company' to male visitors to Thailand. I quickly folded the well-bound folder so as not to offend Mrs. Jenkin's sensitivity. The taxi driver thought I was a quick decision-maker!

"So, who is the lucky lady?" he asked in a conspiratorial tone.

To put him off, I whispered, "I'm on duty as a personal physician to this Duchess from Kenya and I'm not allowed to indulge in such activities."

"No problem," said the driver undeterred. "You can make a choice now so that next time you come to Bangkok alone, I can line her up for you!"

"Let's not rush into it. You might have some new faces when I come again."

I thought I had very diplomatically closed the matter when we heard a feminine voice purring from the back seat. "I hope you have a similar brochure for female visitors as well. After all, what's sauce for the goose is sauce for the gander." The taxi driver burst out laughing almost colliding with a bus.

The surgeons' conference lasted a week during which time I was fully occupied and saw very little of Mrs. Jenkins. I had set aside a couple of days free after the meeting to do some shopping for Marie and the children, and some sightseeing. Mrs. Jenkins had mentioned that she was a regular visitor to Thailand and so I turned to her for advice. Instead, she took me under her wing and showed me the sights of that fascinating city. She arranged a tour of the Grand Palace and a visit to see the Emerald Buddha. She took me to various temples filled with incense and candles where I saw devotees putting golden leaves on the reclining Buddha as an offering to their God.

It pays to be naughty – sometimes!

Everywhere, gentle, small Thai men and petite, smiling women welcomed the visitors with folded hands and bowed heads.

We went to watch bamboo dances, cock fights, an elephant parade and ate ethnic Thai food, sitting on the floor in the traditional lotus position. We were taken to see the floating market outside the city where we saw children with snakes round their necks, ready to be photographed with the tourists for a few *bahts* – the local currency. Luscious green paddy fields and wild orchids lined both sides of the road. The floating market itself consisted of a long, meandering water canal on which were little boats loaded with wares and cute little restaurants where food was being cooked on charcoal braziers.

On my last evening there, I invited Mrs. Jenkins for dinner at the Oriental Grill to thank her for organising my tours and accompanying me. She financed for all the tours and would not let me share the cost. "Thank you so much," I said repeatedly.

"Don't thank me," she replied. "Thank my husband who slogged day and night and did not live long enough to enjoy the fruits of his labour."

In conversation over dinner, I discovered that she was on one of her two six monthly annual furloughs. From Bangkok, she was going to Pattaya, the famous Thai beach, then travelling to Hongkong, Kuala Lumpur and Penang for another beach holiday. She was scheduled to go to China and take a cruise on the Yangtze River. As we were sipping our Thai soup, she, without any warning, darted a question, "Did you, ultimately, take up the offer that the taxi driver made while he was driving us to the hotel?"

"Of course not!" I said, not hiding my indignation.

"I can understand. After all, you are a married man and don't want to betray Marie. You mention her frequently in the *Surgeon's Diary* and all your readers know how deeply you love her." Then, with a wicked twist of her face, she added, "You might also be worried that I could inform her!" She then took the soup bowl to her mouth as the locals did and emptied it. "I have no such compunctions. I don't need to because, after all, I'm a widow and I'm a free woman." By now, we were on our main dish – sizzling prawns and fried rice. She waited till the waiter finished serving. "You are my doctor and I don't like to hide anything from you. I might as well tell you that I have two boyfriends back home." As she saw the astonishment on my face, she added. "That way, I keep young."

"But why two?" I asked.

"I like to have an extra. You know, women of my age get tired and it's nice to have a spare wheel!" There was a pause before she resumed.

"I like to travel. I don't only do sightseeing, but I like to meet and mingle with the local people. And I mean "mingle" with them thoroughly. I don't like to simply scratch the surface."

There was a glint of mischief in her eyes as she continued, "You know, that taxi driver came to see me the next day and told me about a gallery of men in Bangkok available to women like me. Needless to add, I made the most of what the driver had to offer and the experience was unforgettable." As we were enjoying the scrumptious Thai sweets, she posed the fatal question. "As I told you, I'm a healthy girl but this time I noticed a slight bleeding after my indulgence. Could it be serious?" I was caught off guard and took a little time to articulate a suitable response. "It could be something simple like an infection but the bleeding could also portend a more sinister condition like a growth in the neck of the womb."

"So what do I do?"

"I think you should consult a gynaecologist."

She was pensive for a while. Three days after I arrived back home, she called. "I'm in Nairobi. The bleeding persisted

It pays to be naughty - sometimes!

so I cancelled my holiday. Can you please refer me to a gynaecologist?" I did and my professional colleague and friend found an early cancer of the cervix. He removed the womb. "One of the earliest I have seen. I told your friend and patient that she can consider herself cured," he told me.

A month later, Mrs. Jenkins came to see me with a handsome gift. It was a Thai silk tie. "Thank you for not charging me exorbitant professional fees," she said. Then, with a sinful smile, she added, "sometimes being naughty helps. Hadn't I been naughty in Bangkok, my cervical cancer would have gone unnoticed and it would have spread. It was discovered early and I'm now cured."

3
Tragic relief

Doctors are known to make very bad patients. I can only think of three reasons for it. They have been on the serving counter all their professional lives and do not like to be on the receiving end. Two, they know the complications of every medical procedure and surgical operation, and are firmly convinced that they will develop them all. Third, interestingly, doctors cannot take pain. They shirk at the sight of needles, drips, enemas, stomach tubes and other painful and sometimes undignified procedures.

The fear of developing all the complications in the book reminds me of my long-standing anaesthetist, who broke his thigh bone a couple of years ago. The fracture was plated by a competent orthopaedic surgeon. A week later, the patient was found to be safe on crutches and was officially discharged. To everyone's surprise, he declined to go home and asked if he could stay for three more days. He strongly believed in the power of the planets and the stars. Before arranging any important social functions, like an engagement date, marriage or entertaining a business proposition like buying a new property, he always consulted the family astrologer to find out if the stars were propitious for such an undertaking. I attributed his reluctance to go home to some extra terrestrial impediment. However, my curiosity was overwhelming and, in view of my long-term professional relationship with him, I asked him why he was not keen to take a discharge when he was fit to do so. As much as his explanation was flabbergasting, it proved my point. "You remember the good old days when we had no bone specialists and you used to plate fractures?" As I nodded in agreement, he went on, "I recall anaesthetising a patient who had fractured his femur which you plated." As I was wondering what he was driving at, he added the punch line. "Everything was fine until the tenth day when he developed a clot in his lung and died. I just wanted to be in the hospital until I crossed that critical point!"

Sohrab, my professional colleague and long-time friend, underwent all these vicissitudes and more. He and I first met when we were undergraduate students at the Grant Medical College in Bombay. He was a local boy who came from a wealthy Parsi family. Parsis are the most Westernised group of the Indian society. They derive their origin from Persia, a country they fled centuries ago because of religious persecution. They migrated and settled in India through hazardous trade routes. In no time, they made their mark in business and industry and produced icons like Tata. He was responsible for, among other enterprises, opening the first Indian airline under the banner of Air India.

Strangely enough, like the Jews and the Ismailis, the Parsis are highly insulated as a community; their commercial contacts and their philanthropy made them internationally recognised. Incidentally, the most unconventional thing about them is their awesome burial traditions. They leave their dead on top of a tower and let vultures and other predatory birds devour them. The Tower of Silence in Bombay was one such facility, into which non-Parsis were hardly allowed. However, Sohrab managed to smuggle me into this forbidden territory, proving, beyond doubt, the intensity of our friendship.

The two of us befriended another medical student from Kabul with whom we associated closely, earning the title, "The Three Musketeers" in the college. The idea of three young men being that close did not create any misgivings, nor did it raise eyebrows. This was because the student fraternity in those days was strictly divided on gender lines. Boys and girls did not mingle socially.

Our daily entertainment was a walk in the evenings on 'Marine Drive', which was the in-place for college students. It was a delightful walk by the edge of the Indian Ocean, where university students from various colleges – segregated gender-wise – walked and talked animatedly.

At one end, the scenic drive went through Chowpati, the famous Bombay landmark with a patch of sand on which hawkers sold local snacks like *chevda*, *bhel* and *pani-puree*. It ended on Malabar Hill, the elite residential area of Bombay which, when illuminated at night, looked like a set of glittering gems and was appropriately called 'The Queen's Necklace'. At the other end, the drive projected into the sea at Nariman point, named after a Parsi philanthropist, as many spots in Bombay are. On Sundays, the three musketeers went to see new releases of Indian movies. They were screened in cinemas which had recently been air conditioned and, therefore, provided a novel experience and welcome comfort.

The commonest topic of discussion at the cinema was what we wanted to do after graduation. Sohrab was crystal clear about his future career. "I want to be a heart specialist." When I told them that my ambition was to be a surgeon, his immediate reaction was, "Surgery is a manual science and requires only a good pair of hands. Medicine, especially cardiology, is cerebral and needs greater brain power."

Not to be easily cowed, I put him right straightaway. "You know the latest definition of a surgeon? He is a physician who can also operate! It implies he has both a good brain and dexterous fingers."

Imdad, the 'third man', also had a unique specialty but was not sure if he could practise it in his country. "I want to be an obstetrician and gynaecologist", he said. "But, as you know, in this speciality, every woman who consults me undergoes an internal examination. However, Afghanistan is a strictly Islamic country. Women, as a rule, wear a burqa. I would be lucky to see their faces, let alone carry out a vaginal examination!"

"I shouldn't be too upset about not becoming a gynaecologist," Sohrab quipped, "the gynaecologist can only do five operations, one of which is abortion, generally considered both immoral and illegal!"

After we passed the final exams, Imdad went back to Afghanistan, which, later, went through a severe political turmoil. As a result, we lost touch with him. Sohrab and I stayed in contact and followed our dreams – with one difference. Sohrab did become a heart specialist but, instead of becoming a cardiologist – a heart physician – he became a heart surgeon! I ascertained this when we ran into each other in Dewsbury, Yorkshire. When I went there as a Surgical Registrar, I met Sohrab. "How come?" I asked sarcastically. "You thought you had a better brain than me and, therefore, you plumped for cardiology. Poor me with a lesser brain, banished to manual work like surgery.'"

His witty reply confirmed my feeling that he should have made a good politician! "Of course, I had to have a superior brain to become a heart specialist. But then, while on my surgical internship, I discovered that I also had a deft pair of hands. I then remembered what you said one evening when we were sitting on Nariman point. A surgeon is a physician who can operate. That meant that if I had both, a sharp brain and manual skill, I had the perfect combination to be a surgeon. I, therefore, decided to become a heart surgeon."

"Good," I felt vindicated. "A surgeon is like a woman with both beauty and brain. The only difference is that, instead of beauty, a surgeon's other attribute is a pair of skillful hands."

We had both attained our goals, again with one difference: I became a general surgeon, married an English girl, Marie, and came to Nairobi. Sohrab became a heart surgeon, also married an English girl, Maureen, but settled in the country of his wife. Nevertheless, our friendship continued unabated.

The scope of heart surgery was expanding rapidly and consultant posts in that specialty were coming up fast in the UK. Sohrab walked into one and made a name for himself. At about the same time, incidences of heart disease were rising in Kenya caused by changing lifestyles. People could now afford rich food, full of cholesterol. They led sedentary lives with no time for exercise and incidences of diabetes and high blood pressure were rising. These were risk factors which made people more prone to coronary artery disease. Initially, the Asians were the more common victims but soon the Africans caught up with them, as they did in every other sphere of life. Therefore, coronary bypass was gaining ground as an effective operation. It was a clever way to short-circuit the blocked coronary artery by grafting a vein above and below the block, creating a new channel to conduct blood supply and, thus, provide normal nourishment to the heart. Soon the innovative procedure became 'bread and butter' surgery for heart surgeons. Not surprisingly, Sohrab, with his innovative approach and sharp intelligence, became a *fundi* at it and reaped all the benefits. With our friendship flourishing, if anybody asked me to refer them to a doctor for a coronary bypass, I naturally gave his name. With increased interaction between the two of us, our wives too became good friends. On our visits to the UK, we invariably met over lunches and dinners and updated each other on personal and family matters. Sohrab and Maureen came to Kenya a couple of times and we took them to our game lodges and our beautiful beaches.

It was about ten years ago when calamity struck Sohrab. He told me about it when we met at his house in St. John's Wood – a very desirable residential part of London. "One night, I suddenly found out that I couldn't pass urine. Maureen rushed me to the hospital where I work; they passed a catheter. You can imagine the embarrassment of having all the young nurses and doctors you have trained inserting a catheter into you and doing a rectal examination to feel your prostate." I could see the mortification he must have felt, visible on his face. "I'm fifty – a bit young for prostate but there was no doubt. Worse still, the blood test showed that my PSA was very high, arousing suspicion of prostatic cancer." He was referring to a prostate specific antigen which goes up in the blood when one has prostate cancer and can easily be checked by a simple blood test. He paused, knowing that this was a nasty turn his life had taken. The brief pause gave my jarred shock absorbers time to recover. "My surgeon did a TUR on me." Sohrab used surgical jargon. This meant that the surgeon chiselled out the prostate and widened the passage to enable Sohrab to pass urine spontaneously. This technique did not require a cut on his abdomen. Of course, the report on the prostatic scrappings was cancer. Sohrab sighed. "It is a vicious type of cancer I need to undergo – both radiotherapy and chemotherapy. In addition to that, I need Zoladex injections which, as you know, reduce potency and libido to zero." Being a professional colleague, he was candid.

I comforted him and Marie did the same to Maureen. Over the next few months, on our visits to the UK, we witnessed Sohrab suffering the unpleasant side effects of chemotherapy.

He lost his hair and his skin became coarse and pale. Worse still, he lost his oomph. I suppose drug-induced erectile dysfunction at fifty, and its unspoken effect on Maureen, must have weighed heavily on his mind. Once the chemotherapy course was over, he recovered a part of his original self but the disease continued to take a toll on him. "The damn thing has spread to my bones," he complained the next time we went to London. "Look at my X-rays." He threw a large brown envelope in my lap. I held them opposite the window. They were typical of metastasis from prostatic cancer – solid sheets of white replacing the normal spongy trabeculation of healthy bones. His pelvic bones, spine and skull were teeming with those opaque shadows. "They are bloody painful," he said with agonising transmission of the excruciating pain.

"There are so many things for pain these days," I cheered him up. "In this day and age, there's no need for anybody to suffer any pain."

"That's what I tell my patients," Sohrab replied, "because I believe what I say." Not hiding his disbelief and disillusion, he added. "You only realise the hollowness of these claims when you suffer the pain yourself."

Thereafter, it was Maureen who kept us in touch with subsequent happenings. The first time she saw me alone, she gave me the disturbing news. "The pain is really getting Sohrab down, so much so that last month he attempted suicide." I sat there listening, feeling numb and sick. "I found him sitting in his BMW, with the engine revving and a hosepipe going through a chink in the window."

"No," I stifled a scream.

"I managed to yank the pipe from the window and turn the engine off in time," Maureen added, tears streaming down her face. "Suicide is an abomination no Parsi would stoop to. It's believed that even the vultures would not touch the corpse of a person who committed suicide."

"How are you?" I asked Sohrab when I went into his bedroom after listening to the ghastly details. I was determined not to touch on the issue of his attempted suicide. He looked gaunt and wan. "I'm on Morphine tablets to ease the pain," he replied. "Now they are talking about connecting a morphine pump to my vein so that I can regulate the dose of morphine to control my pain better."

I wished I could do something to liberate him from his unbearable pain. As a surgeon, I'm used to disease and death staring in my face all the time. It's a duel I constantly fight. Many a time, I emerge as the winner. But some battles can't be won. In the case of Sohrab, I had lost professional objectivity as well which, like thick skin, all surgeons develop in time. I sat like a helpless onlooker, feeling the pain my friend was going through. In the end, he found his own salvation and relief in an unconventional but equally tragic way.

A few months later, one evening, our phone in Nairobi rang. It was Maureen. "You've lost a good friend," she said, "and I have lost a wonderful husband." She was choking with emotion. It was not possible to comfort her. She had lost her composure and could not speak coherently. We could not converse any further and had to hang up. "Sorry," was all I could say before doing so. "Marie and I will join you in London, as soon as we get a flight."

"In the end, the pain overwhelmed him and he shot himself." Maureen said as we sat in a Thai restaurant where we had taken her for lunch after our arrival. It was Sohrab's favourite and we often went there during his lifetime. "He brought me here for dinner and treated me to all the dishes he knew I liked," Maureen continued. "I could see he was in pain but he went on pumping Morphine into his system and made out as if he was in high spirits. We reached home. By now, we were sleeping in adjacent rooms. He didn't want me disturbed by his groans and moans. Two hours later, I heard a gun shot and rushed into his room. This time, he had done a good job. He had shot himself in the heart.'

As Marie and I jerked up, she produced a note. "He left this on his bedside table," she said, handing it to Marie. It was a brief note; *Couldn't take any more pain. I love you darling. So long – till we meet again.*

"The next morning," Maureen concluded, "a beautiful bouquet of flowers arrived. It was our 25th wedding anniversary. There were 25 carnations – my favourite flower – one for each year we spent together."

4

Rich man in a dhoti

Since the time of Hippocrates, medicine has been considered a noble profession and vocation. The Hippocratic Oath is partly based on this assumption. So when I was forced to put my brass plate up and join the rat race of private surgical practice to make a living, I had great difficulty in accepting the concept of imposing fees for my professional services. I would have been much happier if the matter of fees was disconnected from my professional work.

The ideal was within our grasp when I worked as a full time surgeon at the Aga Khan Hospital in Nairobi, many years ago. I strongly urged the expatriate administrator and the Board of Governors that the full-time system be further developed in the main specialties, with a provision of generous emoluments for the incumbents. That way, there would be no conflict of interest and academic development of the broad specialties and research in the main branches of medicine would proceed without distraction or hindrance. I also argued that, with such a system in place, it would be easier to integrate with the medical school, which was in the offing at the Kenyatta National Hospital. The expatriate consultant staff at the time, deeply steeped in full-fledged private practice with very tenuous sessional attachment to the Aga Khan Hospital, successfully opposed the idea. Therefore, when my brief full-time contract came to an end, I only had one choice; to accept three sessions a week. The sessional income was meagre and it was inevitable that I threw myself to the lions in the jungle of private surgical practice. The private income was essential to keep my head above water. I consoled myself that I was ahead of my time and was floating an idea whose time had not yet come. Its time did come, however, many years later, when the Aga Khan Hospital was aspiring to be a post-graduate teaching hospital and was facing stiff opposition in dismantling an entrenched system of sessional consultants and establishing full-time teaching departments. Ultimately, they did but, by then, I had established myself firmly in private practice and had also obtained an honorary attachment to Kenyatta National Hospital as a consultant surgeon, and to the University of Nairobi as a senior lecturer in surgery. I reckoned that I had the best of both worlds.

At this point, I must confess that I have thoroughly enjoyed the healthy combination of an honorary attachment to a teaching hospital and earning my bread and butter from the private sector. The former appeased my academic bent of mind. I also satisfied my deep-seated desire to teach the undergraduate and postgraduate students and get an opportunity to mingle with the younger generation. It had two distinct advantages: in some ways it gave me a sense of eternal youth and also an illusion of immortality by passing on the little surgical talents and skills I possessed to the future generation of doctors and surgeons. I was leaving surgery in safe hands. The private practice, on the other hand, gave me enough income to live comfortably, educate my children, travel extensively, save for both a comfortable retirement and a rainy day and still leave something for my son and daughter to remember me for! But I found that the proportion of academic activity was far less compared to the time and effort I devoted to my private work.

Rich man in a dhoti

If I had another life to live, I would simply reverse the roles. I would like to be a full-time professor of surgery, running an academic department, teaching, conducting research and examining candidates. However, it would have to be in an institution which paid their academic staff an international salary scale, enough to fulfill their worldly needs so that no one would have to resort to private practice. The limited private practice, which sometimes comes with such appointments, would only serve as an icing on the cake!

It is in connection with the monetary aspect of a surgeon's life that I recall the case of a dhoti-clad Indian gentleman who was referred to me by my cardiologist colleague. The poor dhoti came into the equation because my professional colleague, for good reasons, described the patient by the type of apparel he wore. "In fact, if he comes to see you wearing the same worn out dhoti that he came to see me in, you will understand the reason for this phone call," Dr. Karanja told me on the phone, when he rang me about Pandit Rahul. From what I gathered, Dr. Karanja had been treating him on a long term basis for a chronic heart problem. "When he developed a swelling in his scrotum, he came to see me," the doctor explained. "Now I'm no expert on scrotal swellings, but, from what I gathered during my undergraduate days, I think Pandit Rahul has a hydrocele. I'm ringing you for two reasons," the doctor continued. "One is that I've checked his heart and can assure you that he's fit for surgery." He paused before touching on the more delicate point. "The other reason is that the man has always pleaded broke and has regularly asked for a discount on my professional fees. He wants me to make the same plea to you on his behalf."

"Discount on professional fees?" I asked in disbelief and then added in a light vein. "He must think that we are *dukawallas* and wants to treat us as he does with the poor ladies in the hawkers' market where he probably haggles endlessly when buying his *bhogas*."

Dr. Karanja laughed and, to drive his point home, referred again to Pandit Rahul's tatty dhoti. When the patient entered my consulting room, my eyes were riveted on his dhoti – for two reasons. One, his disease resided behind it and, secondly, I wanted to confirm the observation Dr. Karanja had made about its condition. On both scores, he was right.

The swelling was the size of a *mdafu* and its contours could not be easily concealed behind the fine muslin. The dhoti was threadbare and tattered, highly diagnostic of its antique value! Pandit Rahul looked nervous and, to put him at ease, I first talked about his name. "Pandit in Hindi is equivalent to *mwalimu* in Swahili," I said. "If my memory serves me right, the Oxford Dictionary defines Pandit as a person who is learned in Sanskrit, philosophy, religion and jurisprudence. The great Indian leader, Jawaharlal Nehru, used the name Pandit as a prefix to his revered name." I could see that my prelude relaxed the stress lines visible on his face.

"Perhaps my ancestors belonged to that hallowed category," he replied, raising his arms and pressing his palms together to greet me with a *namaste*, in the traditional Indian style. "I'm only a small trader."

With the background information from Dr. Karanja, I could easily see what he was driving at. Small trader indicated only one thing – he was preparing the ground to negotiate for a hefty discount. "Right," I said. "Let's get down to business. What's your problem?"

Pointing shyly at the dhoti, he said, "This large swelling on my private part is the problem."

"How does it bother you?" I asked – rather foolishly.

"Bit of a burden, sir," he blushed, "and also too big to be hidden by the largest underwear on the market."

"Do you mind taking off your clothes?" I asked. He unknotted the dhoti at the top and as it fell down, I could see a large hydrocele – a collection of fluid in the space between the two layers of the sac that covers the testis. The condition requires an operation to remove the fluid and obliterate the space to prevent fluid from collecting again.

"Dr. Karanja tells me that your heart is fit enough for the surgery," I told him. "When would you like to undergo the operation? It's neither urgent nor serious, so it can be planned to our mutual convenience."

"The sooner the better," Pandit Rahul said. "I have carried it for too long and it forces me to walk with my legs wide apart."

We settled on a date. "Where would you like to be admitted?" I asked. "As you know, we have excellent general wards and a variety of private rooms – going up from the very modest to the five-star category. It all depends on how much money you want to spend."

"In my case, sir, it depends on how much I can afford," Pandit Rahul said obsequiously, "the cheaper the better."

"No problem," I assured him. I rang the central booking office and arranged a bed for him in the general surgical ward, to come in on a Monday two weeks from then, for surgery on my Tuesday operation list. I asked Dr. Karanja to manage his heart condition while he was in the hospital, especially when he was in the operating theatre.

Once Rahul was admitted, I went to see him for a final preoperative check-up. It was late in the evening and I found that he had two visitors; his wife and daughter. The wife was very much in her husband's mould. She wore a white sari, made of coarse material, which predated her husband's antique dhoti. She had a red mark on her forehead and round her neck was a *mala*, which is a chain of large holy beads. The daughter, on the other hand, was a complete contrast and looked like a glamour puss. She looked more European than Indian. There was no *tilak* – the red dot on her forehead – which her mother wore. Instead, she was made up to the nines, with mascara, eye shadows, long artificial eye lashes, bright red lip stick and long manicured painted nails. Even to my eyes – utterly uneducated in women's fashion – it was obvious that the young lady had a good taste in fashion. I was convinced that her blouse, skirt, shoes and wrist watch all carried a designer's label.

I went over Pandit Rahul very carefully, confirmed that he was fit for surgery, reassured him, his wife and daughter and left. As I came out of the ward, a sweet fragrance of Chanel perfume followed me. I turned back. The daughter had come out of the ward to talk to me. She asked a few questions about her father's surgery and then said. "You probably don't know that he's a workaholic and I wondered if you can keep him in the hospital for a few days after surgery for rest." Looking at my puzzled face she added. "If you don't mind, please tell him that a week's rest in the hospital is mandatory after the operation."

"I will be telling a lie," I said, "considering that, sometimes, we do this operation as a day case."

"I know," she said with a winsome smile. "Please do it for me," she added with a hint of seduction in her whispering tone.

"In return for this favour, please clarify one thing for me," I said. "Pandit Rahul introduced you as his daughter but I don't see any resemblance or connection."

"Oh," she replied. "I stayed in France for a few years and was taken in by the fashion and style of that lovely country. It wasn't difficult because, unlike the British, French culture is so addictive. In the process, I became disconnected from the family fold, my own roots, and fully adopted the French way of life. And, one more thing about my dad," she added, quickly changing the subject, which I could see that she was not very keen to dwell on, "He will say he can't afford to stay, but just ignore it."

"That's strange," I said. "When he came to see me, and before he even told me what was wrong with him, he informed me that he could not afford much and that's why I see him lodged in the general ward."

"Well, let me put it this way: he's careful with his money and is not a spendthrift."

Pandit Rahul's surgery was uneventful and he readily complied with my advice to stay longer in hospital. On one of my postoperative visits, I saw a new face by his bedside. Judging by his accent, I thought he was a French man, also elegantly and expensively dressed. I put two and two together and concluded that he must be connected in some way to the daughter.

Then, during that week, two surprises came my way. One was my secretary informing me that Pandit Rahul had requested to be moved to the most expensive wing in the hospital for the remaining days. The second was a phone call from Dr. Karanja, "you remember me telling you to lower your fee for our mutual patient? There's no need to do so," he advised me. "In fact, if you can bend your medical ethics sufficiently, double it."

"What's going on?" I asked.

"Let Rahul tell you what he told me. Coming from the horse's mouth, you will find it more interesting," Dr. Karanja explained.

The next day, when I went to see Pandit Rahul in the platinum wing of the hospital where, he opened up. "I'm sure you remember meeting the French guy in my room." As I nodded, he continued, "He is my daughter's ex." Then, pointing at the richly upholstered arm chair, covered with real leather, commensurate with the daily charges of his private suite, he added. "Please, sit down because it is a long story." I released the Sister who had accompanied me and sat down.

"Saroj wanted to be a fashion designer and got a chance to do the course in Paris. She first went to Sorbonne and while there, she met this chap, who called himself an artist, learning to paint. He swept her off her feet. He introduced her to his Bohemian friends and their artistic way of life. Our daughter was fascinated by the sheer novelty and fell for it. They soon moved into the Latin Quarters, not far from River Seine. One fine morning, she announced to us that she wanted to marry the man. We had no choice. We had to accept Jacque or lose Saroj. Being our only daughter and child, we gave in. We did warn her though that marriage is a complex institution and she, therefore, needed to be careful." Rahul paused and contorted his face as if he was tapping his receding memory. "After the wedding, we got to know Jacque better. We had to chew our own words. He charmed us too.

"My wife and I realised that we were getting on well and decided to invest in real estate in our daughter's name. She was determined to settle in France. We thus invested in real estate in Paris and on the French Riviera. It never occured to us that they could part ways. We were also ignorant about the laws of France that stipulated that a husband would claim and get half of his wife's assets in that country in case of a divorce." I sat there, flabbergasted and wondering what was coming next. "In a couple of years, the infatuation wore off and the bubble burst. Consequently, they separated and he took us to the cleaners." There was an expression of dismay on Rahul's face. It reminded me of the picture of Dorian Gray as seen at the end of Oscar Wilde's classic novel, a prefiguration of his own tragedy. Rahul took a grip of himself and continued. "The chap came to see me yesterday." It occured to me that the mental connection I had made of the Frenchman whom I had seen the previous day, with Pandit Rahul's daughter was correct. "He's on holiday in Kenya with his new wife. When he heard of my illness, he came to see me, for old time's sake, as he put it. In conversation, he told me that he now owns a chalet in Switzerland, a villa by Lake Como in Italy and has just bought a house in Lamu facing the sea. He drives a Mercedes Sport 600. As he was flaunting his riches, I asked him where he got the money from. I knew him as a young, impecunious artist struggling to make a career when he was courting my daughter. He glibly replied, 'From the divorce settlement. If I might say so, it's all your money, thank you very much. I'm enjoying the largesse and putting the money to good use!'" I could see Pandit Rahul's face turning red with rage as he continued, "The crook gave me food for thought and I said to myself, What the hell am I doing, counting every penny when all my hard-earned money is being squandered by this con man who, obviously, married my daughter for her money? Seeing and listening to him brag about his unearned illicit wealth, I decided to reorient myself and spend some of my money on myself for a change. So as a start, I moved to this luxury accommodation and rang Dr. Karanja to charge me full fees from now on. I also told him to advise you accordingly."

5
Surgical mishaps

When I first started writing, I thought of using a pseudonym. There were three good reasons for it. Firstly, I needed some anonymity. In the case of my fictional work, I was not sure how my readers would react to the torrid love scenes which are an integral part of my fictional novels. As for the factual *Surgeon's Diary*, I was uneasy about how my patients would feel about their surgeon writing about them. Even though I, effectively, camouflaged their names, ethnicity and locations, there was always a possibility – however remote – that an odd patient might identify himself or herself with the story.

Secondly, I wanted some relief from the name Kodwavwala, a cross I have carried all my life. I acquired it at birth because my family hailed from Kodwav, a village in Saurashtra in Western India. In my culture, it was, and still is, traditional to acquire surnames after the place one was born in or had some connection with. Over the years, I became acutely aware of the difficulty everyone, including myself, experienced in writing, spelling and pronouncing Kodwavwala. When I had an opportunity to relinquish it, even part time as it were, I grabbed it.

Finally, my father, Dawood, had worked very hard in his time to get me into a medical school and make me a doctor.

I, therefore, wanted to honour his name. And so the pen name Yusuf Dawood made its debut.

Over the years, however, my double life as Dr. Jekyll and Mr. Hyde has been uncovered but, by then, it did not seem to matter. Both my readers and patients, and the public at large, accepted the split personality with considerable relish. As the saying goes, the pen is mightier than the sword, and so it proved in my case. My pen is, obviously, sharper than my knife and Dawood is better known and indeed more popular than Kodwavwala. I do not count it as an aspersion on the latter but a happy endorsement that my pen has touched more people than my knife!

What I did not reckon with, at the time, was the financial implication of the assumed name, until I went to deposit my first royalty cheque. It was in the name of Yusuf Dawood and the bank teller, quite rightly, refused to deposit it in my account which ran under the name Yusuf Kodwavwala. She proposed that I ask my publisher to give me another cheque. Knowing how difficult it was for an unknown writer to extract money from companies which published creative writing for the literary prestige it bestowed on them rather than the income they derived from it, I was reluctant to take that option. "Open an account in the name of Yusuf Dawood", she suggested, looking at the long queue forming behind me. That is precisely what I did. With a surgeon's income which fulfilled all my needs, I did not have to draw any money out of the writer's account and, over the years, it grew into a nice egg nest. It was time I did something with it rather than just let it laze in the bank. Thus, the Rahima Dawood Foundation was born, initially in Kenya, and the author's largesse was transferred into its newly opened account.

In time, the Marie Rahima Dawood Foundation was formed in the UK. The aims of both charitable foundations were to promote health, education and excellence in East, Central and Southern African regions, specifically targeting Kenya. In both cases, tax exemption was obtained from the inland revenue of both countries in which the Foundation was established.

One of the very first projects sponsored by the Rahima Dawood Foundation, in association with the Royal College of Surgeons of Edinburgh, was that of a travelling fellow. The idea originated from a travelling fellowship financed by the Royal College of Surgeons of England, called the Arthur Sims Travelling Fellow. Under its terms of reference, an eminent surgeon, selected by the English College, would travel to the Commonwealth countries to deliver surgical lectures. For some reason, his travel was confined to the White Commonwealth. The Rahima Dawood travelling fellowship was inaugurated to correct the omission and restore the balance. As a result, every year for the last 22 years, a Rahima Dawood Travelling Fellow visits our region for three weeks in November – December. The remit of this eminent surgeon, headhunted on an international level, is to lecture at medical schools and hospitals in the nine countries that constitute COSECSA: The College of Surgeons of East, Central and Southern Africa. Incidentally, the College is an offspring of ASEA, (Association of Surgeons of East Africa) which, after 50 years of sterling service to our region, decided to convert itself into a training and examining institution. The final assignment of the Fellow is to deliver an eponymous oration at the annual conference of our College, held in the capital city of one of the constituent countries. The topic for the Fellow is chosen by the College Council, based on a burning issue in the region at the time. Breast cancer, surgical research, antibiotics, laparoscopic surgery, HIV and Aids, children's surgery, urology and burns are some of the subjects already covered.

As everybody knows, operative surgery is fraught with dangers, most of them caused by the disease for which surgery is carried out. Some, however, are a result of surgical mishaps, out of which a few can be attributed to human error. Examples of human error include removal of wrong organs, limbs, toes and fingers. Cases have been recorded where a right, healthy kidney was removed instead of the diseased left. That left the patient without a functioning kidney and the only recourse was kidney dialysis or a kidney transplant.

There are also instances where wrong operations were carried out. In one country in our region, a patient scheduled for a brain operation ended up with surgery on the knee and vice versa. Most people have heard of a surgeon leaving a swab or a surgical instrument inside a patient's belly. Finally, administration of wrong drugs and mismatched blood transfusions are not unknown. All these accidents result in litigation, whereby the patients, justifiably, bay for the surgeon's blood and claim enormous financial compensations. These few unfortunate cases cast aspersions on our noble profession and inflate the premiums imposed by the insurance companies. This has led to a fall in the number of doctors wanting to take up high risk specialties like obstetrics, trauma and orthopaedics.

'Safe surgery' puts in place strict measures to minimise these errors, which, unfortunately, capture headlines in the press. These alarming reports overshadow the fact that an overwhelming majority of operations are safe and without any adverse consequences.

Talking of surgical mishaps, one that occurred in Great Britain during the Suez crisis, perhaps, changed the course of history. Though the political details of this unhappy episode captured the headlines both in the British and the foreign press, for reasons of medical ethics and the rule of confidentiality enforced on the profession, the medical details remained a secret.

Surgical mishaps

For many years, Anthony Eden, the handsome British Foreign Secretary worked in Churchill's shadow and was dubbed his political heir. It was rumoured in political circles that he even married the old man's niece to improve his chances of succeeding him. However, soon after Eden became the prime minister, two things happened: Col. Nasser of Egypt nationalised the Suez Canal and, in defiance of American advice, conveyed by the then Secretary of State, John Foster Dulles, Britain and France, under a flimsy excuse, invaded it. Unknown to the public, about the same time, Eden developed gall bladder trouble, which necessitated its removal. Naturally, the operation was carried out by the most renowned biliary surgeon in London. It was an easy gall bladder to pluck and was removed in record time. The next morning, the prime minister was deeply jaundiced. His bile duct, the passage that conducts bile from liver to the intestine was inadvertently tied. Eden underwent repeated surgeries, some at Lahey Clinic in USA to undo the damage but he never recovered fully. In the process, he lost the will to fight Nasser and retain his position as prime minister; Britain lost the Suez Canal!

Nearer our time, a Spanish surgeon was fined, suspended and sentenced to one year in prison for committing a fatal surgical error. Stella Obasanjo, the wife of the then Nigerian President Olusegun Obasanjo, consulted him for a liposuction procedure intended to reduce the fat around her waist. It was a simple, cosmetic procedure. Unfortunately, in the case of the Nigerian First Lady, the needle meant to be inserted in the wall of her belly punctured her colon and liver. The former resulted in faecal discharge from the colon setting up a fulminating peritonitis. The latter caused a serious haemorrhage from the liver and she died within six hours.

Nearer home, a couple of years ago, I remember Maryann Muthama, a forty five year old lady, who also underwent a horrifying experience. Maryann was a beneficiary of women's empowerment and a quaint mixture of the traditional and modern African woman. It was evident, in her personal history, that she started life from humble beginnings but, with common sense and education, which she obtained by distance learning while working as a bank clerk, she had now become a woman of substance. She had bought out a dry cleaning business, where she was in charge when the Asian owner decided to emigrate to Canada. In appreciation of her sterling services, he sold it to her for a song and even helped her obtain a loan from the bank. Within a short time, by dint of hard work and with a bit of luck, as she put it, she expanded her business and now owned a few branches in Nairobi and its environs. "I managed to send my only daughter to US and my two sons to the UK to study," she said as she gave me her family history. "They all found jobs and their partners in their land of adoption and are happily settled there," she added.

From the moment she entered my office, she looked both uncomfortable and embarrassed. After many years at the game, surgeons develop a sixth sense and I felt that she was suffering from a complaint that she was shy to express. We exchanged polite greetings and I tried to put her at ease before asking the stock question. "So what's your problem, Madam?"

"I see blood in my motion," she replied hesitatingly, explaining why she looked nervous.

"How often?"

"Every few days."

"Any constipation or diarrhea?"

"Mostly constipated."

"How much do you bleed?"

"Varies, can range from a tablespoon to a small cup." She sounded less tense now.

"And the colour of the blood?"

"Bright red," Maryann replied.

"Sounds like piles," I said after obtaining some more relevant details from her. "Let's check you up."

I told her that I needed to carry out a rectal examination, which involved both the insertion of my gloved finger and an instrument in her back passage. Having assured her that it was an uncomfortable procedure but not painful, I put Maryann in the correct position to carry out the test. "Fine," I said when I finished, "dress up and let's talk about it."

As Maryann, still smarting from the uncomfortable and embarrassing examination, sat in front of me, I confirmed to her my diagnosis. "Yes, you have haemorrhoids, commonly known as piles."

"What are they?" she asked.

"Piles are dilated, thin tortuous veins in the anal passage."

"And how does one get rid of them?"

"By surgery." Looking at her face which was asking for an elaboration, I added. "During the operation we dissect, tie and remove these abnormal veins so that they don't bleed when you go the loo."

"It's supposed to be a very painful operation. Isn't it?" she expressed the fear that most patients associate with piles surgery.

"It's because we work around the anal sphincter which goes into spasm and causes pain. But I use a technique of injecting a long acting local anaesthetic into the sphincter at the start of the operation. This relaxes the muscle and almost eliminates the pain," I tried to reassure her.

I could see that she was not fully convinced and continued to harp on other people's experience in the matter. Based on their stories, it was obvious that she dreaded surgery for her haemorrhoids. I saw the long list of patients my secretary had scheduled for me to see and tried to bring the consultation to a close. "Piles is not a life-threatening condition," I said. "Take some time over it, think about it and come back when you are ready."

A month later, Maryann came to see me again. I thought it was to book a date for surgery. Instead she asked, "Have you heard of the haemorrhoid gun?"

"Yes," I said. "It is a new instrument and uses a new technique whereby one can tie the piles without much cutting."

"A surgeon whom I know has just come back after having attended a hands-on workshop to learn the new technique. He claims that it's less invasive and relatively less painful." I could see Maryann was falling for this innovative technique because of the pain-free inducement offered to her. Pain is something we all like to avoid and Maryann was no exception.

"No problem," I said. "If you are happy with the surgeon and his experience in the new technique, please go ahead. Call me when you are admitted and I will visit you in the hospital with a bunch of red roses," I added facetiously.

As they say, many a word said in jest come true. The call did come but under very different circumstances. It was the gun-toting surgeon who rang me at Maryann's behest. "Maryann seems to have developed severe peritonitis and needs an urgent exploratory laparotomy." The surgeon said using surgical jargon to describe a procedure where we open and literally explore the abdomen to find out what is going on. "I will feel comfortable and confident if a senior surgeon like you were with me when I do it," he said and proceeded to give me more technical details.

I rushed to the hospital and went straight to see Maryann. She was desperately ill but wanted to give me her side of the story. "Apparently there was excessive bleeding while the surgeon was working with the haemorrhoid gun and the procedure took a long time," she said. "But I was told that it was successful and I could go home the next day which was yesterday. Within a few hours of the operation, however, I developed excruciating pain in my tummy. I could feel it hardening like an ironing board. I told this to the surgeon when he came ready to discharge me. He examined me and, by the expression on his face, I gathered that there was something seriously amiss. 'I think we need to take you to the theatre immediately and open your abdomen,' he said, Maryann added, her face in a painful contortion. "It was at that point that I asked for you to be called in," she added.

The inside of Maryann's belly was like a battlefield. There was a hole in the upper rectum caused by the notorious gun which, for lack of better term, could be described as having misfired. Faecal contents of the colon had poured into the belly through this vent and caused fulminating peritonitis. There was only one choice, since closing a hole in the large bowel or rectum never works. Due to the pressure exerted by faecal contents, it reopens within hours, allowing more faeces to flow freely again inside the belly. "I think we have to do a colostomy," I whispered in the ear of the surgeon. This meant bringing a loop of the colon out on the skin surface so that the faeces could discharge outside the body. Naturally, Maryann was beside herself when we told her what we found inside and what we did. Though I had warned her of the possibility, she was hoping against hope that it would not come to pass. The shy young lady, who was bashful at me doing a straightforward rectal examination, was now saddled with the indignity of passing stools in a bag attached to her skin. In all the vicissitudes she had faced in her eventful life, this was something she did not know how to tackle.

"Fancy coming for a minor operation and ending up with a life-threatening emergency, major abdominal surgery and a colostomy," she lamented.

Surgical mishaps

"It is only temporary," I comforted her. "Once the hole caused by the gun has healed, we will close your colostomy. In time, the whole thing will sound like a bad dream."

"More of a nightmare," Maryann sounded bitter and dejected. Quite justifiably I thought, because her trials and tribulations were not over yet.

Three months later I caught up with her again. "I have decided to go to the UK for my corrective surgery. My two sons think that they would be more at ease if I was near them while all this is going on," she said and, taking a hard look at me as if trying to read my thoughts, she added. "I hope you don't mind. Believe me, it's not lack of confidence in you."

"You don't even have to mention it," I comforted her. "I would do the same in your position."

On her return, she gave a full account of the last stages of her ordeal.

"The surgeon there discovered that though the hole in my gut caused by the gun had healed, in the process it had left a severe narrowing of the passage. That had to be gradually stretched by an instrument inserted from below. Then, when the surgeon went in my abdomen to close the colostomy, he found it a mess because of previous faecal peritonitis. He closed the colostomy but gave me a safety valve by bringing a loop of my small intestine out. He said it was necessary in case a leak sprung up at the level of my closed colostomy. I carried that cross until my colostomy had completely healed, as verified by a barium enema. Eventually, the surgeon decided to close the loop of small intestine he had brought out and put it back. A whole year to my piles operation, I passed my stool from the normal passage for the first time."

"Pole sana," I said. "All is well that ends well."

"It was hell – one whole year in a purgatory," she said ignoring my statement of solace.

Surgical mishaps

To close this sad saga, I recall a Rotary meeting where a renowned lawyer and I were indulging in a friendly sparring match. "You surgeons have one distinct advantage over us," he said. "Your mistakes are buried six feet deep in the ground. Ours are flung six feet up in the air for all to see." How wrong he was! Our mistakes haunt us for a long time.

Surgeons are neither divine nor infallible and, therefore, should not be allowed to get away with impunity which they sometimes do courtesy of their gracious patients.

6
Comprehensive insurance against all risks

As usual, Marie and I went to Mombasa for the Easter weekend. While we were there, we bumped into a 'learned friend' who had established a law practice at the Coast but had now retired. In our established conversation, he told me how much he enjoyed reading the *Surgeon's Diary*. "Your writing reminds me of Somerset Maugham," he added.

"Not surprising," I said, "considering that I read all his books when I was a young medical student. It's likely that his literary style rubbed on me and seeped into my pen."

However, Maugham was not my only role model. I suppose the seeds of creative writing were sown by the writing of many doctor-writers I had read in my youth. In my college days, I read Oliver Goldsmith, who was born in Ireland, studied law in London and medicine in Edinburgh, but did not practise either! Instead he turned to writing and became one of the most versatile British writers of the 18th century. He went on to create classics like; *The Vicar of Wakefield* and *Citizen of the World*. He remained in a state of impoverishment most of his life but it was mainly self-inflicted because he gambled most of his money or gave it away in recurrent fits of generosity. Many years later, when I went to Dublin, I saw his statue along with that of Oscar Wilde outside the Trinity College. I found the

Comprehensive insurance against all risks

two historical statues emotionally fulfilling because I had also read Oscar Wilde. The Picture of Dorian Gray was obviously a prefiguration of this remarkable writer's own tragedy and *De Profundis,* written in jail, was a confession that came out of the crucible of his life.

There were two other doctors–cum–writers who had made a great impact on me when I was in my most impressionable years. One of them was A. J. Cronin. My introduction to the writings of this humane doctor and writer came about in an unusual way.

Janmohammed, my eldest brother and mentor, took me to watch a film in Bombay as a treat when I was struggling to obtain a seat at the Grant Medical College. It was an English film and, for the comfort of its British viewers, it was screened in Metro Cinema, an air conditioned facility which, in itself, was a novel experience for me. The film, *The Keys of the Kingdom,* was based on Cronin's novel by the same name. The film moved me so deeply that I read most of the author's work. *Adventures in Two Worlds,* an autobiographical account, in which Cronin relates his interesting cases and narrates how he successfully blended his two roles – of doctor and writer – proved an inspiration. The second one was Sir Arthur Conan Doyle, whose central character became more famous than the man who created him! Doyle's powers of observation, in my view, were a result of his training as a medical student on how to elicit signs and symptoms from patients and interpret them. Finally, though I did not use Roget's Thesaurus until my children gave it to me as a birthday present after being firmly convinced that writing had become a second string to my bow, I did know that Dr. Peter Mark Roget had practised as a physician in London.

Reverting to Maugham, he started his life as a doctor. While he was a medical student at St. Thomas' Hospital in

London, he went into the slums of the city to conduct home deliveries during his midwifery term. Based on his knowledge of the squalid conditions he saw there, he wrote his first novel; *Liza of Lambeth*. It received favourable reviews from literary critics and Maugham quickly changed from medicine to writing. There is another likeness I share with him. Like my *Diary*, some of his work was written in first person.

Amongst his many novels, my most favourite is *The Razor's Edge,* where the art of making the author an all-pervading character in the book has been taken to a perfect level. In this novel too, Maugham has created a remarkable character by the name of Elliott Templeton. He has depicted him as a snob and a bore. Within these two parameters, however, the author has made him very interesting and likeable.

Elliott lived in the South of France which, in those days, was the playground of the rich and decadent of Europe and America. His only purpose in life was to be a socialite and, in the process, host and attend fabulous parties. In connection with this trait, there is an amusing incident in the book. Elliott Templeton is very upset at not being invited to Princess Novandu's fancy dress party, a highlight of the season on the French Riviera. Elliott tells Maugham how sore he felt about being left out. By this time, Elliott was almost on his death bed but still craving for an invitation to the Princess' party. Knowing how much it meant to him, Maugham managed to sneak an invitation card out of Princess Novendu's secretary whom he knew and sent it to him by post. A couple of days later, when Maugham went to see Elliott, he was beaming. "I have had my invitation," he said. "It came this morning."

"You see your name begins with a T and the secretary has evidently just reached you," Maugham fobbed him off.

As it happened, death claimed Elliott before the party but, being the perfect gentleman that he was, he wanted to send

Comprehensive insurance against all risks

a R.S.V.P. to the princess before he died. He was too weak to write so he dictated it to Maugham. With his eyes closed and a mischievous smile on his face, he said. "Mr. Elliot Templeton regrets that he cannot accept Princess Novendu's kind invitation, owing to a previous engagement with his Blessed Lord." Soon after, Elliott died a happy man, still holding the purloined invitation card. At the end, where Maugham sums up all the characters in the book, he aptly describes Elliott as a 'sad Don Quixote of a worthless purpose'.

In our line of work, we are constantly confronted by patients who are coming to the end of the road. The most painful part of a surgeon's job is to inform them that the end is nigh. Having had the misfortune to do so on patients with terminal or incurable illness, I find their reactions both interesting and intriguing. Some are in disbelief and denial while others demand for a second opinion, or a desire to tie up loose ends. There are those determined to fight till the bitter end, those who exhibit fear, withdrawal, remorse at one's past actions and their consequences, concern for those who will be left behind, an attempt to find solace in God's will, complaints about the wrong timing, an urge to mend ways, revival of faith and, finally, relief from the bondage of life and earthly encumbrances.

In this connection, I clearly recollect the reaction of Najib, a patient of mine, originally from Zanzibar but now settled in Nairobi. Before he came to see me professionally, I had met him at a few social functions. "We must stop meeting at other people's houses," he once said to me. "I must put the matter right and invite you home." Like many such 'threats' it was never carried out. Notwithstanding that, I always enjoyed talking to Najib when I met him at sundowners and dinners. One needs to be an expert in small talk to enjoy these functions and Najib was an expert at it. Once in a while though, in the light-hearted atmosphere teeming with captains of business

Comprehensive insurance against all risks

and industry, diplomats and politicians, he would come out with a profound statement. "If there is no God, we will have to invent one" or "If God created the world, which we now know is millions of years old, how is it that the oldest religion is no more than 5000 years old? Buddha and Moses can trace themselves to roughly that time span in human history. Christ is only two millenniums away and Prophet Mohamed is even more recent."

In these flashes of his profound thinking, three things became evident to me. Najib was well read, possessed an articulate mind and had a good command of the English language. Sometimes, he even recited English poetry and came out with some interesting quotations.

Naturally, I was a little disconcerted when this worldly, wise man lay on my couch seeking a surgical opinion. "It was quite an insidious onset," he said when I asked him what his problem was. "I was feeling a bit off colour, nothing definite, and I don't know why, but I decided to see my GP."

"That's what your doctor said in his phone call to me." I replied.

"It was he who noticed a yellow tinge in my eyes and started a barrage of investigations. At the end of it all, he frankly said I had cancer of the pancreas and referred me to you."

Apart from giving me medical details, Najib was quite cagey about his personal and family history, except disclosing that he had inherited a number of family properties and had never had to work for a living. "My job is to manage a string of residential and commercial properties and collect rent," he said, "I'm not sure if you can call that a job," he added.

My examination and additional investigations led to the same conclusion and I operated on him with a diagnosis of cancer of the pancreas. As most of these cases turn out, he had an inoperable tumour. The cancerous pancreas was adherent to the aorta and vena cava, the two largest pipe-like blood vessels in the human body. Any attempt to dissect the pancreas off these massive structures ran the risk of poking holes in them and losing the patient on the table in a couple of minutes. Following the wise adage that discretion is the better part of valour, I did a palliative procedure and came out.

Next day on my rounds, Najib asked me point blank what I found inside his belly and what I did. When I told him the details of my findings and what was safely feasible to do, he asked. "What is this palliative procedure?"

"Cancer of the pancreas blocks your bile passage and gives you jaundice. I did an operation to find another route for your bile. This will relieve your jaundice," I explained.

"The cancer is still inside?" he asked.

"I'm afraid so because any attempt to remove the advanced cancer might have proved fatal on the operating table."

He took a little time to absorb the brutal disclosure and then asked. "So how long have I got?"

"Difficult to quantify, but may be six months at the most."

"Will I have any pain?"

"Unlikely," I said. 'The jaundice will improve because of the short circuiting procedure which I have carried out. In time however, the liver will be affected by the cancer and will fail progressively.'

"Out of the six month period you are giving me, what part of it will I remain fit to travel?" he asked.

"At a rough guess, three months."

"Good enough," he said in a smugly satisfied tone.

Next day when I went to see him, he had news for me. "As soon as you remove my stitches and certify me fit to travel, I'm off."

"Where to?"

"I don't know," he replied. "But I will send you cards from all the places I visit."

The first card was from Khatmandu; *Went on the 'Angel's flight' today. It is a scary flight in a small aircraft which hops from one peak to another in the Himalayas.* Najib wrote. *Somehow going through the clouds, which looked like a flock of sheep from above, flying high, high up in the air, gave me an exhilarating feeling. I felt close to God - if there is one - than I have ever been.*

His last remark did not surprise me in view of what he had said on the subject when we had socially met before.

Next message in the form of a long letter came from Benares – now called Varanasi. *Went to the bank of the Ganges early morning today and saw cremations by the dozens. Some had just started with flames rising high in the air and others were smouldering, with the dead reduced to ashes. It was an awesome sight for me but was treated calmly by priests walking around in their saffron robes. They seemed to take death as a logical end to birth with no reason to mourn for it. The Hindu philosophy of reincarnation teaches that death frees one from the bondage of life and might, ultimately, take one to a state of nirvana when one is finally relieved from the cycle of rebirth and becomes a part of the absolute. I also saw thousands of pilgrims, bathing in the Ganges, ostensibly to wash their sins, praying with their long outstretched arms to the rising sun. It was their devotion to a god they could not see which was so remarkable, especially to a man who is not sure of His very existence!*

This too did not surprise me because it was in line with his thinking.

And then there was a change of continent and the next message was from King David Hotel in Jerusalem. *Went to Bethlehem and visited the manger where Christ was supposedly born. Also walked the path Christ walked with the cross on his back.*

To complete the picture, saw the site where he supposedly rose from the dead. All seemed and sounded so unconvincing. Pondering on Judaism, which is the official state religion of the country I am in, it seems so futile to continue waging a war with all the neighbouring countries on the basis of their religion which is based on such flimsy grounds!

A few days later, a card, terse and pithy arrived from Rome. It read; *Today I am at the Vatican and have just seen the window from where the Pope blesses the congregation at Easter and Christmas. The Vatican is a state by itself and, obviously, an endorsement of the faith his followers have in him and in the religion he represents. Incidentally, the Pope also visited the Trevi Fountain. Traditionally, if one puts a coin in the Fountain, they are bound to return here. From what you told me, it is unlikely to happen in my case, but put a coin anyway. Who knows, the small investment might prove you wrong!* I could see the wicked smile on his face as he wrote the tail end of his this message.

The next one was a rather long letter written on a Niagara Falls Hotel headed paper. It was the first disclosure about his family life. *My ex-wife has lived here since she left me a few years ago. We met and married in Canada where I studied for a few years and from where she originally came from. She accompanied me home to Zanzibar but could not put up with my polygamy, which I thought was my birthright. Even though she was the senior wife and her co-wives treated her like a queen, the idea of sharing her man officially with other women offended her feminine dignity and her self-respect and proved an anathema. Her culture, and her upbringing in a foreign land, would not allow her to accept the situation. Eventually, she left. Luckily, we had no children. On her return home, she met a compatriot, a strict monogamist, married him and settled in Niagara Falls. We have been regularly communicating with each other and remain good friends. So I thought I would come, make peace with her and officially bid her goodbye. All forgotten and forgiven!*

The last missive from Mecca was very brief. *Visited the Ka'aba and did seven circumlocutions of the black stone. P.S. I am afraid the three months of pain free life is coming to an end. I am also feeling homesick. It will not be long before I will need to come in the hospital for terminal care! Before I do so, however, I wish to have a few days by the beach in Jeddah. I have visited it before and found it fascinating. All the rules of purdah and abstinence from the two pleasures of life which mankind enjoy can be violated with impunity there by the sea. Though my failing health might not allow me to avail of either, it would give me a special satisfaction to defy Allah on His own home ground!*

It was while he was resting in the hospital bed, after his long, arduous and interesting safari, that I asked him what motivated him to take that journey, and how and why he came to choose the places he visited. I was interested to hear what he had to say but it also gave us something to talk about. After all there is very little one can say on a daily basis to a patient who knows he is dying.

"Well, you see," he said. "In my lifetime, nobody has convinced me about God's existence in one way or the other. And so I had to go out and find it myself."

"And did you?" I asked.

"Yes and no," he replied. What follows is a gist of what he said over the next few days during my daily rounds to see him. His observations were not as coordinated as I have made them out. Some days he was quite coherent and on other days either because of pain or obfuscation, his narration was neither clear nor concise. To give my readers an articulate account of what was said, I will paraphrase it, but still try to retain Najib's own words, as far as possible.

No, I did not find all the answers but learnt a lot about the origin of different religions and their founders. I was convinced of one eternal truth, which is that all the prophets, the so called emissaries of God, were great men. They were great thinkers and religious leaders. They looked at the ills of their contemporary societies and decided to reform it. They knew that they needed an almighty God to enforce their innovative philosophy and so went ahead and created Him. They also had to bring in the concept of heaven and hell for the same reason. It was based on the age-old policy of carrot and stick, something that human beings have acknowledged from the time they evolved into homo-erectus. A moral code had to be introduced and the prophets did that with relish. The emphasis of values differed with the times in which these prophets lived but the core values remained the same. That is why all religions have the same moral code. What separates them is the rituals.

"Buddha, historically and chronologically the first to arrive on the scene 5000 years ago, harped mainly on reverence for life and non-violence, amongst other requirements of a clean life. And so Buddhism was born and is still practised by almost one fifth of the world's population. Then came Hinduism, not identified with any particular prophet but associated with characters and mythology in the two great epics, Ramayana and Mahabharata. Later on, Moses peddled the Ten Commandments because they were very relevant to his time on earth and he left Judaism as his legacy. To the chagrin of the Jews, Jesus arrived on this earth and brought Christianity with him. He added the element of crucifixion and rising from the dead to add the 'miracle effect'. This was engineered to raise himself one notch higher. He needed that additional fillip to pronounce himself the Son of God. Prophet Mohammed emerged a few centuries later and announced that Allah is neither begotten nor does He beget, thus exploding the myth of the Father and the Son. He founded and propagated Islam and conveyed the message of Allah to the new converts in the form of the Holy Koran, which was ostensibly transmitted to him by angel Gabriel, while he sat in a hypnotic trance in a cave near Mecca."

Comprehensive insurance against all risks

All this was food for thought for me, someone who had studiously avoided getting into the labyrinthine and getting totally lost!

It was on his last day on this earth that Najib made his final confession in an entertaining way. "Finally, to answer your question as to why I made the trip during the sunset of my life, I wanted to pay my respects to the headquarters of all recognised religions. I didn't want to take any chances and burn in hell the rest of my days – if indeed the concept of heaven and hell was real. I decided to reconcile myself with all religions and all gods. That way I secured a comprehensive insurance against all risks and was covered for all eventualities."

It was the last time Najib made me laugh and left me craving for more! Unfortunately there was no more, for that night, he passed away, peacefully, in his sleep.

7
From a jaundiced patient to a liver specialist

I first visited Cambridge many years ago and fell in love with it. I was then working as a house surgeon in a London Hospital in preparation for my fellowship in surgery when I took a day trip to the university town. I have two distinct memories of that first visit. One, the town swarming with young boys and girls on bicycles and noticing that, like the animals in our game parks, the cyclists has the right of way on the roads in Cambridge. The other is a stroll I took on what is popularly known as 'The Backs'. This is a walkway by the Cam River, after which the town is named. The backs of the famous colleges, some of them almost a thousand years old are a sight to behold as one takes a walk in the town. The reflections of King's College, founded in 1441, and Clare, dating from 1326 in the still waters of the River, made a picture postcard and remained framed in my mind for many years to come.

My second visit was in connection with buying equipment for a recently approved Intensive Care Unit – ICU. I was the Executive Director of The Aga Khan Hospital in Nairobi and had managed to persuade the Board of Governors to invest in this innovative way of looking after seriously ill patients. ICU was then a new concept based on a sort of socialist policy – providing care to patients based on their needs. It became obvious to both clinicians and administrators that most patients need minimal routine nursing care and monitoring. They could be taken care of in the conventional wards. However, the seriously ill needed extra care, close observation and ready means of resuscitation. To this end, specially trained nurses and doctors and a battery of modern equipment were required. A separate unit had to be allotted to these patients who were in dire straits with the medical and nursing staff working on them under very stressful conditions. This, appropriately, came to be known as Intensive Care Unit. Patients were lodged there during the time they required intensive care and then transferred to ordinary wards where they would receive routine care.

I had personally sampled a rudimentary ICU in Brompton Chest Hospital in London, where I had been flown from Nairobi, a few years earlier after developing a collapsed lung. I underwent a major chest operation and was kept in the newly opened ICU for 24 hours after surgery. I was quite impressed with the specialised extra care I received during the critical hours after my major surgery. By now, ICU had become an essential part of every first class hospital, certainly in the Western world.

To bring the Aga Khan Hospital in line with other centres of excellence, I put up a proposal at a hospital Board meeting and, after a lengthy explanation on my part to justify the capital expenditure, it was unanimously approved.

An instrument company in Cambridge won the tender to equip the unit and I was invited there to check and choose the high-powered gadgets. While there, I had a very interesting day at the Addenbrook's Hospital with Prof. Calne, the liver transplant pioneer surgeon in the UK. I watched him actually carry out the complex procedure. He was a swarthy, small, modest, soft-spoken man and, as he did the liver transplant, Mozart's famous symphony was playing softly in the background. For me, this was a novel experience, because I prefer pin drop silence when I am operating. Prof. Calne was a lover of classical music and, before scrubbing for the operation, he slipped a cassette into the record player, provided by the hospital authorities for his exclusive use. The symphony seemed to soothe his nerves and fortify his concentration. After the operation, a meeting was held in the department of surgery chaired by Prof. Calne, which every member of the liver transplant team was supposed to attend. At this meeting, recently published research papers on the subject of liver transplant were discussed and all aspects of the operated patient and his post-operative management were thoroughly thrashed out. This, too, was a novel experience for me.

Somehow, Prof. Calne and I took an instant liking for each other, perhaps, because it was a meeting of minds. After the meeting, he invited me to lunch with him in the hospital cafeteria. It was during lunch that he suddenly darted the question. "Have you seen anything of our beautiful town?"

"What with sorting out the ICU equipment with the local manufacturers and learning something about liver transplant from a world authority like you, I haven't had much time."

"Well," he said, peering above his glasses, "it would be a great omission on our part if we sent you back to Nairobi without showing you this academic showpiece of Britain. It is the oldest university town, certainly in the English-speaking world." He then adjusted his glasses and added facetiously, "Oxford sometimes claims that honour but then they claim to win the boat race when they lose it by a foot! I have an idea," he continued. "Today is my secretary's afternoon off. If she has not arranged a date, I'am sure she can take you round."

"That's putting her through a lot of trouble," I said.

"Not at all," Prof. Calne said. "She will be delighted to do what she did before she came to work for me. She was a tour

From a jaundiced patient to a liver specialist

guide. She knows the history of this town and its colleges like the back of her hand."

The professor was right about his secretary. Apart from her knowledge of the subject, Liz had a passion for her work as a tour guide and also for Cambridge, where she told me she was born and grew up. She first acquainted me with basic rules of the place as we entered the college grounds. She made me laugh when she said; "Only Fellows are permitted to walk on the lawns. If the chap walking on the lawns is not a Fellow, he's a foreign tourist who can't read English!"

She first took me to Queen's College, built in red brick and pointed at its sundial. "Sir Isaac Newton designed it. The clock not only shows the hours but also the moon faces."

We were now walking on what Liz called the mathematical bridge. From above, I could see punters gliding on the calm waters of the River as Liz continued to talk about it. "It was originally built on a mathematical formula with no screws and bolts," she said. The bridge was long and, from where I stood, I could see some screws and bolts at the far end. When I brought it to her attention, she explained; "Some bright spark of a mathematician, in the last century, took the bridge apart to see how it hung together without screws and bolts and then could not put it together without having to use them!"

Next, I found myself inside the King's College Chapel, with its very high ceiling in a stern gothic style. On the walls were various coats of arms. The glass windows told the eternal Christian story, starting with Virgin Mary in the barn at one end and finishing with the Crucifixion at the other. The organ was playing as Liz led me into the main chapel to show me Reuben's original painting on wood of the Adoration of the Maji adorning one of the walls.

Finally, we walked over to the world renowned Trinity College. Prof. Calne must have told his secretary that I was

From a jaundiced patient to a liver specialist

a writer because Liz took me to the library where I saw some fascinating historical documents. One was the original manuscript of *Analysis of Matter* written by Bertrand Russell, the great English philosopher. There was also the first edition of *Winnie the Pooh*, the 1605 copy of Shakespeare's *Hamlet* and the original letter written by Lord Byron from Greece in May, 1810. The masterpiece, from my point of view, was a letter written by Dr. Livingstone on 20th October 1859, while he was still on his African safari. There were also Ruskin's letter from Venice, manuscripts of Milton's poems and Newton's Principia. As Liz led me into court, she remarked. "This is the biggest college court in England and this college has produced a large number of thinkers and intellectuals. To name a few, Sir Isaac Newton, Milton of *the Paradise Lost* and *Paradise Regained* fame, Sir Francis Bacon, Lord Macaulay and Lord Byron are, indeed, products of Trinity." Then, with a strange smile on her face, she added, "Even Prince Charles took a degree in archaeology from here."

My day with Prof. Calne proved an essential prelude and contact when, a few years later, I was confronted with a liver problem which could not be treated in Nairobi. It was in the days when the country lacked specialised paediatric surgeons to cater to the surgical needs of children. The 'general surgeon' needed to be a jack of all trade!

In that role, I was escorted to the nursery by my obstetrician colleague, Dr. Hilda Bennett. "I have a newborn girl whom I had to readmit in the nursery yesterday." She said to me, as she walked me to the ward, "She was jaundiced at birth and we all thought it was the usual physiological jaundice of newborns. The parents were very keen to take her home and so I let her go. Naturally, I kept an eye on the infant." Dr. Bennett obviously had a high level of suspicion. "In the next couple of weeks, the baby would not breastfeed and her weight dropped to six pounds and three ounces from the seven pounds she weighed at birth. The mild yellowish tinge had now turned to deep jaundice."

We were now in the nursery and I could clearly see the description on the newborn was correct. I went over the tiny baby carefully and saw the few investigations available in those days for such cases. "Looks like biliary atresia," I said to Dr. Bennett in the hearing of the parents.

"What's that?" the mother asked anxiously.

"It's the under development of the ducts that connect the liver to the gut. The liver produces bile, which normally flows to the gut where it's required for digestion of food. When the ducts, which are the conduits for bile, are either not developed at birth or get blocked for some reason in adult life, the bile is retained in the liver and gives jaundice."

"And what do you do about it?" the father asked.

"Treatment depends on the cause. In this particular case, the best we can do is to attach the gut to the liver and hope that the bile will seep directly into the intestine." I then added the precautionary rider, "Unfortunately, the results are very poor, but in this case we have no option."

At that point, the mother broke down and started crying. "Am I going to lose Olivia? I had to wait ten years to have her, and now you are implying that she will soon be taken away."

"I haven't said that," I gently corrected her.

That evening I rang Prof. Calne and apprised him of my dilemma and the solution I had in mind.

"Damn difficult problem," he remarked.

"Shall we fly her over to you?" I asked eagerly. I sounded like a man in a hurry to pass the buck.

"Not yet," he said. "I think you should proceed with Jaurez's operation for now." He was referring to a procedure first described by a spanish surgeon whose name it bore. It involved attaching the gut to the base of the liver like a sucker foot, thus connecting the two organs and giving a channel for the bile to flow. "If that succeeds, you have solved the problem," he concluded.

"And if it doesn't?"

"Then you will have to bring her here because she will need a liver transplant," the professor replied.

I carried out the very rare operation with trepidation and, though Olivia showed a dramatic improvement immediately after surgery, she soon relapsed. "Feeding is still a problem," the mother complained. "She takes an hour to empty one breast, yet her tummy is enlarging."

I discovered that the 'big tummy' was a result of collection of fluid in the abdomen, another sequel of blocked liver. I watched Olivia for a couple of months and, registering no improvement, told the parents, "Olivia needs a liver transplant."

I had gathered, in the course of my interaction with Olivia's family, that her father worked for a multinational British company, which took care of their medical expenses. "I have contacted Prof. Calne in Cambridge. He's a world authority on liver transplants and is prepared to take Olivia's case." The company insisted that I accompany the family to Cambridge.

After assessing Olivia, the specialised liver transplant team focused on Olivia's father, Ron. It became apparent to me that they were after a part of his liver to transplant into his daughter's belly. They investigated him extensively to make sure that it was the right shape and size from which a slice could be safely taken. Luckily, it was also a match.

On the day of the operation, I felt sorry for Judy who, in a span of a few hours, suffered two wrenches. She first had to bid farewell to her husband who went to the operating theatre to give a part of his liver – a procedure which took full five hours.

Then it was Olivia's turn. I could see tears glistening in her eyes as her baby was taken away from her. I watched both the operations, one on the donor and the other on the recipient – one after the other.

Olivia's operation lasted eight hours, at the end of which the professor, myself and a host of doctors and nurses transferred her from the operating theatre to an incubator. It was quite a sight to see so many people surrounding the tiny creature, cocooned in wires and breathing through a ventilator. Ron was in the adult ward while Olivia was in the children's special ICU; the poor mother kept floating between the two. I left the next day to come home but was told later by Judy that she took daily pictures of her daughter and took them to Ron to show him how their daughter was progressing.

In time, the parents came back to Nairobi with their healthy, jaundice-free baby and worked here for five more years before returning back to their country. By then, Olivia had grown into a bonny girl and with regular follow-up to monitor her progress, I had grown very fond of her. I felt a wrench when she, with her parents came to bid me good-bye. As I always do in such cases, I said to the parents. "Just send me a Christmas card every year and tell me how Olivia is doing." They kept to that commitment and I have been receiving Christmas cards every year from them since. Apart from the usual greetings, all that the cards said was – Olivia is blooming. In the last one, the message was longer. The parents informed me that Olivia had qualified as a doctor at the age of 25.

"What does she want to specialise in?" I sent an eager enquiry.

"She has already enrolled in late Prof. Calne's unit to train as a liver transplant surgeon!" came the equally quick reply. From a tiny patient in that unit to a trainee surgeon - indeed the wheel had turned a full circle!

8
High intelligence fused with profound love

"This girl will be a miracle," said Prof. Borthwick, the visiting neurosurgeon from Newcastle upon Tyne, with his usual literary flair. "I'm connecting the centre of her love with the focus of her intelligence."

It was in the days when the country lacked home-grown neurosurgeons. Arrangements were, therefore, made with various neurosurgical centres abroad to send specialists to our teaching hospital. While here, they conducted brain operations on our patients and, in the process, trained our aspiring young surgeons who wanted to specialise. My role in the theatre, when I heard those poetic words of Prof. Borthwick, was two-fold. I was attached to the teaching hospital as I still am, and was part of this programme. Secondly, I had a close family relationship with little Susanne who was being operated upon by the professor and was instrumental in arranging her surgery.

Susanne's father, Simon and I climbed up our respective professional ladders together. He was a stockbroker and had put his brass plate up about the same time that I did mine. We first met when he came to see me with a lemon-sized lump on his head. He entered my office wearing a trilby hat and when I asked him what was wrong with him, he simply took it off and

High intelligence fused with profound love

pointed to the lump. "Doesn't bother me in any way except that my wife doesn't like the look of it," he said. "Over the years she has convinced me that the lump is unsightly. So I just cover it with my hat." Then, with a naughty smile on his face, he added. "To please my wife, sometimes I wear the trilby when I am in bed!"

"Is it growing?" I asked looking at the lump.

"Yes," replied Simon. "It was the size of a pea but now it has matured into a lemon."

"It's nothing serious," I said after examining the lump. "It's a sebaceous cyst." Looking at Simon's puzzled expression, I added. "Our skin needs some natural moisturizer and lubricants and so we have been provided with sebaceous glands. The sebum secreted by these glands does the job admirably and saves us a lot of money, which we would have to spend on buying artificial creams and lotions. Once in a while a gland becomes blocked, sebum collects inside and causes a swelling which we call sebaceous cyst."

"And the treatment?" Simon asked.

"Removing it," I said and looking at the horror on Simon's face, I elaborated. "It can be done under local anaesthesia as an outpatient."

This was quickly arranged and done. Surgery was uneventful and, a week later, he was due to have his stitches removed. "This is a painless procedure," I tried to reassure Simon. As happens with most of my patients, Simon was not convinced. So, to divert his mind from his perceived fear of pain, written all over his face, I engaged him in a conversation which proved profitable to us both. While I was removing his stitches, I picked his brain on stocks and shares. "As a full time surgeon, with a young family to support, one never has enough money to invest," I said. "Also one is scared of riding into the unknown without expert guidance," I added. "Having now plunged into the rat race of private practice, I am hoping that in time, I may have some extra cash to plough in."

"Played cautiously and carefully, there is a lot of money to be made on the stock market," replied Simon. 'The people who come to grief are the ones who believe in DIY - do it yourself. After all, it is a science and we stockbrokers are there to give advice.'

"For which you charge a commission," I said.

"Only when we buy and sell on your behalf. But it is worth it because it's a minefield out there and you can burn your fingers if you are not careful," Simon cautioned me. "We don't charge for advice though," he added.

On his visit for the final check up, he brought the names of some public companies listed on the stock market. "They have a good track record and their share prices will appreciate. Since there is no capital gains tax in Kenya, we advise professional people like you to go for capital appreciation rather than income." Simon gave me free advice, knowing fully well that once he got me interested in it, he would reap a lot in broker's commission.

Thus started a long, healthy barter relationship. I became his adviser on everything medical and he became my sole stock broker with both of us receiving hefty discounts from each other on our respective professional fees. So naturally, when his wife Eunice became pregnant, he asked me to recommend a good obstetrician and I gave him the name of Dr. Mati. The pregnancy progressed very well under his antenatal care and, whenever I saw Eunice in the hospital for various tests and visits to her obstetrician, I would tease her. "Pregnancy suits you. We must find some way of keeping you perpetually pregnant!"

"Simon will shoot you if you do! He is already finding this one cumbersome," she replied, her face bashfully breaking into a million-dollar smile.

High intelligence fused with profound love

It, therefore, came as a shock when, one early morning, Dr. Mati informed me that Eunice needed a Caesarean section. "There is cephalo-pelvic disproportion," he added meaning that the head was too large for the normal pelvic passage. In view of my close relationship with Eunice and Simon, I joined Dr. Mati in the operating theatre. I was horrified to see that the problem was caused by the newborn's abnormally large head caused by hydrocephalus, otherwise known as 'water on the brain'. To explain the condition in lay terms, the brain normally secretes cerebro-spinal fluid which circulates under the coverings of the brain and spinal cord. This fluid has a normal channel of circulation, absorption and elimination. If this channel is blocked at any point, the fluid collects inside, expanding and enlarging the baby's soft skull to the outside and inwardly pressing on the brain and shrinking it. The latter can hamper brain development.

And so began a long and sad medical journey for the young couple and their lovely daughter, Susanne. "There is an operation whereby a chamber of the brain is connected to a chamber of the heart so as to drain the fluid and bypass the obstruction," I informed them. "If you like, I can arrange for the surgery during Prof. Borthwick's next visit to Nairobi. One never knows how much good the operation will do, but it's supposed to cut down the size of the head and let the brain grow." As on previous occasions, they took my advice without hesitation.

Surgery, appropriately called shunting, involved connecting the two chambers, one in the brain and the other in the heart by a tube with a special valve mechanism which allowed the fluid to flow in one direction only – from the brain to the heart. If, by any chance, it reversed its flow, the valve would shut down.

It was while Prof. Borthwick was carrying out the shunt operation that he spoke those lofty words "This girl will be a miracle because I'm connecting the centre of her love to the focus of her intelligence." He was obviously referring to the channel he was creating between Susanne's heart and brain.

Over the years, my portfolio with Simon was growing fast and so was Susanne. Like the missed heart beats, I developed when the market changed from bullish to bearish, Simon and Eunice kept worrying as Susanne grew. "The world is so competitive these days and people with high IQs have difficulty in making a career. So, if Susanne's brain doesn't develop well, what will she do?" Simon lamented to me.

"And to make matters worse," Eunice expressed her fears. "She has to find a husband. Who will look at her if she has a huge disfigured head with very little brain inside?"

"She might not grow to be Madame Curie," I said to Simon, "but I doubt she will be left with serious mental deficiency," I said to Eunice. "When I see some eminent people's wives, I have noticed that they were neither picked for their intelligence nor for their beauty!"

In the meantime, Susanne grew normally, quite oblivious to the grumblings about her and around her. All her milestones were naturally delayed but she arrived there. Better late than never seemed to be her life slogan. She crawled, sat, stood, walked, and talked later than other children. However, when she did, she carried them out quite well. After surgery her head stopped growing and as she grew, the asymmetry of her big head with her small face disappeared. In fact, she developed a lovely face and figure. Academically too, she was in the middle stream as it were. She scraped through her eleven plus which was the mode of primary education then and, eventually, obtained seven in 'O' levels. Eunice was very keen that her daughter should proceed to 'A' levels. "I want her to be a doctor like

High intelligence fused with profound love

you," she said to me, "and for that she needs good grade 'A' levels in science subjects."

"Did you want to be a doctor?" I asked her.

"I did," Eunice replied.

"Is it possible that you are subconsciously pining for Susanne to fulfill your failed ambition?"

"Could be," she reflected

"We haven't discussed the matter with Susanne," Simon nodded in tacit agreement but added his own view point.

"It would be interesting to know what she wants to do with her life," I suggested.

"You know, because of our system of extended families, we don't appoint god-fathers for our children," Eunice said. "But we consider you as her god-father because you have known her and have been associated with her for as long as we have."

"That's true," I agreed. "In fact, I have known her since before she was born. I distinctly remember the day when Simon conveyed the good news to me when you became pregnant," I replied.

"Why don't you tell her what a wonderful life a doctor has?"

"I won't do that," I said, "because, as you know, one man's food might be another woman's poison." Looking at her crestfallen face, I reckoned that I had reacted badly. So to amend, I added, "but I'm happy to discuss with Susanne what she wishes to do."

To everyone's surprise, Susanne had a ready reply. "I want to be a physiotherapist," she said unequivocally.

Since 'O' level was an entry point in the US unlike 'A' levels in the UK, and since Eunice's sister had moved to San Diego from Nairobi, Susanne was sent there to do her four year course. That is when the miracle that Prof. Borthwick had predicted all those years ago started to materialise. She met a nice young man there, an Afro American, and fell in love with him. She kept both her parents posted with all the happy developments. Five years later, Eunice proudly announced to me. "Susanne has finished her internship and, before she starts working in the hospital there, she and Arnold have decided to get married. And guess what," she said, her big eyes eyes wide open, "they will have a civil marriage in San Diego and will then come home to celebrate a traditional wedding."

The celebrations were arranged over two functions, one at their beautiful home in a salubrious suburb of Nairobi and the other at one of the best hotels in the city. The former was adhered to the tradional Kikuyu where all members of the immediate and extended families of Simon and Eunice and their close friends were invited. The latter was a 'sophisticated' affair where all Simon's business associates and clients attended. It turned out to be more of a PR exercise and a marketing gimmick. Happily, Marie and I were invited to both.

It was the Gikuyu traditional function that fascinated us most. In our time we have been to quite a few Gikuyu weddings but this one was different. Even the Agikuyu found it interesting because it revived old traditional rites which older folks had forgotten and the younger generation had never witnessed. Since the bride was a local lass and the groom hailed from US, the ceremony was conducted in both Gikuyu and English.

The first one to appear on the stage was the master of ceremony, dressed in a traditional costume made out of animal skin. He called the friends of the two families to act as proxies for the parents of the bride and the groom. Then emerged the bridegroom, who addressed the bride's father, "During my last visit to this village, I selected a bride for myself. Could you please bring her here?"

The bride's father called his wife and told her what the boy wanted. "I don't quite know who he is referring to but let me

High intelligence fused with profound love

call some family members and he can tell us if she is amongst them," replied the wife.

To the amusement of us all, two old ladies dressed in long African gowns came on the stage for the groom's scrutiny. The groom looked at them very carefully and said, "They both are very beautiful but the one I'm looking for is not among them."

Another call from the bride's mother brought forth two little girls, beautifully dressed and walking demurely. "They are also beautiful," said the groom, "but the woman I am looking for is not with them."

"Are you sure you have come to the right village and the correct household?" the bride's father asked.

As the groom nodded, hiding his smile at the ongoing charade, the bride's mother came to his rescue. "Some girls have gone to the river to fetch water. Let me see if they are back."

Enter a bevy of six girls covered from head to foot confusing the young man completely and leaving him bewildered. He summoned his best man to help him and between them they identified the bride.

At this point the MC, wielding his authority, inquired. "Has the dowry been paid?"

"Yes," replied the bride's father.

"What about the animals?"

Responding to the MCs question, two herdsboys, accompanied by a pretty lady, supposedly their mentor, arrived on the scene. "Have they looked after the cows and goats that the groom's family left the last time they were here?" the MC asked.

"Yes," replied the pretty woman.

"Are you sure that that the cow did not have a broken neck or diarrhea?" the MC wanted to be sure.

"Quite sure," the two herdsboys replied in unison.

High intelligence fused with profound love

As the bride's father handed an envelope to the two boys, a Gikuyu lady sitting between Marie and me explained. "That's the fee for their services."

By now, all the 'financial transactions' were over and the MC said to the bride, "You are now a part of the bridegroom's clan. But don't forget that you will always belong to your parent's clan because that's where you came from. So from today, you should consider yourself a child of two clans and an offspring of two worlds."

The formal ceremony was now over and, as if to signify its end, food and drinks were served. On this occasion, Arnold was surrounded by family members and apart from a brief introduction, hastily carried out, we had no opportunity to talk to each other.

At the sundowner and dinner at the hotel a couple of days later, Eunice made me very proud when she introduced me to him. "This is the godfather that Susanne never had."

"Ah," Arnold beamed. "I have heard a lot about you from Susanne. She gave me her whole medical history and told me how you arranged surgery to treat her hydrocephalus."

"And what's your line of work?" I asked Arnold.

"I am a nuclear physicist," he replied.

I gasped. "That's a career that requires an IQ of 150 plus."

I was wondering how a high flying egg-head like him was attracted to a girl of slightly below average intelligence. As if he read my thoughts, he replied. "Yes, mine is a highly cerebral line of work. So naturally I was looking for a contrast. As they say, opposite poles attract. Susanne is so loving and affectionate and I fell instantly in love with her." He then took a thoughtful pause. "What better than a fusion of high intelligence with profound love?"

As I drove home, I realised that Prof. Borthwick's prediction had come true. The centre of love had indeed been connected to the centre of intelligence in holy matrimony!

9
The chicken or the egg

In the first quarter of 2010, discussions on Kenya's new constitution had reached fever pitch. The Committee of Experts had drawn a draft, which was then discussed extensively by the Parliamentary Select Committee, sitting in Naivasha. It was then brought to the floor of the August House for discussion by members of parliament. As widely expected, bitter wrangling continued amongst the coalition partners, mainly on the subject of the powers of the Executive – specifically about the President – and devolution. It was obvious that positions were taken, not on the basis of what was good for the country but what was in the best interests of the political parties. There were, however, non-partisan issues and the public debate on the proposed constitution revived controversy about when actually life begins – whether at conception or at birth. It also brought into sharp focus the related topic of abortion.

In connection with the divergent views expressed, I recalled the case of Dr. Carol Njunge. I had no intention of influencing the political debate nor did I want to be judgmental; I simply related Carol's heart-breaking story as it unfolded. In the process, I wanted to show that we doctors face the same conflict on a regular basis and have neither a ready answer nor a common point of view.

High intelligence fused with profound love

As the bride's father handed an envelope to the two boys, a Gikuyu lady sitting between Marie and me explained. "That's the fee for their services."

By now, all the 'financial transactions' were over and the MC said to the bride, "You are now a part of the bridegroom's clan. But don't forget that you will always belong to your parent's clan because that's where you came from. So from today, you should consider yourself a child of two clans and an offspring of two worlds."

The formal ceremony was now over and, as if to signify its end, food and drinks were served. On this occasion, Arnold was surrounded by family members and apart from a brief introduction, hastily carried out, we had no opportunity to talk to each other.

At the sundowner and dinner at the hotel a couple of days later, Eunice made me very proud when she introduced me to him. "This is the godfather that Susanne never had."

"Ah," Arnold beamed. "I have heard a lot about you from Susanne. She gave me her whole medical history and told me how you arranged surgery to treat her hydrocephalus."

"And what's your line of work?" I asked Arnold.

"I am a nuclear physicist," he replied.

I gasped. "That's a career that requires an IQ of 150 plus."

I was wondering how a high flying egg-head like him was attracted to a girl of slightly below average intelligence. As if he read my thoughts, he replied. "Yes, mine is a highly cerebral line of work. So naturally I was looking for a contrast. As they say, opposite poles attract. Susanne is so loving and affectionate and I fell instantly in love with her." He then took a thoughtful pause. "What better than a fusion of high intelligence with profound love?"

As I drove home, I realised that Prof. Borthwick's prediction had come true. The centre of love had indeed been connected to the centre of intelligence in holy matrimony!

9
The chicken or the egg

In the first quarter of 2010, discussions on Kenya's new constitution had reached fever pitch. The Committee of Experts had drawn a draft, which was then discussed extensively by the Parliamentary Select Committee, sitting in Naivasha. It was then brought to the floor of the August House for discussion by members of parliament. As widely expected, bitter wrangling continued amongst the coalition partners, mainly on the subject of the powers of the Executive – specifically about the President – and devolution. It was obvious that positions were taken, not on the basis of what was good for the country but what was in the best interests of the political parties. There were, however, non-partisan issues and the public debate on the proposed constitution revived controversy about when actually life begins – whether at conception or at birth. It also brought into sharp focus the related topic of abortion.

In connection with the divergent views expressed, I recalled the case of Dr. Carol Njunge. I had no intention of influencing the political debate nor did I want to be judgmental; I simply related Carol's heart-breaking story as it unfolded. In the process, I wanted to show that we doctors face the same conflict on a regular basis and have neither a ready answer nor a common point of view.

Chicken or the egg

Carol Njunge joined my surgical teaching unit, first as a fifth year medical student and later, as an intern. In both instances, she was like a breath of fresh air. As a student, though she gave an inkling of her real self, she was shy and hesitant because of her relatively junior status. However, she showed her mettle when she qualified as a doctor and returned to my unit as an intern. She asked questions on the ward rounds and, more often than not, she was not satisfied with the answers. She had obviously done her homework, having obtained the latest information from the journals and the Internet, and always provoked a healthy discussion. In the process, she kept members of my team and me on our toes. She did not accept dogmas and always asked for scientific evidence. I could see that she was genuinely hankering after truth and seeking knowledge. Her second attribute was equally endearing. She was hardworking and always around when needed. She, therefore, developed a warm affinity for her patients and, to her, they were not merely bed numbers but Njoroge, Liz, Otieno and Jessica. She thus became the darling of the patients and the nursing staff who all adored her.

About the end of her six-month internship, she came to see me in my office. "I wonder if you can recommend some time off for me to the director before he transfers me to the medical unit for my second term of internship."

"I can't imagine you ever taking a holiday. There must be a special reason!" I commented.

"My dad thinks he has spent enough money on my education and he wants a return on his investment. He's looking for bride price."

I realised that it was Carol's way of telling me that she was getting married. I was so pleased for her and even a trifle envious of the young man who was soon going to be her husband. In

Chicken or the egg

my heart, I hoped that the lucky man realised the value of the diamond he was tying the knot with.

The wedding was a lovely occasion and I had to drive a few miles out of Nairobi to attend it. After the church ceremony, we all drove to a large farm, which belonged to Carol's father. There was a richly decorated marquee, in which the bride, groom, both families and close friends sat. Marie and I felt very proud when we were escorted there by the colourfully attired ushers. There was another large canopy for the guests and one reserved for the *totos*. Long speeches were delivered by men and women from both sides – the groom's and the bride's. At about three in the afternoon, *nyama choma*, maize, samosas and, to give it a local flavour, calabashes filled with *pombe* came round. Just before sunset, the wedding cake was cut by the newly-weds and Marie and I decided to leave. From the mood of the assembled guests, I reckoned that the drinking and dancing would go on late into the night.

When Carol resumed work, her surname had changed to Eliud and she made sure that she was addressed as such. Just to make sure, I suppose, she incessantly kept twirling her newly acquired engagement and wedding rings as she talked.

Three months later, Carol, now working in the medical ward, came to see me again. "I will soon need some leave," she said bashfully.

"This married life seems to have gone to your head," I said teasing her. "You took leave between terms for your wedding for which I had to plead hard with the director. Now you are after more holidays. How am I going to justify it?"

"You won't have to," she replied, still blushing a little. "When the time comes, I will be entitled to it."

The penny dropped. "Are you talking of maternity leave?" I asked guessing that this was Carol's way of telling me, in her special code, that she was pregnant. "Congratulations," I said.

"I'm so pleased for you. I suppose, with marriage and family, the question of specialisation is out."

"Oh yes," she replied. "Mind you, I never had any plans. I just love to be with patients and specialisation would have put a distance between us."

There was a tinge of disappointment in my voice as I said. "You would have made a very good surgeon."

Our mutual happiness at Carol's announcement, however, was short-lived because, two months later, she rang me. "I need to see you urgently," she said.

"Come now," I said hearing the anguish in her voice.

Carol looked distraught as she entered my office. "I want you to examine me, please," she said and flopped in the chair.

"Which part of your body?" I asked, noting that her stress levels were atypically high.

For the first time, Carol smiled. "In your area of speciality."

"Alright," I said. "Take your upper garments off and sit on the couch. While you are doing that, just tell me what has driven you so fast to me."

"A lump in my breast," she said. "I discovered it in the bath this morning. I'm afraid I can also feel a tiny gland in my armpit."

I lost the smile on my face and realised the drawback of being a doctor. One knows too much of medicine to miss anything. As I examined Carol, the revelations of her disease were like an icy hand on my heart. Very little was spoken between us because we both knew. I tried to look at her face but she had covered it and had turned it towards the wall so that our eyes did not meet. As my student and intern, she was a bit shy and did not want to meet my gaze as I was examining the most sensitive and intimate part of her female anatomy. I carried out all the usual tests which proved that Carol had cancer in her right breast. She was 30 and three months pregnant – all poor prognostic signals. When it came to discussing the treatment with her, I found the responsibility too heavy for my lonely, stooping shoulders and called my gynaecologist, radiotherapist, and chemotherapist colleagues to sit with me. Since she was primarily my patient, I started the ball rolling. "Carol," I said, "you know as well as we do, what needs doing."

"I don't," she snapped. "I have lost all objectivity."

"Alright," I said, thinking that if I started the discussion on the premise that I wanted to save her breast, it might be less traumatic for her. "We can remove the lump and save the breast but you will need chemotherapy and deep X-ray therapy. In connection with that, I'm sure Dr. Olunya, our gynaecologist has something to say."

Dr. Olunya cleared his throat, trying to find the right words. We could all feel his anguish at having to say what he had to. "As you know all these treatments are going to be harmful to your pregnancy. To put it bluntly, we can't safely offer any of them unless your pregnancy is terminated."

"Are you here to obtain my consent for an abortion?" Carol sounded shrill and then added without hiding her indignation. "It looks to me that you all are conspiring against me."

Dr. Olunya ignored the cruel accusation and grabbed the leading question. "To answer your question, yes we are seeking your consent for an abortion."

"Out of the question," Carol said. "How do you justify it?"

At this point, our chemotherapy and radiotherapy colleagues came to Dr. Olunya's rescue. "To achieve any hope of a cure, you need both chemo and radiotherapy and they cannot be given unless you are relieved of your pregnancy. They both will induce abortion anyway and if you escape that, you run the risk of delivering a baby with severe birth defects!"

Carol turned to me. "What if I allow you to remove my whole breast?" Obviously she was prepared to lose her breast to save her unborn child.

"Even then," I said. "In our present state of knowledge, we would still want you to have adjuvant chemotherapy and possibly radiotherapy too. Also, pregnancy promotes the cancer growth in the breast and, to arrest that, the foetus must be removed from your body."

"What's the legal position?' Carol asked.

"If continuation of pregnancy is harmful to the mother's health, we are allowed to terminate it. That is the current legal position," Dr. Olunya replied. "Of course, to play safe I would have to seek a second opinion, which shouldn't be difficult in your case."

Carol took a long pause. When she spoke it became evident that she had fully articulated her thoughts. "What you are telling me is to snuff this unborn baby so as to prolong my life and give me some semblance of a cure?"

"I think it's wrong to call your three months pregnancy a baby. That puts our medical discussion on a wrong footing. It should be called a baby only when it's born because that's when life starts. Life does not start at conception; it starts at birth." The chemotherapist stated his view without mincing his words.

"How can you say that?" Carol raised her voice. "I can feel this little thing growing inside me. How can I bring myself to murder what my husband and I conceived with love? Moreover, I strongly believe that, at conception, my baby acquired the same rights I enjoy."

"Unfortunately, it is either the chicken or the egg," the radiotherapist spoke. "Letting the egg to survive at the cost of its mother is letting the tail to wag the dog. In my view, the foetus has no rights until it is born and its umbilical cord is severed.

Until then, it is a part of the mother and the part cannot be allowed to destroy the whole. What would the situation be if a girl was raped and conceived as a result?" he asked and then replied in a persuasive tone. "Let me tell you about a true and historical incident which occurred in England after the last world war. A young girl was gang raped by soldiers and became pregnant. England had the same law on abortion as we have now. The poor girl did not qualify for a legal abortion because continuation of pregnancy did not endanger her health. As often happens, a courageous gynaecologist by the name of Alec Bourne heard of her plight and openly carried out an abortion on her. Naturally, he was hauled up in court and it became a sensational case. It aroused a great deal of public interest. Finally, he was acquitted by a majority vote of the jury. His defence was that continuation of that pregnancy would have been detrimental to the girl's mental health. This case proves that doctors should be allowed to make a decision on medical grounds and in your case there is overwhelming medical support for termination of pregnancy."

Once again, Carol took her time and conveyed her decision and her reasons in very clear terms. "I will not agree to an abortion and will only accept treatment which is not inimical to my baby and one that does not stipulate removal of my baby from my body until it is viable. Secondly, our understanding of breast cancer is incomplete and there are many unknown factors in the equation. I'm, therefore, not fully convinced that abortion will improve my chances. Thirdly, my child has no say in this decision we are making on his life and death and no opportunity to defend himself. Finally, I have had a happy thirty years while my baby has not even seen the light of day. If it's a question of him or me, his right to live must supersede mine!" It did not escape my attention that Carol had even determined the sex of her unborn baby. To her, it was not only an individual; it was also a boy!

At that point, I thought that we all were getting dogmatic and emotional and straying away from the main issue. "We don't have to make a decision here and now," I intervened. "Let us sleep on it and meet again tomorrow. A good night's rest and a quiet think may lead us to a correct decision.'

As I drove home that night, I could see that the matter was not cut and dry. These were matters touching on law, ethics, religion, uncertainty about when life actually begins, human rights and above all, our private beliefs and our own conscience.

It was a restless night and I jerked up when my phone shrilled. It was Dr. Olunya. "Carol has been admitted with abdominal pain and vaginal bleeding. Her cervix is wide open and the products of conception are protruding. She's now a case of inevitable abortion and needs an emergency D & C to evacuate her uterus. I'm taking her to the theatre now." He sounded physically rushed and emotionally wrenched.

I saw Carol very early in the morning. She was crying uncontrollably and was inconsolable. I sat by her side to try and comfort her. "I'm sure my baby heard our discussion yesterday, felt very unwelcome and decided to commit suicide," she said between sobs. As I held her hand tenderly, she added. "He took your advice and gave his own life so that his mother could live."

10

Wedding ceremony or burial service

Surgery can be broadly divided into two categories – elective and emergency. In the elective type, the patient consults a surgeon for a problem which may have been present for some time. Classical examples of this type are hernia, hydrocele, breast lump or gall stones. There is reasonable time to examine, investigate, plan surgery and carry it out. There is enough space for things to move in an unhurried, deliberate and properly planned manner. Because of the adequate pre-operative preparation, this type of surgery is likely to develop fewer complications. It is, therefore, preferred by everybody concerned.

In contrast, emergency surgery is a different kettle of fish. In this case, the patient suddenly develops an acute serious illness. Typical examples are burst appendix, perforated stomach ulcer, acute cholecystitis or inflammation of the gall bladder.

The other group of emergency conditions is caused by severe haemorrhage, internal or external. Ruptured tubal pregnancies and injuries to multiple organs like the liver and spleen are good examples of internal bleeding where the haemorrhage is not visible. External bleeding occurs where a large artery of a limb is torn or a patient vomits copious amounts of blood or passes it per rectum from a bleeding duodenal ulcer.

Then, there are surgical emergencies which are manifested by severe pain as happens in colic caused by stones in the kidney or gall bladder and acute intestinal obstruction. All the emergencies arising inside the belly go under the omnibus term of an acute abdomen. Sometimes they are so severe, sudden, and life-threatening that they are deservedly called abdominal catastrophes. In all cases, certainly in severe haemorrhage and perforation of an organ, time is of the essence. There is no opportunity to carry out elaborate investigations and decisions are made mostly based on clinical judgement.

For these reasons, emergency surgery is more challenging and taxes the surgeon's clinical acumen and operative skills to their very maximum. At some stage, I was asked if I would like to be relieved of the yoke of emergency work. The offer was too tempting because this type of surgery entails disturbed nights and working during unearthly hours including weekends. It can be stressful, both to the surgeon and his family. There is also more risk of error and medico-legal claims for compensation. Along with a couple of other surgeons of my vintage, I declined the offer because I enjoy the excitement and the challenge and, above all, the very gratifying results. There is no greater satisfaction for a surgeon than to see a patient going home after being at death's door! I also felt that if emergency surgery can be served better by surgeons with long experience, senior surgeons should not shy away from it just because it is more difficult and demanding.

Over the last two decades, road traffic accidents have entered, with increasing frequency, into the complicated orbit of emergency surgery. They started as a trickle and have now become a torrent.

Wedding ceremony or burial service

As a surgeon who has been in practice for almost half a century, I have been called upon to treat hundreds of accident victims. Many survived, thanks to the surgical intervention but, sadly, we also lost a few. Naturally, I cannot remember all the fatalities that I encountered but the death that followed a road traffic accident on the Nairobi-Naivasha road a few years ago will be etched in my memory for as long as I live. This is because it resulted in unusual social implications and caused great repercussions on the life of Ngengi Mungai and the two families which were involved.

I met Ngengi under rather unusual circumstances. He had applied to a private charitable foundation for a scholarship to pursue his master's degree in pure and applied mathematics. I happened to chair the panel of trustees who were assigned the invidious task of interviewing the many applicants who had applied for the bursary. With the funds available, we could only choose a few, making the whole exercise extremely competitive. "Where will this higher degree in maths lead you to?" I set the ball rolling, remembering one of the important criteria laid down by the foundation's policy makers. We were enjoined to select candidates whose qualification would lead them to a self-sustaining career. "What sort of job would you apply for after passing M.Sc. maths?" I elaborated.

"I will teach Maths," replied Ngengi.

"Teaching is not a very highly paid occupation," one of the other trustees on the panel intervened.

"I enjoy Maths and I enjoy teaching. It will, therefore, be a source of double satisfaction," Ngengi replied smiling. "I will also do some research and, who knows, I might discover a theory which might change the world." He looked round and seeing us receptive, felt emboldened to continue on the theme. "As you know the theory of relativity, enunciated by Albert Einstein, had its roots in mathematics," Ngengi's voice sounded melodious.

Hearing this, one of the panel members introduced a new angle. "Of course, if you rise to the position of professor of mathematics, in theory, you could be within a heartbeat of the state presidency, as one George Saitoti did a few years ago!"

"That's highly unlikely," Ngengi replied, "because I'm not interested in politics. I am really a scientist."

"I agree with you," a lady member on the interviewing committee contributed. "Just today, I had an occasion to read former President Ronald Reagan's famous quote. He said that politics is supposed to be the second oldest profession after prostitution and it bears a very close semblance to the first!"

The interviewing committee seemed to be in a wickedly hilarious mood and I decided to bring it back on track. "Looking at your application, you come from a very modest background. So how did you manage to attain your B.Sc. without any financial support?"

"My mother has been mortgaging the family silver to help me achieve my goal," Ngengi replied. "The last document she handed over was a title deed of a tiny piece of land which was dished out to people like us before the last election."

Ngengi clinched the bursary due to his performance at the interview, his easy and endearing manners and his very high grades in B.Sc.

As per the rules laid down by the donor, thereafter, we received regular reports from the university about Ngengi's progress. We were impressed with the grades in his first year and he, therefore, sailed through when he approached us for a bursary for the second and final year. "I hope you realise that one of the things we expect from our alumni is that, after successfully achieving their academic goals with the help of our Foundation, and once they start earning, they will extend the same charity to those who need it. That way we all can perpetuate the vision of our Foundation." As chairman, I exhorted Ngengi at the final interview. We felt confident that he was going to comply if and when his fortunes changed.

I did not see Ngengi thereafter until two years later when we met under very sad circumstances. It was about 3 am when my phone rang. "I have a girl here with severe multiple injuries," Dr. Joyce Mbwana, the Casualty Officer said. "She was involved in a road accident on the escarpment, coming from Naivasha to Nairobi." Dr. Joyce Mbwana was one of a rare breed of trainee surgeons on my unit, studying to obtain the post-graduate degree of M.Med surgery and aspiring to specialise in general surgery. Rare because, when lady doctors look for specialties, they go for "soft landings" like radiology and pathology. The more daring ones plunge into obstetrics and gynaecology, presumably because they consider it an anatomically familiar territory! Few lost sheep wander into paediatrics – again for their sentimental attachment to children. Surgery, for some reason, has been a male domain. It was, therefore, refreshing to see Joyce break the mould. She was a worthy pioneer because she had the makings of a good surgeon – sound diagnostic judgement and pretty pair of hands – functionally speaking!

I was quite confident that Joyce could deal with most major surgical emergencies and was wondering why she was calling me. "I doubt if she will make it," she said as if she read my thoughts. "There are some special social features associated with the case and I need your endorsement before I give up." Knowing Joyce as I did, I did not want her to labour her point any further.

"Do all what is necessary. I'm on my way," I said.

"I'm taking her to the ICU," replied Joyce. "She certainly needs life support."

As usual, the Intensive Care Unit was a hub of activity. All beds were occupied, with patients attached to various gadgets, cardiac monitors, intravenous drips and oxygen tubes. To enliven the atmosphere, bleeps were constantly going on. Doctors and nurses were working round the clock and consuming mugs of coffee. With all the gadgetry, there was an almost robotic feeling in the place.

Joyce led me to our patient's bed. I read her sketchy notes, made in a hurry. Laboured breathing, deeply unconscious, pale, paradoxical movements of the chest, multiple fractures, blood stained urine obtained on catheterisation – were the essential findings. It was obvious that through these headings, Joyce wanted to collectively convey one message. This was to make the last few hours of the patient's life relatively painless and her passage out of this world as smooth and easy as possible. Having endorsed that decision and having put it behind us, I asked Joyce, "What's the other angle which you talked about on the phone?'

Joyce took a little time to reply. "The patient is due to be married next Saturday and the couple has arranged a church wedding."

Well, I have suffered a few shocks in my surgical career but this one felt like an electrocution. I looked at the watch on my wrist – it carried the date and day. The dawn of Thursday was gently breaking. "The bridegroom is sitting outside waiting to see you." I faintly heard Joyce. Her voice sounded as if it was coming from a different planet. I followed her like a zombie in the waiting room reserved for patients' relatives. I jerked visibly when I saw the bridegroom. It took me a little time to recognise him. It was the way his two interviews had gone which made the recognition easy. Without saying a word, Ngengi handed me an envelope. Inside was the wedding invitation. I read it and reread it. True enough, Ngengi was scheduled to wed the dying accident victim in two days' time. "I'm sorry Ngengi," I said, both my emotions and my words broken. "I don't think she will make it to the church."

Wedding ceremony or burial service

True and loyal to his pure science, the mathematician had obviously done his sums. "She will – may be in a different role," he replied, sounding forlorn but firm.

Joyce and I looked at each other as we moved away. "I don't know what he means," I whispered to her.

"I did tell him that the outlook was grim but in view of the strange circumstances of the case, I had asked for a second opinion from you. Based on that, he probably made some plans, while waiting for you," Joyce concluded.

We did not have to wait long to see what the plans were. The bride-to-be passed away the next day and I personally informed Ngengi.

He shed a few silent tears and then said. "Over the last twenty four hours, the two families, our friends and I have been thinking. We have decided that the wedding ceremony committee will convert itself into a funeral committee. The ceremonial funeral will take place tomorrow, which is a Saturday, the exact day the wedding was planned." He then turned to me and Joyce. "All of us would feel greatly honoured if you both attended the ceremony. You have played such an important role in the last few hours of her life and did your best to save her. The ceremony will be at her parents' home in Limuru." It did not escape Joyce's attention and mine that the burial and funeral were now referred to as a ceremony.

It was an eerie feeling to witness a burial conducted on the lines of a wedding. It was an odd mixture of joy and sadness, happiness strangely laced with tragedy. Residents of the area, famous for its lush fields of tea and coffee plantations turned out in large numbers to bury the bride, one of their own. Jessica was dressed in her bridal gown, net, shoes with bridal flowers around her. Ngengi and his best man wore black suits which, obviously, had been tailored for the wedding. Charged with

Wedding ceremony or burial service

high emotion, the guests watched the ceremony conducted with both dignity and gravity.

Finally, the pastor addressed the gathering. "This is the first time I have conducted a burial service which was initially planned to be a wedding ceremony. In our faith, when nuns take their final vows, we consider them wedded to Christ. Similarly, this celebration of Jessica's life is her marriage to Christ. Although she is not with us today, her presence is keenly felt, in fact, she is the chief guest."

11

Sharing credit with Allah

Most women who come to see me with a lump in the breast are on tenterhooks and the 'Lady from Lamu' was no exception. She was given her special title by my secretary who announced her unscheduled arrival in my office between escorting a patient out and ushering the next one in. "I have a lady from Lamu sitting in the waiting room," she informed me. "She has no appointment with us today but is carrying a letter from a doctor who, she says, trained under you. We have a very tight schedule but I told her that, if she is prepared to wait, I might be able to fit her in. Is that alright?" she asked.

"Of course," I replied, "if she has travelled all the way from Lamu and has a letter from a doctor whom I allegedly mentored, we must see her." Then, to humour her further I added, "Your lady from Lamu reminds me of Florence Nightingale, who was affectionately called 'The Lady with the Lamp'. She was given this endearing title by soldiers who fought in the Crimean War, in appreciation of the sterling nursing services she provided on the battleground." I could see my secretary looking harassed from unscheduled patients disrupting her well-organised appointment list of the day. She was, therefore, unable to register, let alone appreciate, my historical remark.

At the end of a long morning session, when she did enter my consulting room, I realised that the title of 'Lady from

Lamu' was very befitting. The lady in question was dressed in strict Islamic fashion, with a black *bui bui* concealing her body, except for her face and hands. On her bare hands, I could see intricate flame coloured designs left behind by the henna paste she must have used recently in preparation for a special celebration. She handed me the doctor's letter without saying a word. What struck me most was the date on the referral letter. It was dated three months ago. "Considering that you have a lump in the breast, I am surprised that you sat on it for three months before seeking treatment," I expressed my displeasure at the lady whose name, according to the file in front of me, was Maryam.

"Let me explain," she smiled to mollify me. "Initially, I was scared to death. By the time I plucked up enough courage to come and see you, the holy month of Ramadan was upon us. With fasting during the day and praying and reciting the *Tarawihs* at night, there was no time to worry or even think about the lump. Then came Idd and all the festivities that go with it." She said it all with such religious fervour that I found difficult to remonstrate even though I felt like telling her that in cases of breast diseases the prognosis depends on how early the diagnosis is made and how soon the treatment starts.

I took an elaborate history and asked her to go in the examination cubicle, undress and lie on the couch. A few minutes later, when I followed her, I found that she had only taken her *bui bui* off. In all other respects she was fully dressed! I soon realized that it would have to be a 'keyhole' examination conducted in a piecemeal fashion. Finding unusual features in both her breasts, I went back on my history taking. "How long did you say you have had this lump?" I repeated. Just as well, because this time her reply was more informative.

"Difficult to pinpoint the exact duration," she said. "When I turned forty four, a couple of years ago, I found that both my breasts had become lumpy. I went and saw a surgeon in Mombasa, who said that most women in my age group notice these changes as they approach menopause. He even gave it a name; I think he called it fibrocystic change. He told me not to worry but be vigilant and examine my breasts regularly."

"That was the correct advice," I endorsed the Mombasa opinion. "There's quite a bit of hormonal flux immediately before and after menopause and it can cause this condition. But it can also trigger something sinister, so it is better to be extra vigilant. A regular examination helps you to pick a different lump which might not be a part of the fibrocystic change."

"That's exactly what happened, Doctor," Maryam replied. "Recently, I found a new lump in my breast which stood out from the usual lumpiness. So to answer your question, if you want to know when I discovered this new lump, I can honestly say – about four months ago, a month before I went and saw my own doctor in Lamu. On the other hand, if you are asking how long I have had the fibrocystic lumps, the answer is a few years ago."

Further history was marked by the same perspicacity on Maryam's part. "You are right," I said as I examined her. "You do have lumpy breasts very suggestive of fibrocystic changes. But this lump on the right is markedly different," I added as I palpated the isolated lump. "This one does feel suspicious."

That alarming remark naturally raised Maryam's stress level and, as a result, she bombarded me with what I thought were irrelevant, hypothetical, and premature questions. In the process, it also became clear to me that she had obtained considerable knowledge on the subject, perhaps from the Internet. "Let's us take one step at a time," I tried to calm her down. "We need to obtain a firm diagnosis on this lump by doing certain tests."

"And what will you do if it is cancer?" she asked.

I thought it was an uncharacteristic remark on her part because cancer, in general, is considered an accursed term and shunned by most people when talking subjectively about their own illness. Once again I attributed it to her condition of stress. "We will cross that bridge when we get there."

I felt that in her present ruffled mood, any further discussion would only prolong her agony. I ordered the necessary tests and, as both Maryam and I had suspected, they came positive for breast malignancy which needed a mastectomy. I knew that she had many questions to ask and this time I answered them patiently. Once again she had obviously gone on the Internet and had also talked to various people and the main thrust of her interrogation was related to fibrocystic breasts.

"I understand that it's considered a pre-malignant condition," she threw down the gauntlet.

"I wouldn't go as far as that," I replied. "The risk of malignancy is slightly higher in a fibrocystic breast than in a normal breast."

"Since you are taking out the right breast because it has proven cancer in it, why don't you also remove the left which has potential cancer?" She came out with what was really worrying her.

"I think that would be an over-kill." I realised that it was wrong term to use in the context of our discussion and corrected myself. "That would amount to an over reaction." I now wanted to soothe her frayed nerves and added. "The slightly higher risk of the left breast developing malignancy does not justify its removal."

"But I don't want a bomb ticking in my body. It can go off any time."

"I think that is a gross exaggeration of the situation and out of all proportion to reality. Our statistics do not warrant such a drastic action."

Sharing credit with Alllah

After a long persuasive session, I shook her off her misguided perception and carried out a right mastectomy. The operation was uneventful and after completion of other necessary modalities of treatment, the long follow-up started. I saw her every few months. "How long will this go on for?" she once asked.

"We are friends for life," I said. "In the case of breast malignancy, the follow up continues until the surgeon retires."

"Or the patient dies." Maryam completed the sentence with a sense of fatality.

Thereafter, every time she came to see me, Maryam's left breast featured prominently in my examination and her interrogation.

"Are you sure nothing is happening there?" was her constant refrain.

"None at all," was my usual reassuring reply.

"I wish you would take it off and relieve me of my anxiety," she would insist.

And then she forced my hand. "A friend of mine," she said, on her unscheduled urgent visit, "had a similar problem– fibrocystic breasts. The one on the right developed cancer and her surgeon removed it. She begged him to remove the left side but, like you, he wouldn't. She now has it on the left and it has spread to her lungs and liver and she has been certified terminal."

There was no holding her back this time. "I have never removed a perfectly normal breast," I said.

"But it is not normal," she said forcefully, visibly shaken by this nasty turn of events in her friend's case. "It's fibrocystic and I can't sleep wondering what changes are occurring there while I'm asleep.'

I had no choice. I consulted two other surgeons and a psychiatrist.

The last word

"She will go mad if you don't remove the other breast," my psychiatric colleague said.

So I carried out the operation and all was well for three years. She had obviously developed cancer phobia and attributed all her minor complaints to her breast disease. On her last visit, she complained of cough. "I have this cough," she said, "which I can't shake off."

"Do you produce any sputum?" I asked.

"No, it's dry," she replied.

I examined her thoroughly. Her chest was flat with two fine linear, symmetrical surgical scars. "Most of my patients with breast cancer have one of my autographs across their chests. You were greedy so you have two," I said with good humour as I brushed my hand over her rib cage. While I did so, she identified a point of tenderness.

"This is your rib," I explained. "It can now be felt and is tender because the breast cushion is not there any more."

"But then the other ribs are not tender." She had her rebuttal ready.

"Okay," I conceded. "In view of the cough and this rib being tender, let us do a chest X-ray. It will clear our doubts over both the issues."

I thought I had very cleverly shelved the issue which, for me, was a non-issue in any case. However, the X-ray report shocked me. Appearance in the left 7th rib is suggestive of metastasis. A biopsy is strongly indicated. This in lay terms meant that there was a likely spread of Maryam's breast cancer into her rib and I should send a piece of diseased rib to the pathologist for confirmation. I had two concerns; Maryam and myself! She would hit the roof if she saw the report and my professional reputation would be in tatters. Seriously doubting the credibility of the report, I looked at the name and signature of the radiologist underneath. He had been recently introduced

Sharing credit with Alllah

to me as a new staff member in the X-ray department, relatively a junior person. As I always do, I looked at the X-ray films myself and was not convinced about the lesion in the rib. I went to the senior radiologist to discuss the films and he agreed with me. "That rib is perfectly normal," he said. But the damage had been done and my fears proved right. True to character Maryam had insisted on knowing the report from the first radiologist and he had told her that he was not happy about it, but that she should discuss the matter further with me. So when she came to see me she was tearing her hair.

"I have already discussed your X-rays with the chief radiologist and he is quite sure that the rib is normal and certainly has no evidence of spread from the breast malignancy."

But Maryam remained adamant that the disease was now widespread. "Alright," I said more to placate her. "Let's repeat the X-ray after a fortnight and review the matter."

"Let's make it a month." As she saw the surprise on my face at her wanting to delay it, she added. "I'm due to go for Hajj in a week's time and will be away for a month."

"Fine," I said. "Here is the X-ray request form. Please get it done two days before you see me so that the films and report are with me before you come."

As planned, she collected an X-ray request form from my secretary two days before she saw me and the X-ray films were delivered to my office a day before her appointment. As per my usual routine, I had done a preview of the films just before Maryam was due to see me. In this particular case, there were two compelling reasons. Both my curiosity and concern impelled me to open the large X-ray envelope as soon as it arrived in my office. I was a bit anxious too and wanted to see a disease-free rib, both for the sake of Maryam and also to preserve my own reputation. The gods were kind to both of us and the rib looked

The last word

perfectly normal. So when Maryam entered my consulting room, I was well prepared to brag about my expertise.

But Maryam quickly threw cold water on my idea. "I'm convinced that the first X-ray specialist was right," she asserted, "there was something going on in that rib of mine."

"So how do you explain the new X-rays which are reported normal?" I said sounding slightly agitated.

"I'm coming to that," Maryam replied calmly. This time the fiery, anxious, frightened woman was as cool as a cucumber. "You have to perform Hajj to understand it all. As you put the Ihram on and fulfill all the formalities of the Pilgrimage, you feel as if you are face to face with Allah. As you witness the Kabah being washed by the Saudi King, walk between the two hills, al-Safa and al-Marwa, do the circuit of the Black Stone, mingle with two million other pilgrims from all over the world in the plains of Arafat and pray in front of the Mount of Mercy, from the top of which Prophet Mohammed preached his last sermon, and finally start stoning the devils in Mina, you feel in communion with Him. So of course I wasn't going to let the opportunity slip between my fingers. I made a passionate plea to my Allah and you see the result."

"What's that?" I asked with my mouth gaping.

"He simply removed the metastasis from the rib and that's why the X-rays look normal now."

I didn't want to disillusion Maryam. She was so happy with her version of events and I thought that if I tried to change her belief, I would be committing sacrilege. Also, I did not mind if, once in a while, the credit went to Allah. After all it is not infrequent that He cures the patient and I take the credit!

"I have brought something small for you from Mecca," Maryam said as she got up to go. "Unfortunately, my luggage did not arrive with me but the airline has assured me that it will be here on the next flight from Jeddah."

"Many thanks," I was blushing with embarrassment. "Don't worry. Please bring it when you can."

Two days later my secretary announced Maryam's arrival. "The lady from Lamu is here again. She seems to be making a habit of suddenly appearing without prior appointment."

"Oh," I said. "Please send her in quickly. She won't stay long."

"I won't take too much of your time," Maryam said, politely declining to sit down. "Your waiting room is full and your secretary is a bit cross with me." She said as she opened the gift parcel and started handing me the items. "These are dates from Arabia. I bought them from a shop outside the Prophet's Mosque in Medina. They are for you to eat and if your faith is as strong as mine, you will live to be a hundred. The other gifts are the *Tasbih*, the Islamic rosary and a bottle of holy water from a well in Zam Zam. They both are to be used when you are confronted with a difficult problem like mine. Pray on the Tasbih and give a sip of Zam Zam water to the patient. They will work miracles as they did in my case."

Before I could even thank her, she had gone!

12
Severe attacks of the midas touch

As a writer and a surgeon, I have had my fair share of both writer's cramps and the midas touch. The former is a well known phenomenon which all men and women of letters occasionally suffer from. Contrary to popular belief, authors do not get inspirations. In fact, writing is a lonely vocation and puts the self-discipline of the scribe to the most stringent test. A writer has to lock himself into a familiar spot where one hopes that there will be a smooth and unimpeded coordination between the part of the brain where literary creativity lies and the pen or personal computer. In my experience, on some lucky days, there is an avalanche of words; they start to flow so fast that my pen can not keep pace with them! They are like revelations coming down from the creative imagination of an author's mind. On those rare occasions, I have learnt to strike the iron while it's hot and squeeze every drop out of my brain until it runs dry. As Socrates, the great Greek philosopher, said, 'Every time a writer dips his pen in the inkpot, he leaves a piece of flesh behind.' He must have been right because, after frenzied writing, I feel a sense of both, great achievement and utter exhaustion. At other times, I face a literary desert. I learnt, by experience, not to give up too quickly when the mind refuses to produce anything authentic. Perseverance sometimes pays off after a lazy lap, cramps might disappear with a surprisingly pleasant outcome.

The midas touch, on the other hand, only afflicts doctors. According to Greek mythology, Dionysus, the god of wine, being under obligation to Gordius, offered to grant his son, King Midas any request he might make. Midas, in his greed, requested that whatever he touched should turn to gold. The request was granted but, to his dismay, Midas realised that 'all that glitters is not gold'. He soon found out that when he tried to sip his usual wine, a cataract of gold poured out of a golden cup and when he tried to eat, he found a lump of gold stuck inside his mouth. Even his clothes turned into gold. In his distress, Midas begged the god to take back his gift. Dionysus told him to bathe in River Pactolus, which the wretched Midas did to lose his golden touch which had turned into a curse.

When a surgeon develops the midas touch without asking for it, the situation is worse. What he touches does not turn into gold but it becomes cold! I was advised by my seniors that when I develop the midas touch, as I would sometimes in my professional career, I should take a short break and not let a patient come within 100 miles of me! At the end, the midas touch would disappear as spontaneously as it came. I would then regain my clinical acumen and operative dexterity. My surgery would then be devoid of post-operative complications and life for me and my patients would, once again, be rosy.

My most memorable midas experience is associated with Ngugi, one of my patients. It all started with a lady scribe inviting me for dinner at the historical Muthaiga Club. The club was established in 1912 and is due to celebrate its centenary in 2012. She was doing a write-up on me and thought that an interview over dinner in the salubrious ambiance of Muthaiga

Club would induce me to readily part with my secrets. While we were on our first course, she decided to add salt to her French onion soup. In doing so, she accidentally knocked the salt cellar on the table and spilt some salt on the table cloth. She quickly pinched some grains of the spilt salt and tossed them across her shoulder. Seeing the bewilderment on my face, she explained. "Spilling salt on the table is a bad omen in my culture. However, one can exorcise oneself by throwing a few grains over one's shoulder."

Just before our main course was served, the waiter, in a white crisp uniform, approached me. "There is a phone call for you at the reception desk," he said. The club did not allow members, or their guests, to carry their mobiles inside the club house. I had, therefore, given my whereabouts to the teaching hospital where I was on call that evening.

"I have a man here with what looks like a volvulus," My Registrar, Dr. Opar, a senior trainee surgeon, said on the line. He was referring to a condition where the colon – usually the pelvic colon – twists upon itself, blocks its blood supply as a result and becomes gangrenous. "He is in bad shape. I have arranged an X-ray, ordered blood and I'm in the process of organising the operating theatre," Dr. Opar concluded.

"How long will all that take?" I asked.

"At least a couple of hours, sir. In the meantime, I have started him on IV fluids and antibiotics."

Since I was allowed some time and did not have to rush, I finished my dinner in a leisurely manner and gave the lady all the material she needed for her article. After dessert, we went in the TV room for coffee. Oddly enough, a funeral in Venice was airing on the National Geographical Channel. I was dismayed but after getting over the initial shock of being confronted with such a morbid programme, I got quite absorbed in it. I had never seen a funeral on water. A big gondola carrying a wreath covered coffin was bobbing up and down on the waters of the canal. Other gondolas carrying mourning relatives followed like cars chasing a hearse on the road. Traffic on the canal, however, continued unaffected. In other gondolas nearby, lovers holding hands were enjoying the view of St. Mark's Square, a couple of appropriately attired Italians, accompanying them on the ornate gondolas, offering champagne to celebrate the occasion and serenading them with music from their violins. Judging by the illuminations visible in the square, I surmised that it was evening in Venice, with the sky lit with beautiful colours.

My thoughts were interrupted by the dining room waiter. He requested me to take a phone call at the reception. "The patient's condition seems to have suddenly deteriorated and the anaesthetist thinks we should go in quickly," Dr. Opar sounded anxious.

"Fine," I said. "I 'm on my way."

As I drove to the hospital, the heavens opened up and there was a big downpour with lightening and thunder. My windscreen wipers, working at maximum speed, could hardly keep pace with the lashing rain. I had to slow down to a creeping pace. Near the All Saints' Cathedral, I saw an old man drenched to the skin trying to hitch a lift. Disregarding all security precautions, I stopped the car and opened the door.

"Hop in," I said, "where are you going?"

"Kibera," replied the man looking like a drip dry shirt left on the line to dry.

"What do you do there?" I asked just to get some sort of conversation going.

"I'm a grave digger," replied the man shivering in his wet clothes, his teeth chattering from the cold.

I froze in my seat. Salt spilt on the table, funeral on TV, now an undertaker in the car with me! Was I receiving a message in triplicate?

"I think the chap has perforated his gut." Dr. Zipporah, my anaesthetist greeted me with these fateful words as I entered the surgeon's changing room.

"Let's get into the operating theatre and quickly remove that gangrenous colon. He will feel better without it," I said.

"I'm ready," she replied. "He doesn't need much anaesthetic," she assured me. "He's halfway there already."

I didn't bother to ask her what she implied by 'there'.

Surgery, in Ngugi's case, was a difficult procedure. Inside was 25 inches of gangrenous gut. It was like wet blotting paper, tearing wherever it was touched. With great difficulty, we removed the dead colon. As we handed it to the sister and heaved a sigh of relief, Dr. Zipporah purred in my ear. "I can't feel his pulse," she said. Then a louder and more sombre announcement followed. "I think his heart has stopped." Undaunted by the most feared calamity which can befall a surgeon in the operating theatre, all of us, doctors and nurses girded our loins and quickly went through the drill laid down for what is called 'Cardiac arrest' procedure. Dr. Zipporah stopped all anaesthetic drugs and pumped pure oxygen full-blast into the man's lungs. I started massaging the heart by kneading on his chest bone to mimic the action of his lifeless heart. Dr. Opar lowered the head end of the operating table so that blood gravitated to the patient's brain to prevent brain damage while the arrested heart was not actively pumping blood into his head. The theatre Sister injected a barrage of drugs in the patient's arm to flog the heart into normal activity. All this happened in a span of 60 seconds but it felt like eternity.

Before my own heart ground to a halt, under stress at the distinct possibility of losing a patient for the first time in my career on the operating table, Ngugi's ECG, which was flat, started flickering. The waves on the cardiac monitor rose as did my morale. Soon, Ngugi's heart started beating and he came back to life. To me, crucifixion and resurrection were no longer a Biblical story. They were real and visible.

As I drove home, in the early hours of that morning, having put the patient in the ICU, I could not shake myself off the salt, the funeral in Venice and the cemetery – the unholy trinity I had witnessed at one go. As I put my head to rest, I thought that I had received enough punishment from forces that I did not understand, for sins that I had not committed! Little did I realise that Ngugi still had three shocks up his sleeve in store for me.

Later that morning, as I was reviewing Ngugi in the ICU, I noticed a tinge of jaundice in his eyes. "Looks yellow," I whispered to Dr. Opar as the retinue of students and nurses moved away from his bed with me. All the terrible causes of post-operative jaundice floated through my mind when I suddenly remembered. "How much blood did we give him? With the perforated gangrenous colon to remove and the cardiac arrest to boot, I lost count," I said to Opar.

"He received three units – all cross-matched on emergency basis."

"Oh well," I comforted myself and my staff. "It could be the blood transfusions in which case the jaundice will start fading out. Let us do his liver function tests just to make sure."

The results were a relief, but short-lived. On the fifth day, Ngugi sprung a leak in his anastomosis – the junction where I had joined the two ends of his healthy colon after removing the gangrenous pelvic segment.

One of the dilemmas of this particular surgery is whether to join the colonic ends as I had done or give the patient a temporary colostomy. The latter option would involve bringing his colon out to the surface for passage of his motion after excising the dead pelvic colon, at the emergency operation, then, after a few weeks, go back inside his belly and join the two ends of the colon. Finally, when the newly formed joint is fully healed, a third separation would be required to close the colostomy. Considering how strongly colostomy – even the temporary variety – is resented in our culture, and to spare Ngugi an inordinately prolonged three-stage procedure, I had decided to do an anastomosis at the emergency operation.

There were enough surgical indications to decide on that course of action and it was, not bravado or foolhardiness on my part. But now, the junction was leaking faeces and colostomy was a distinct possibility. We put him on the usual measures usually taken to let the junction rest and heal. It meant 'nil by mouth', intravenous fluids and a tube to continuously suck his stomach contents. Going by Ngugi's record up to date, I had little hope of success and Drs. Zipporah, Opar and I stayed with him, on the threshold of the emergency operating theatre, ready to pounce on him with my scalpel if his condition deteriorated. For a change, there seemed to be a silver lining in the dark cloud that Ngugi had thrown over all of us. To every one's surprise and delight, the quantity of leaked faeces gradually diminished and four days later, ceased altogether. I thought my ordeal had come to an end and I had been let off the hook.

On the contrary, it was not to be. One day before Ngugi was due to be discharged, a day I was looking forward to, Dr. Opar rang me at three in the morning. "I think Ngugi has burst his abdomen." He sounded very despondent. He was referring to a condition where the operation wound suddenly opens up and the abdominal organs spill out. "As you know, he developed a mild chest infection and was coughing. Just a few minutes ago, he had a heavy bout of cough and broke all his stitches. The Sister called me and I'm with the patient."

I knew Dr. Opar was competent enough to close a burst abdomen but I did not think it was fair to pass the buck to him

Severe attacks of the midas touch

in the case of a patient who was disaster prone. As a seasoned surgeon, I could weather the storm. If anything went wrong after Opar's surgery, it would be a nip in the bud in the career of a budding surgeon. I struggled out of bed and wearily drove to the hospital. En route, I was praying that there would be no rain, no thunder, no lightening and above all, no grave digger from Kibera waiting for a lift! In the theater, I was met by Dr. Zipporah. "Chap is not giving up. Is he?" she remarked.

"Now you know why a majority of surgeons die from heart attacks. This chap has certainly caused a few clots in my coronaries," I said.

I met Ngugi in the anaesthetic room and he seemed to be quite unaffected by all these complications. In fact, he was grinning from ear to ear, as if he was sadistically enjoying the experience. As Dr. Zipporah pumped Pentothal in his vein, he waved at me. I was wondering what that unusual gesture from a patient portended. Was he waving a goodbye? This time my fears were unfounded. His wave proved innocuous because the repair of his burst abdomen, in contrast to the first operation, was uneventful. As we came out of the theatre, a new dawn was breaking. "I hope this new day heralds a new surgical course for this poor patient," I mused.

"And for us too," remarked Dr. Zipporah.

It did but, by then, I had had enough. I was now convinced, beyond reasonable doubt, that I was suffering from a severe attack of the midas touch. I remembered the advice of my 'elders' when I was a surgical *toto*. It was time to take a break. Luckily, Easter was round the corner. I got home and said to Marie. "Let's go to Mombasa for Easter."

"That's two days from now," she reminded me. "We have no flights booked and no hotel reserved. In all my 50 plus years with you, you have never made such a rash decision. You book your flights and hotel a year in advance. You pack your suitcase at least a month before."

"Extreme situations call for extreme measures and sometimes exception proves the rule," I said. "We can drive. I'm told Mombasa Road is now in good shape except for a small patch from Athi River to the Machakos turn-off. It would be a nice experience and a happy reminder of our younger days when we packed the kids in the back of the car and drove to Mombasa. As for the hotel, the manager of our favourite North Beach resort has often told me that he would move out of his house if we suddenly arrived and the hotel was full. It would be nice to check him out!"

We were at the coast in no time, trying to shed off the midas touch. A patient would have to travel three hundred miles to see me. I was thus completely out of danger! This was three times the distance recommended by my seniors, when they advised me, many years ago, on how to get rid of the malignant midas touch. The hotel was full except for the presidential suite, which the manager unhesitatingly allocated to us without charging us extra when he heard my story.

I swam morning and evening during our stay at the coast hoping that it would work like midas' dip in River Pactolus, which he took to wash off his curse. I relaxed and tried to unclog my coronaries. I enjoyed writing this blow-by-blow account of my safari to hell in Ngugi's company! Obviously, he found it too hot and came back!

13

Arresting a population explosion

Eliud was about ten when his parents brought him to see me. To this day, I can clearly visualise the expression on their faces. There was a shade of embarrassment on the couple's face. The reason dawned on me when I started asking questions as to what surgical problem had driven them to see me. I can also vividly remember the little boy that Eliud was at the time. He was shy, a little underdeveloped for his age with childlike innocence written all over his face, and a bit unsure as he stared at my white coat. When I said hello and greeted him, he asked. "Are you going to give me an injection?"

"I don't give injections," I replied. "In fact I haven't given an injection for so long, I wouldn't know how to give one." He, still, continued looking at me with deep suspicion. "Just look round," I said. "Can you see a needle or a syringe anywhere?" He looked round and not seeing any of the two items, he felt a little reassured. "Now tell me what is wrong with you," I said.

My question was greeted with stony silence. I repeated my question and addressed it to all three, hoping that one of them would respond. Instead I saw Eliud's eyes glued to the floor, the mother coyly looking at the ceiling and the poor father left holding my question. I could see that both the parents and Eliud felt shy to mention the complaint, which had brought them to my office. After an interminable silence, the father spoke. "It would be easier if you looked at the problem rather than us talking about it."

"Alright," I said to Eliud. "Go behind the screen and let me examine you." Not knowing his complaint, I was wondering which part of his anatomy I should focus on. I needn't have worried because as I went behind the screen, I saw Eliud literally with his pants down, exposing the site of his pathology. As I was silently absorbing it all, the parents joined me.

"He was born like this," the mother said. I was now in full possession of the diagnosis because it was staring me in the face. Eliud's scrotum was empty and underdeveloped and his tiny curled penis was lying like a shrivelled worm on the sharply defined scrotal raphe. There was no sign of a testicle on either side. I felt the scrotal bag and confirmed that the testes were not in their usual place. I then, carefully, palpated both his groins and could feel tiny lumps in the middle on both sides. They were oval soft and tender, a finding which drove me to the conclusion that Eliud was a case of undescended testes, with the testes lying in the groin. They had descended up to that point where, for some reason, their descent was arrested.

"Cough please," I said to the *toto*. As he complied readily and vigorously, I could see small swellings appearing in both his groins. They confirmed the clinical diagnosis of hernias which usually accompany undescended testes.

"If he was born like this," I asked, "why did you wait so long before bringing him to see me?"

"Well," the father explained. "We heard so many views on the subject, traditional and otherwise. First we were told that it is a curse and we must exorcise the boy. Then the local herbalist gave us herbs to apply on the scrotum. "These will entice the testes to come down," he said. Another person said that we had given him a wrong name. He should not be called Eliud but should have been christened Alice, implying that he was in fact a girl. A doctor in the local hospital advised us to wait. She said that, at puberty, the testes will grow and will fall down in the right place by gravity." The father continued. "In the meantime Eliud was having problems at school. He became withdrawn and morose and first we thought that he didn't like school and contemplated changing it. But then we realised that he worked very hard at his homework and brought excellent results in his exams." The mother was watching her husband intensely as he related the problem with some empathy. "I, therefore, tried to take him into my confidence," the father continued. "After a long time, he came out with it. He was being teased by his classmates because, in the changing room, the difference in the appearance of his scrotum from other boys of his age was pretty obvious."

"It was my mother, Eliud's grandma, who brought the matter to a head." The mother intervened with some pride in her voice at the fact that the old granny really put them on the right track. "Recently, when we celebrated Eliud's tenth birthday, she told us; 'If nothing has happened until now, nothing will happen even if we waited for a hundred years,' she said, 'we need to do something about it.'"

"We went to the local doctor, who was your student, and he asked us to come and consult you." The father concluded the story.

"Fine," I said. "Let me now explain the surgical side of the problem to you so that you can take informed interest in your son's illness." Judging by the healthy curiosity on their faces, I thought I owed the parents some medical explanation of their son's condition. "The testes develop higher up near the kidneys when the male baby is developing in his mother's womb. Normally, they start descending from about the third month of pregnancy and they are in the scrotum by the time the foetus is seven months old. Sometimes, one or both fail to descend completely. They remain high up, usually in the groins and fail to come in the right place even at birth. That is exactly what has happened in Eliud's case. I can feel both his testes in his groins."

"So what do we do?" the mother asked.

"We bring them down by a surgical operation."

"What happens if we don't?" the father shot the question.

"There are many reasons why we should bring them down surgically," I explained. "The most important one is that a testis lying in the wrong place does not produce sperms and, therefore, if both are left where they are, Eliud will not be able to father a child."

Suddenly I saw Eliud's eyes open wide. The usual curiosity of a boy of ten at the mention of siring children and his usual interest in the "bees and the birds" and "where babies come from" was aroused and I could see his ears pricking! "The sperms need lower temperature for their production than what is prevalent inside the body. That is why nature has provided men with a scrotum in which the testes normally dwell. The scrotum, being exposed to the outside, has a cooler temperature than the rest of the body. So for Eliud's testes to start producing sperms at puberty, I must bring them down in the scrotum now so that they grow in the right environment," I concluded and waited. Since no response came, I proceeded with my didactic discourse. "The second important reason to bring them down is the fact that an undescended testis is more likely to develop malignancy in later life than the testis in the correct place. "Finally," I concluded, "a testis lying inside the abdomen is more prone to injury than one which is in the scrotum, because the scrotum is mobile and can easily move out of harm's way."

Arresting a population explosion

The patience I showed in explaining the details paid dividends. As I have frequently noticed, in problems connected with children, the mother makes a decision and does so quickly. "Let's take the doctor's advice and proceed," the mother said.

"What does the doctor advise about the timing?" the cautious father asked.

"The ideal time to operate on these boys is when they are one year old. So in the case of Eliud, we are already late by nine years," I replied. "However, now that he's going to school and, as you say, a very keen student, fond of the school and brings good results, we can time the operation so that it does not unduly disrupt his schooling. When is the next school holiday?" I enquired, looking at the calendar on my desk.

"The school will soon break for Easter," the father informed me, "can we line it up then?"

"I think we can," I said looking at my diary.

"Now that we have decided on the date, may I ask about the outlook?" the father spoke again. "Considering that there is a delay of nine years, as you put it, what are the chances of Eliud fathering a child?" Looking amusingly at his wife he added. "I'm asking this question because my wife is too shy to ask but she wants to know if she will ever be a grandmother!"

"It's difficult to predict precisely." I wanted to be honest. "Ten years is a long time for testes to be hibernating in the wrong temperature. But as you know the testis is a lively, resilient structure and has a habit of bouncing back!" I deliberately said it all in the hearing of the little lad because it was important for him to know all aspects of his congenital problem.

At operation, I explored both groins and found the testes, situated quite high up on both sides. Surgery was, therefore, difficult and finicky but happily not hazardous. I freed each one of them, gently, lengthened the spermatic cord without jeopardizing the blood supply of the testes or damaging the vas

Arresting a population explosion

deferens which conducts the sperms. I managed to bring them down to the bottom of the scrotum. I then narrowed the tunnel through which I had brought them down so that they could not retract back where they had lain comfortably for the last ten years. Luckily, everything went off very well on the operating table and Eliud's post-operative course was uneventful. He and his parents went home happy.

As per our normal procedure, I followed him up for a couple of years. I was very gratified to see that the testes, having arrived in their normal and natural abode, put a spurt in their growth and size. As a result, Eliud's secondary sexual characteristics like the growth of his beard, pubic hair, genitalia, the masculinity of his body and the change of voice all developed quickly and with a vengeance.

I was a little sad when it was time to discharge him because over the years, I had grown fond of the little boy. I had also noticed an interesting change in the boy in that period. I knew the surgical benefits of orchidopexy, but was surprised at the psychological boost my operation had given Eliud. He looked more confident and walked with a spring in his gait. He developed a very handsome figure. I concluded that the shy little boy had turned into a virile young man under my very eyes. I discharged him with my usual valedictory advice. "You don't need to make a trip to come and see me any more. But if there is ever a problem, you know where I am." I bade farewell to him and his grateful parents and, as I closed Eliud's file, never expecting to see them again, I added with some nostalgia in my voice, "Keep in touch."

Eliud did, almost fifteen full years later. One fine morning, I saw this young man walk into my office with an appointment to see me. "Do you remember me?" he asked.

"The face is familiar but give me some clues, to help me make the connection." I gave my stock reply which I use when put under similar embarrassing situations.

Arresting a population explosion

Like he had done as a little boy, he started unzipping his trousers – with one difference! This time he did not even wait to be told to go behind the screen. His brazen exposure jolted my distant memory. I could see that his surgically descended testes had made up for lost time and the man was very well endowed! "And, sir," the handsome hunk of a man said, "the development is not only anatomical; it is also functional!"

Still staggering under the 'blast' as it were, I took a little time to regain my poise and, at the same time, study him. He was six feet tall and looked like an improved version of Sydney Poitier. He had acquired a Yankee accent and, as I discovered later, also their candour and confidence. "So what have you been doing all these years?" I asked him when I recovered my speech.

"Oh I did my 'O' levels here," he replied, "and went to Cornell University. Having done a basic degree in humanity as required, I went for a second degree in computers and I am here now as an IT expert."

"Have you self-designated yourself as an expert as many expatriates do or have you got a high powered job to prove it?" I was laughing.

"Oh no," he replied exuding self-assurance. "I have started my own business!"

"And how is it faring?" I asked.

"I can't complain."

"And how are your parents?" I asked.

"Sadly, my father died while I was in the US, but my mum is fine."

"Have you made her a grandmother yet?" I enquired remembering what his father had told me at our first meeting.

"Not officially," replied Eliud.

Looking at the puzzling furrows on my forehead at his brutally frank reply, he changed the subject and disclosed the real purpose of his visit. "Doc," he said sounding rather abrupt, "I'm in trouble." As I stared at him in dismay he reiterated the point. "In deep trouble."

"What is it?" I asked wondering what could have gone wrong with my orchidopexy operation, or what was ailing this successful looking young man.

"I have impregnated a woman," he said.

"What's so unusual about that?" I asked. "Millions of men help equal number of women to conceive everyday in this world." I was being facetious.

"But this is unplanned."

"Ah, now you are talking," I said. "Why did you have to go and do something like that?"

"I was only trying to find out if the operation you carried out fifteen years ago on me was successful," he said looking all innocent. He reminded me of the boy who was hauled up in a court of law charged with the murder of both his parents. In mitigation he pleaded that he was an orphan then!

"But there are more scientific ways of finding that out," I said. "A semen analysis would have given you the answer."

"I could have, but I took a biological test instead of a laboratory one. It is more interesting," he said unashamedly. "I now realise that your success has caused my downfall," he added. "What do I do?"

"There is only one honourable way out," I said.

"And what's that?"

"Marry the girl."

"I was hoping you will suggest a surgical solution, not necessarily an honourable one," Eliud sounded quite serious.

I do not quite know what actually transpired after that but within two months the wedding bells rang. I was invited and met Wairimu at the wedding. She was like a little doll, pretty and petite. Eliud was not amused when I wished them a large family. As Eliud looked daggers at me, I whispered in his ear. "The more children you have, the greater will be the success rating of my surgery!"

My blessing literally bore fruits for within ten years, Eliud and Wairimu had five children. Every other Christmas, Wairimu presented Eliud with a child. When Eliud came to see me he was on his knees. "Doc," he begged. "Push these testes up where they were before you interfered with them."

"I can't do that," I said.

"Doc, you have got to do something!" He then looked hard at me and confessed. "Five is only the official tally. You would be horrified if you saw the unofficial account!"

"Why don't you use a condom?" I asked.

"You know the analogy of eating a chocolate with the wrapper on," he laughed heartily.

"What about a coil or pills for Wairimu?"

"And lose control?" he asked looking offended at the very suggestion.

"Don't you trust her?" I edged him on. Not surprisingly I had become quite fond of this rogue.

"Of course I do," replied Eliud, "but why put temptations in anybody's way. You are a writer so you must know what Oscar Wilde said about temptations." Looking at my eagerness to see him quote one of my favourite authors, he added, "The best way to resist a temptation is to yield to it." As we both laughed uproariously, he continued, "I understand that women became more promiscuous after you doctors provided them with the means to control their pregnancy."

I could see that he was winning me over. I thought hard on the matter. "The only recourse is to tie your vasa," I said. "But that's almost irreversible and, at thirty, you are too young to undergo permanent sterilisation."

"Doc," Eliud said persuasively. "You have to judge the age of a person, not only by the years he has put in his life but also by the intensity with which he has lived that life."

"You know I have never done this operation for a person of your age," I frankly expressed the reason for my hesitation.

'In everything in life Doc, there is always a first time," he replied pushing a piece of paper across the desk.

"Here is the consent from Wairimu and myself," he said.

Having consulted a couple of my peers to cover the legal and ethical aspects of the case, I carried out the 'deed' with one solitary cause for satisfaction. I could not curb his promiscuity but, hopefully, I had arrested the population explosion Eliud was causing in the country!

14

A regretted delay

My life as a surgeon is quite varied, which makes it very interesting. It extends far beyond seeing patients in my office, conducting ward rounds, carrying out surgical operations and, finally, teaching and examining undergraduate and postgraduate students. In addition to all these assignments, which fall within the orbit of most surgeons who also teach, I am often called upon to make reports on victims of accidents. In this connection, I get a lot of referral work from insurance companies and lawyers to assess temporary and permanent disabilities in cases of road, traffic and industrial accidents.

With a disproportionately high fatality on our roads, and many more maimed and disabled, the insurance companies are inundated with claims from victims of various types of accidents. Naturally, the lawyers want to obtain the maximum compensation for their clients and similarly, insurance companies want to make sure that the claims are genuine. This is where a surgeon comes in. His job is to obtain correct history of the accident, confirm the injuries caused and residual problems left behind, on the basis of which, he or she can assess permanent and temporary disability and guide the litigants and the court accordingly.

In my role as an expert witness whose duty is to make an impartial assessment, I come across interesting cases. Due

A regretted delay

to human nature, the victims sometimes try to exaggerate the residual complaints or concoct amusing symptoms in an attempt to obtain a higher compensation than they deserve. In the process, they provide me with juicy tit-bits.

For example, I saw a young lady recently who told me that while she was digging in a flower farm in Isinya in the Rift Valley, she sustained a large wound on her big toe which needed 27 stitches. Looking at the size of the toe I did not think there was enough room for 27 stitches even if they were to be put like sardines in a tin. I let it pass and asked her. "What are your present problems?"

"I cannot wear high-heeled shoes because of the pain in the scar," she replied.

I drew her attention to her *maridadi* stylish, high, platform shoes lying on the floor beside my examination couch. "Ah," she explained. "I only put them on because I was coming to see you!"

Occasionally, insurance companies have to cope with prodigious number of casualties. In this connection, the case that takes the cake is a series of patients I was asked to examine recently. They were travelling in a bus which rolled over near Voi, on Mombasa Road, injuring all the passengers. Since these compensation cases are accommodated between my surgical consultations, I can only examine one or two at a time. It therefore, took roughly two months to assess 46 patients. I rang the legal advisor of the insurance company to ask how many more I was supposed to examine. 'You have already examined far too many!" she said. "The capacity of this bus, according to our information, was thirty two and that included passengers who were standing. Going by your figure, it seems that relatives and friends of passengers travelling on the bus literally got on the bandwagon too!"

A regretted delay

Over the years, I have found that one popular ruse employed by women is to complain of a miscarriage resulting from a traffic accident. The pregnancy is invariably of a very short duration and the abortion is managed at home – both happenings difficult to verify. They even have the temerity to bring supporting medical certificates. In a similar vein, men complain of another disability not easy to corroborate. They complain of inability to perform sex as a result of the injury. Again it is difficult to find a reliable witness to this very private and intimate activity. As one of my lawyer friends remarked, this disability can only be verified by the wife of the victim or a lady of twilight hired for the purpose by the lawyer of the insurance company. The former would be ruled out by the court on grounds of conflict of interest and the latter would be declared persona non grata!

Apropos of this popular trickery, I clearly remember Ogola and his impotency ruse. He almost got away with it until the bubble burst in the nick of time.

I was called by a gynaecologist to a back street nursing home in the middle of the night. "This morning I did a D&C on a woman who was admitted with an incomplete abortion. She was bleeding furiously and I needed to evacuate her uterus to remove the products of conception to stop the copious uterine haemorrhage. All was well until an hour ago when I was called because the patient's condition had suddenly deteriorated. I examined her and she seemed to have developed fulminating peritonitis." Having said it all rather rapidly, the gynaecologist took a tactful pause. "It is likely that while doing the D&C I pushed the sound too far and perforated her uterus."

Considering the seriousness of this recognised complication of D&C, I rushed to the nursing home. It was located in an insalubrious part of town and I lost my way a couple of times. I was met on arrival and escorted to the unfortunate lady's bed by

A regretted delay

her gynaecologist. Having confirmed the diagnosis, we rushed her to the operating theatre and closed the hole in the dome of her womb. Just before I left the place, the doctor requested me to talk to the woman's husband and explain to him the circumstances of the case. "Coming from a senior person like you, it will sound better and will be accepted without argument," he added.

So I did meet the husband and who did I find sitting in the visitor's lounge? None other than the crafty Ogola. He would have sunk in the ground if he could have found a hole big enough to swallow him. Not a word was spoken between the two of us. He quickly realised that he only had two choices, either come clean about his full potency or confess to being a cuckold husband. The former was naturally less embarrassing! Wisely, he instructed his lawyer to withdraw the case.

The story of Martin is not directly connected with an accident and, therefore, does not relate to either temporary or permanent assessment. Neither is it as hilarious as Ogola's story. Nevertheless, it is an insurance matter, more precisely, life insurance, where an inadvertent delay caused by myself was unforgivable and something I have regretted all my life.

Though I had operated on Martin more than ten years earlier, I could remember his case quite clearly, when he came to see me again, because there was something unusual about it. In surgical circles, appendix, hernia, hydrocele, piles, and other such operations are classified as common or garden type, and are considered 'bread and butter surgery'. The two labels imply that they occur frequently and provide the surgeon with a modest but regular income. Martin's hernia fell in this category and had no reason to remain in my memory for long. However, the special anaesthesia he needed made it a case out of the ordinary.

A regretted delay

His doctor hinted at it when he rang me. "The hernia needs repairing but I'm ringing you because there is more to it than meets the eye."

I knew it would be so because this particular doctor did not refer his straight forward cases to me. He had often explained it on the dubious basis that he would offend my seniority if he asked me to see simple surgical problems. "Martin suffered a very serious heart attack three years ago. Presently, he has a poor chest. I'm not sure if your anaesthetist would want to put him under general anaesthesia. He might be better off under spinal or local."

"Thank you for this information. Let me see Martin, then my anaesthetist and I can plan our strategy," I said.

A week later, Martin was in my office. On a superficial assessment, he had hardly any residual signs of a heart attack. What was more glaring was his laborious breathing. He was of medium build, a little overweight and admitted to smoking 'sparingly'.

"The heart attack was a big surprise," Martin said in his medical history. "This is something that happens to someone else, a friend, a neighbour, a professional colleague. But one morning as I was getting ready to go to work, I was seized with this terrible pain in my chest. It was like pincers squeezing my heart. I was in intensive care for a week and in the ordinary ward for another week. I was then shipped off to South Africa where I underwent a bypass."

"What about your chest?" I asked. "I can hear it wheezing."

"I don't know," Martin said. "For the last two years, I have had an occasional cough. My doctor calls it congestion and thinks that it might improve if I stopped smoking. Also, my heart surgeon advised me to refrain from smoking but somehow I can't shake the habit off." Martin paused and then added with a childish innocence on his face, "The spirit is willing but the flesh is weak." As I grinned at his literary flair, he continued, "It was during one of these bouts of coughing that I noticed a swelling in my groin and went to see my doctor. He took one look at it and said 'operation'. With my history of heart and present chest problem, I did not accept his advice. But, a fortnight ago, the damn thing got stuck and I had to call him home. He said he had worked with you as a house surgeon and had some surgical experience. He gave me an injection of pethidine and, after waiting for an hour for it to work and relax my groin muscles, gently pushed the hernia back. He warned me that next time we might not be so lucky and I would be faced with emergency surgery, perhaps in the dead of night. So here I am, frightened to death but with no other option."

I examined Martin. "There is no doubt that the hernia needs to be repaired but the crucial question is what anaesthesia to give you. Knowing this was the deciding factor, I have asked my anaesthetist to be available," I added. I then called her on the internal hospital line and she arrived from the ward where she was doing a procedure. She went over Martin very carefully in my presence and then gave her opinion. "You are not fit for general anaesthesia. That's for sure. It's not your heart which is worrying me but your lungs. So we are left with two choices. One is local anaesthesia, where we inject a drug at the site of the operation and make it numb. The problem with that is that when the surgeon comes to manipulate the intestine, as he might, you will feel sick and uncomfortable. Also, sometimes the relief of pain is not complete. The other option is a spinal anaesthetic. Here we inject the local at the bottom of your spine – knocking out all the nerve roots. You cannot feel from waist downwards but you are conscious and can talk to us – if you wish. There is no stress on your heart or lungs and a couple of hours later, your sensations and movements come back." I was looking at Mrs. D. Patel with admiration, due to the succinct manner in which she had put the matter.

A regretted delay

"But I don't want to talk or remain conscious," was Martin's first reaction. "I don't want to watch all the gory scenes."

"You don't have to. If you wish, we can give you a little dope and put you to sleep," Mrs. Patel reassured him.

Luckily, the surgery went off very well. Dr. Patel administered the spinal anaesthesia. Martin was attached to various gadgets put up by her and Martin's cardiologist. They made the operating theatre look like a high powered space centre. Though conscious most of the time, Martin was snoring under the influence of a sedative which Dr. Patel had injected. His post-operative progress was also uneventful. Because of all these special features, however, his case remained quite fresh in my memory.

So when, a couple of years later, an insurance agent came to talk to me about Martin's intention to take life insurance policy, I clearly remembered the case. "He has already mentioned his coronary disease and bypass, his hernia operation and his chest condition in the proposal form. We would like you to send us a case summary of what surgery you carried out on him and also the effect it might have on his life expectancy. We are writing to the surgeon in Johannesburg, who carried out his bypass operation, to send us a similar report, we are to get in touch with his chest specialist to do the same regarding his chest condition." I was listening very carefully as the agent continued. "Of course we might have to consider putting a lien on him because of all his previous illnesses and, perhaps, load him."

"What is loading?" I interjected.

"Oh," the agent gasped. "It means we increase the annual premium."

"Fine," I said. "The best thing would be for me to see Martin so that I can review him and asses the latest position."

"I will send you the medical form to fill," the agent said.

A regretted delay

"Once you have examined Martin you can fill it and send it to us. On the basis of what you write, we will decide on the amount of premium and then issue the policy."

For some reason, Martin delayed his visit to my office. When he did come, I was delighted to see him because he was in fine form. "Take your things off and lie on the couch," I said. Naturally, I looked at the hernia scar first. It was hardly visible.

"Yes Doc, you left a good autograph. It is fading by the day and I can hardly see it," Martin complimented me.

"You are very kind," I said. "Now cough so that I can make sure that the hernia has not recurred." Martin coughed gently and there was no visible bulge. "So far so good," I said.

"That reminds me," Martin said, "you know my chest is so much better since the hernia operation. I don't know whether it was your scalpel or the spinal anaesthesia which did the trick but I have no chest problems at all."

"Good," I said. "Let's go over your chest too." I looked at the vertical scar in the middle of his chest left behind by the bypass operation.

"Considering that they split my chest bone, I have hardly any pain there either. My cardiologist did an ECG for insurance purpose and he tells me that my heart is in top form," Martin continued talking.

"Good," I said. "It looks as if you might have to pay normal rate of premium."

Next day the insurance agent rang. "Can I send you the form?" he said.

"Don't rush," I said. "I am off to Cairo tomorrow for a surgeon's meeting. I will be there for a week so I will fill the form as soon as I return."

"Couldn't you fill it before you left?" he pleaded.

"I wish I could," I replied. "But I have so many patients

A regretted delay

to sort out in the hospital before I leave. Don't worry. Send the form next week and as soon as I come back I will fill it as a matter of urgency." On hindsight, that was a wrong decision and I have regretted it all my life!

The surgeon's conference was excellent. As usual there were tours arranged to see the Pyramids, the Sphinx, the Aswan Dam and a couple of days in Luxor. I returned to Nairobi on a Sunday and, on Monday, as promised to the agent, I wanted to fill the form. My desk was loaded with paper work. There were letters to sign, laboratory and X-ray reports to see, messages and a full day of booked patients as well. I scanned the desk for Martin's form. "Didn't the agent send a form to fill for Martin?" I asked my secretary.

"No," she replied.

"Typical," I said. "They rush you so that they capture the business and the client. Then they don't bother to send the form. Get him on the phone for me," I said quite ready to blast.

"Where is the form you wanted me to fill for Martin?" I said, omitting the preliminaries.

There was an interminable silence. "You are a bit late," he said as I felt a knot in my heart. "I don't know how to put it. All his documents were ready and I was going to send you the form. Unfortunately, three days after you left, Martin suffered a massive coronary and died on his way to the hospital."

"Oh no." I was choking. "I wish I had filled that form. It would have made a lot of difference to his young family."

"Well," said the agent, sounding genuinely upset. "We are also sorry for the family. Mind you, the insurance company has saved a large pay out," he added candidly.

"I suppose we all look at death differently, because it has different repercussions on each one of us." I sighed as I put the receiver down.

15

Divine retribution or poetic justice

"How did you notice it?" I asked the usual question I ask all my patients who have lumps in their breasts.

"Not the way your other patient noticed it," Sheila replied, her eyes darting mischievously. Looking at my quizzical face, she elaborated. "Sometimes in July this year, you wrote about a husband playfully touching his wife's breast and accidentally feeling a lump there."

Sheila and her husband, Roger, were our neighbours in Tchui Close, Muthaiga. The Close is a quiet *cul-de-sac* which faces Karura Forest. When we bought the property there, many years ago, the main attractions were the view of the forest and a stream running between it and our garden. We went to sleep at night with a lullaby from the gurgling water of the stream and woke up in the morning with the chirping of the birds. One could not imagine that three miles from the noisy business district of Nairobi, with its fumes and traffic jams, there was this peaceful quiet corner. We, the residents of the Close, considered ourselves very lucky to be living here.

In 1982, the peace of this heavenly spot was shattered. Immediately after the failed coup in Kenya, Karura Forest became an escape route and a temporary refuge for the soldiers who took part in the coup. As a result, it became a danger

Divine retribution or poetic justice

zone. Even after the forest was cleared by the security forces, it remained a den of robbers. They attacked the houses facing the forest, in the dead of the night, terrorising the occupants and forcing them to part with their valuables, sometimes injuring them badly in the process. Something had to be done to combat this nuisance and I took the lead. I invited all our neighbours to our house to discuss how we could work together to prevent these attacks or abort them if they occurred. We laid out an elaborate scheme. If one of us felt threatened or was on the verge of being attacked, the rest of the neighbours could be alerted by the traditional 'jungle telegraph' and jointly follow a fixed strategic plan to repel the robbers. The most effective part of our strategy was to press our security alarm button once we received the signal. Since we subscribed to different companies, within a few minutes, a host of security vans with armed guards would arrive on the scene, all ready to foil the attempted robbery. There were only seven houses in the Close and so, the project was easy to administer and operate. We made our joint security arrangements widely known to everybody in the locality and others so as to warn potential thugs that they would meet concerted resistance if they tried anything sinister. It worked. For all the years we lived there, no successful attack against any resident was ever mounted, once our plan was put in action.

We informally called ourselves 'Tchui Close Residents' Association and met every quarter, in rotation, in our homes. Though, initially, the meetings centred on security issues, in time, they became a social get-together. The quarterly lunch meetings created a bond of common interest, brought us all closer together and such frivolity, as Sheila exhibited in reply to my question, was quite natural. However, there was a tinge of sadness on her face when she looked ruefully at her husband and added, "Roger played no part in discovering this lump."

Divine retribution or poetic justice

I made a note of it and connected it to something that was common knowledge in the neighbourhood. "You doctors keep on telling us in the press that we must examine our breasts at least once a month," Sheila went on. "In addition, as a neighbourly gesture, you gave me a complimentary copy of your self-breast examination guide. Since then, on the first of every month, I stand in front of a mirror and carry out all the manoeuvres mentioned in your pamphlet to examine my breasts. I assigned it the first of the month so that I don't forget. Last week when I carried out my usual check up I found, to my horror, this monster on the left side," she said pointing to the lump.

In my usual history taking, I touched on the subject of her menopause. I did so because malignancy of tumours, modalities of their treatment and the ultimate prognosis differ in breast cancers which occur before and after menopause. Sheila was fifty-three but I had to ask because, with improved nutrition and enhanced lifestyle, these days girls start their menarche early and our women reach their menopause late. "The process started a couple of years ago but I still suffer from its ill effects like mood swings, dryness and hot flushes. It hasn't been an easy time," she added throwing a glance at her husband again.

I gave Sheila a full general examination and then concentrated on her left breast, checked the opposite side, both armpits and the hollow above her collar bones to check for any tell-tale signs of spread. I did feel some glands in the left axilla, the side on which the breast had a lump. I roughly put the size of the lump at 5 cms by 4 cms by 2 cms as expressed in three dimensions. It was rather large. This, coupled with the presence of glands, ruled out lumpectomy and made a mastectomy obligatory. I thought I should prepare Sheila accordingly. "I'm afraid this lump is likely to be malignant," I said, looking at the couple. "We will have to do various tests including a needle biopsy of the lump and the glands for confirmation. If they

Divine retribution or poetic justice

are all positive, as I suspect they will, we must be prepared for a mastectomy." Having got the difficult part off my chest, I waited for a reaction from them. None came but they both looked stunned. To soften the blow I added, "Nowadays, we can reconstruct a breast after mastectomy and so you shouldn't consider the breast permanently lost."

"You mean you will put silicon prosthesis in her chest?" Roger spoke for the first time.

"Oh no!" I replied, bursting with pride at the strides my specialty had made. "We have come a long way from there. Nowadays, we can construct a breast from the woman's own tissues. We use either the muscle covering her belly or a muscle on the back to obtain the mass, swing it where the mastectomy scar is and form a new breast. If a woman opts for the belly muscle, she gets a tummy tuck as well." I sounded like a car salesman, throwing in a few extras to clinch and seal a deal. That closed what I thought was a very unsatisfactory consultation from the counselling perspective.

Notwithstanding that, Sheila's surgery and subsequent treatment went off very well. Whether Rogers was driven by a guilty conscience or by misguided information, I could not tell but he came to see me alone, while Sheila was on the chemotherapy course. "I have come to put the record straight," he said as he shook my hand and sat in front of me. "You must be wondering why Sheila was sarcastic when you asked her how her lump was discovered and was very disinterested when you mentioned a breast reconstruction." I gave a non-committal nod. "I didn't come earlier because I thought you knew. After all, in the locality in which we live, it's common knowledge." This time, I nodded in acquiescence. "There is another woman in the equation and there are three of us in the marital bed," As a writer, I was amused at the way Roger had put it. It reminded me of something similar Princess Diana had said when she was interviewed on British television. In her case, she had increased the pungency by adding that, as a result, the bed was overcrowded!

"It all started when Sheila started the change," Roger continued. "As she mentioned to you, we went through a difficult phase and she drove me into the welcoming arms of another woman, who happened to be my secretary." As Roger looked at my curious eyes, he went on. "It's an old story; as old as the hills. Husband frustrated by wife, cries on the shoulder of his secretary who is in the right place at the right time and willingly gives him what he needs and is sorely missing. Stressed politicians and high powered executives all suffer from it and succumb to the readily available therapy." He went on the defensive. "You will be glad to know, however, that, even in my infidelity, I follow the Islamic injunction which allows more than one wife provided they are all treated equally. Believe it or not, it's possible for a man to divide his love equally between two women. I have provided a house to Lynda with all the luxuries that Sheila enjoys – same furniture, same brand of car and same number of servants." He got excited about how fair he was, thumped the table and raised his voice. "Parity is the watchword in my dealings with the two women in my life, both of whom I love equally with all my heart." His mood suddenly changed as he added, "Lynda is very happy with the arrangement but Sheila has not accepted the situation and never will. To her, Lynda is an intruder."

"You can't blame her," I spoke at last and jumped to Sheila's defence. "She is your first wife and it's natural and normal for her to consider your mistress an intruder."

I thought my stern rejoinder had brought the meeting to a close. Instead, with some embarrassment on his face, Roger pulled his chair close to mine and popped the question which had obviously been troubling him. "Is there a danger that I might transmit Sheila's disease to Lynda?" As I was wondering what he meant, he elaborated. "I cohabit with both these women wholeheartedly and if I might add, with equal zest and wanted to be sure that I couldn't be carrying the disease from one to the other."

"None at all," I replied. "There is no proof that breast cancer can be transmitted from one woman to another through a common partner."

"So you think Lynda is safe?" Roger asked to seek confirmation.

"No woman is safe from this disease as long as she has breasts. Every woman carries the risk of breast cancer. But if Lynda does get it, rest assured neither Sheila nor you can be held responsible for it, certainly not on medical grounds."

Sheila's chemotherapy and radiotherapy courses were uneventful except for her loss of hair as a side effect of the former. She invested in colourful head scarves, caps and hats. She did not care much for the wigs I suggested, though she did use them for special occasions. The whole treatment lasted for about a year and, once it was over, things moved on normally and she only came to see me for routine periodic check-ups. We met regularly at the neighbours' meetings and behaved with each other as if nothing had happened until three years later when Roger rang me. "I didn't think that lightening hits the same house twice," he said in an agitated voice. "I must be an exception because Lynda has felt a lump in her breast.'

A couple of days later, Lynda was in my office. From her appearance, I could see that she was a superb blend of secretarial efficiency and elegance. "How did you notice the lump?" I posed my stock question.

"It was not me. It was Roger who felt it," she replied bashfully, looking at him.

Divine retribution or poetic justice

Once again, I obtained all the relevant details and examined her. As she was dressing up, I wrote my notes: *Suspicious lump; left breast, 5 cms by 3 cms, hard, nodular, tethered to the skin. Can feel a couple of glands in the left axilla.*

As I wrote and drew a diagram to depict the clinical picture, as I always do, it dawned on me that my findings on Lynda were identical with those on Sheila three years ago. I gave the same advice to Lynda as I had given to Sheila and it was equally readily accepted.

Lynda's mastectomy was a success. The detailed histological and hormonal results on her breast specimen indicated that she also required chemotherapy and radiotherapy exactly as her unofficial co-wife had needed. She, too, lost her hair after chemotherapy but, in contrast to Sheila, she bought all the fashionable wigs in the market and used them to maximum advantage. "I have always wanted to try them but never had the urge or the desire. Now that they are forced on me, I have to make the most of them and try all the ones available in the market. My darling Roger doesn't mind paying the exorbitant cost, especially of the different ethnic varieties and the imported ones." Every time she came to see me, she had a different one on and seemed to enjoy the change and the surprise she gave to me and others. I could now see why mistresses have an edge over wives and how they highjack husbands!

Over the next few months, I saw Lynda frequently. In the course of it, she lost her reserve and fear which was very obvious in the earlier part of our surgeon patient relationship. In time, she was ready to touch on the subject of her illicit liaison with Roger. I'm not sure if it was her guilty conscience which impelled her to open up. Whatever it was, I found it fascinating. "You know mistresses are not given the credit they deserve," she said. I realised that Roger had obviously told her what he had told me about her. "Instead of being called marriage wreckers, we should be called marriage rescuers. People like Roger would walk out on their wives were it not for the escape route and the refreshing change we provide. They are thus able to put up with the dull and, sometimes even, unhappy lives they lead with their wives. That way, the wife usually lives in the lifestyle she is accustomed to. She only shares him but does not lose him. In the process, he makes a spinster like me happy. The only difference is that the marital bed becomes overcrowded but nobody is pushed away and there is no need for anyone to fall off either!"

This was a totally new perspective on marital infidelity; I was thoroughly intrigued and equally entertained. More importantly, the trauma of her diagnosis and subsequent treatment was mollified by this extra-curricular discourse, on a triangular metamorphosis of a relationship, traditionally reserved for two.

All the time Lynda was under my care, Roger's constant refrain was, "Please, please – not a word of this to Sheila."

"I'm not in the habit of carrying tales from a mistress to a wife," I said flippantly.

'I didn't mean that," Roger replied. "I meant the diagnosis of breast cancer.'

"My Hippocratic Oath has sealed my lips," I replied.

In the end, it was Roger who summed up the double tsunami he had suffered in his life in a very philosophical way. "Nature took a lead from me and took this matter of parity seriously, something which I had established," he told me when we were alone at the club. "Same side, same size, same spread, same treatment and same result. It's uncanny indeed."

I had a slightly different perspective. Was it divine retribution or poetic justice? Saddling the intruder with the same disease as the rightful incumbent.

16

A false canopy of good cheer

I was in the middle of an intricate operation when I noticed one of the theatre nurses standing opposite me, presumably waiting for an opportune moment to convey an urgent message. I was removing a grossly enlarged malarial spleen from a patient and had encountered some unusual oozing of blood. I had put a hot pack on the bleeding area and pressed on it with my gloved fist in an attempt to stop it.

As I was waiting for this commonly used method to do the magic, my eyes wandered from the field of operation and settled on the nurse. I was so engrossed in the urgent task at hand and ignored her beckoning. One of the most frightening things in the operating theatre is haemorrhage and arresting it takes precedence over everything else. Everybody working in the super-charged atmosphere understands and accepts it without a demur.

"Forceps," I said to the Sister assisting me, as I took the pack out and identified the bleeder. "Can you retract a little more?" I asked my assistant to give me more room inside the patient's obese abdomen. Having caught and cauterised the culprit, I proceeded to isolate the large splenic artery feeding the bloated organ and the equally big splenic vein going out of it. Commensurate with the size of the spleen, they too had

A false canopy of good cheer

expanded. I put clamps on both ends of the two enlarged vessels and cut between them. The spleen was ready to be delivered. The Sister held a kidney tray on which I placed the organ, which had grown to four times its normal size. I then tied the cut ends of both the blood vessels. It was at the end of this hazardous manoeuvre that the waiting nurse caught my eye again.

"Excuse me," she said, "Dr. Kamau is on the phone. He is at a city hotel, where a group of American tourists are staying. One of them has developed an acute attack of piles and he is sending him here to be admitted under your care. He wants to talk to you about the patient."

"That will not be possible for another half an hour. Please tell him that I will contact him when I finish."

As I put the last stitch to close the incision on the skin, the same nurse made a timely re-entry. "The patient has arrived and Dr. Kamau is on the phone again."

Dr. Kamau was a doctor on call to various five-star hotels in Nairobi, a few major industries and some embassies. As a result, he was a very busy and prosperous GP. "I have sent a patient with very painful prolapsed piles, for which I'm sure he will need emergency surgery," he said, "but that is not what I'm ringing you about. It's his other illness about which he has a letter from his psychiatrist in Pittsburgh." He then proceeded to give me a gist of the letter. "Mr. Newton, the patient has suffered from severe depression as a result of marital problems. He and his wife have now reconciled but he is still on a minimal dose of antidepressant drugs. I thought it was important for you and your anaesthetist to know about the medication he is on. He is here on convalescence for his mental sickness and is in a party of holiday makers."

"Thank you for the information." I said. I asked Dr. Kamau about his wife and children and fixed up a round of golf with him over the weekend. I then had a cup of coffee with the theatre staff, changed in the surgeon's room and walked over to the private wing where Mr. Newton had been admitted. As Sister and I entered his room, we saw him standing by the window, looking a little forlorn. Thinking that it was a sign of his depression, I said. "Sit down and tell me about your problem."

"I wish I could," replied Newton. "My piles are too painful." As Sister rushed out to bring an inflated rubber ring on which Newton could sit comfortably, I had a little time to study the man. He was in his forties, thin, slightly balding and had a constant twitch on his upper lip. The twitch kept recurring, twisting his nose into funny shapes. His eyes were set in deep sockets and there was an inconsolable look in them. His face went into strange contortions from the pain of his piles but was devoid of any expression.

As I looked round his room, I saw an IBM personal computer with a list of visible messages on the inbox. As he adjusted himself to sit on the rubber ring without pressing on his painful piles, he gave me his medical history. "I have had piles for a few years. They bled off and on but remained under control with laxatives and suppositories, until I had to go in the funny farm." There was a distant look on his face as he continued. "The drugs they gave me there and the shock therapy didn't do much good to my piles. They started coming out when I went to the comfort station but slipped back in when I had finished." His mouth twitched grossly as he concluded, "By the time I came out of the snake pit, my piles were worse but I kept them at bay with increased fibre in my food and application of decongestant creams." There was a painful contortion on his face as he concluded. "What with the jetlag, the time change and the food on the plane, I had to strain hard this morning and the piles popped out and refused to go back in. Worse still, they have become excruciatingly painful."

A false canopy of good cheer

"Would you mind undressing and lying on the couch?" I asked.

"You are not going to hurt me. Are you?" Newton said with childlike terror on his face.

"If you turn on one side, I will be able to see them." I reassured him as he reluctantly pulled his trousers down and lay on his back on the couch.

"Don't worry," I said after seeing the prolapsed piles staring angrily in my face. "We will soon put you out of your misery."

"I understand that it's a very painful operation," Newton expressed his fears.

"These days, nobody needs to suffer any pain after surgery." I tried to dispel his misgivings. "We have a variety of painkillers, both oral and injectable. In addition, I inject a local anaesthetic in the anal sphincter and that makes the post-operative period totally pain-free." Trying to humour him and relax the anxious taut muscles of his face, I added. "This special technique has given me the dubious distinction of being a surgeon whose piles operation is painless!"

In reply, I saw a wry smile on Newton's face.

I instructed the nurses to arrange the operating theatre for the afternoon and removed his prolapsed piles. The next day, when I went to see Newton, he seemed quite comfortable. "You believe my word now about operating on piles without inflicting any pain on my patients?" I asked, still trying to cheer him up. I could see that I had earned his trust. As a result, he was in a more communicative mood and I stayed with him for a while. "My companions came to see me this morning and made me very jealous," he said. "They had an unforgettable stay in one of your famous game lodges. On an early morning game drive there, they saw 13 elephants, 22 buffaloes, one rhino, a pride of lions, not to mention herds of zebras and giraffes."

A false canopy of good cheer

"Don't worry," I said. "You will soon be out of the hospital. Our game parks are full of wildlife and I'm sure you will see them all when you rejoin your friends. In the meantime, tell me something about your other condition," I asked him euphemistically. I was a little curious about his mental illness. Since Chris Bernard, with his pioneer transplant surgery relegated the heart, hitherto the seat of love and emotions, to the position of a mere mechanical pump, the human mind has gained greater importance. As a surgeon, I was more fascinated by the workings of the brain.

"My wife and I had a big burst-up and she left me." Newton started on his psychiatric trail. "The outcome of this was Newton going down in pieces. My doctors tried to contain me but to no avail. Thus, they certified me and put me in this mad house. The dope they gave me left me numb and I felt that I was walking in my sleep. Then came the shock therapy. They called it ECT, electro convulsive therapy, and it's simply inhumane. It was as if they were trying to grind my brain to a halt and then restart it in another mode. I went through dark tunnels and mazes of winding thorny bushes." His frightened expression matched his description and he seemed to be reliving the dreadful experience. There was that distant look again, the inscrutable face, that groping in the dark, that puzzled look and the incessant twitch of his mouth. "It was like so many trains arriving at the same time, a car running with one forward gear and four reverse gears, a plane taking off with its nose down." He then smiled unexpectedly. "I'm a mechanical engineer by profession, so you have to bear with my funny analogies." I sat unashamedly staring at him. As an experienced surgeon, I had seen every part of human anatomy, inside out–covered and uncovered. Today, I was seeing the human mind, un-skulled and nude. "It was as if the psychiatrist was trying to empty my brain of old wine and pour a new brew which would lead

A false canopy of good cheer

to fresh emotions and feelings, new ties, a whole set of new associations and connections. That electro-convulsive therapy was like changing from AC to DC, from 240 watts to 120 watts."

I could not help being intrigued by Newton's insight into the electro-convulsive therapy, considered a panacea for unrelenting psychiatric illnesses. Suddenly, I remembered watching the film, *The One who Flew over the Cuckoo's Nest*. He looked washed out as a result of his distressing narration. He paused for a while and went into a meditative mood. "Has your wife accompanied you on this trip?" I broke the silence.

"No. After my discharge from the loony bin, though my wife thought I was sane enough to cohabit with her, she and my 'trick cyclist' decided that a holiday on my own would do me good." He then gestured with his long bony hands. "Parting makes the heart grow fonder and all that Shakespearean jazz," he added derisively.

Sister told me that I was wanted on the phone and I reluctantly brought this interesting session to a halt. Three days later, I examined Mr. Newton and told him that he could return to his hotel the next day after I had visited him. As I left his room, a party of American tourists accosted me. "How is our patient?" they chorused in unison.

"He's fine," I said. They were all dressed as proper tourists with khaki shorts, colourful bush shirts and broad straw hats. Their tanned skin revealed their exposure to our beautiful sun. "He should be out of the hospital tomorrow," I assured them.

"Good," said the corpulent lady, "we miss him so much, he is such fun–absolutely the life and soul of the party. Keeps us going, you know."

"Great," I said awestruck at our enigmatic brain, so split and double-faced as it were. Maybe he was telling me the truth because I was his doctor but concealing it from other people, under a false canopy of good cheer.

A false canopy of good cheer

Next morning, Sister and I walked to Newton's room. "What a pity! The man had saved up for this holiday in Africa. He called it the holiday of a lifetime and was so much looking forward to it." Sister said wistfully as we walked through the long corridor.

"I understand they still have one more week," I replied. "Who knows, this may inspire him to come again with his wife and show her our beautiful country. They might even plan a second honeymoon at one of our gorgeous beach hotels."

We had arrived outside Newton's room and Sister knocked at the door. With my unfailing courtesy, I opened the door and gestured the Sister to lead me in. "There are still a few gentlemen around," I remarked. Sister went in first. Suddenly, she let out a scream, covered her face and rested it on my chest. From behind her, I could now see the horror that she had seen. Seated in Buddha style, Newton was hanging from the grill of the burglar proof on the window. I examined the curious contraption he had used. He had joined his belt and tie and hooked the buckle of the belt to the burglar proof. He had made a noose out of the tie and had put it round his neck. There was not enough length for him to stand and take his feet off, because the windows were low. So he had pulled a chair and sat on it cross-legged and then probably pushed the chair from under him. The chair lay on its side on the floor. He must have done it earlier in anticipation of my visit to see and discharge him. His face was blue and cyanosed, his tongue was protruding out of his mouth and I noticed a collar shaped bruise mark on his neck. I touched his skin, it was cold. I felt his pulse. It was absent. I put a stethoscope on his chest. I could hear neither heart sounds nor breath sounds. All I could hear was the Sister sobbing.

I saw on his side table, his personal computer, the first thing I had noticed when I came to see him immediately after his admission. A modem was attached to it. The inbox of his email was open. On his bed, lay a hospital brown envelope. I ripped it open with my hands shaking, and retrieved a note. It read: *Got an email from my wife this morning. It said that, after giving considerable thought, she had come to the conclusion that it would be in our best interests if we parted for good. 'Accordingly, I'm leaving home, which is now yours. In return, I ask you not to contact me.' She said in that fateful message.*

This has sealed my fate and I was left with no choice but to take my own life. Please don't shed any tears but rejoice with me because at last I am at peace with myself.

17
Suffering without bitterness

As I was driving to the hospital the other day, I heard, on my car radio, that, in an attempt to boost church attendance, a priest in Rome was planning a beauty contest for nuns. The announcer then added: 'The priest mentioned that nuns will be able to wear their habit and veil when participating in the parade, though he did not think that any of them would appear in their swimming costumes!'

Having treated so many nuns during my surgical career, I would have liked to be present at this unusual beauty pageant. This is the story of a nun who was referred to me from Singida in Tanzania by another nun who worked as a surgeon in the local hospital. I knew that there was a very large Roman Catholic mission hospital in Singida. It catered to the medical needs of a large population in central Tanzania and also carried out evangelical work. The surgeon-nun often referred difficult surgical cases to me from there and often talked on the radio to me about them. The letter from her, dated the 20th February, 1995, started with the usual greetings and then mentioned the patient. "I refer to you Sister Maria, age 57, who is a refugee from Rwanda. She has been complaining of pain and swelling in her left breast for the last ten days. On examination, there is a mass which is attached to the areola. I'm worried about a possible carcinoma of the left breast and I'm referring her to you for further investigations and appropriate management."

Having had the unique privilege of studying in a Roman Catholic convent school from the age of six, until nine, I have developed a great respect and affection for these pious devout ladies. In case my readers are wondering how I smuggled myself into what is considered an exclusive preserve of little girls, let me explain. When my father obtained admission for my sister into the convent school, in Mangalore in South India, he was so impressed by what he saw that he successfully persuaded the Mother Superior to enroll me there as well. I suppose he convinced her that at the age of six, I was pretty harmless to my classmates! I am very happy that I was accepted there because the convent inculcated in me some enduring lessons by which I have lived all my life. I still have very happy memories of my three years in St. Agnes Convent School and of the Irish nuns who taught me. As a little boy, I was intrigued by their ankle length habits, blouses buttoned high at the neck and large crucifixes hanging across their chests. Their kindly faces were framed in their wimples and flowing black veils, but, above all, it was their kindness, their caring attitude, their purity and their gentleness, which left a lasting impression on me.

Sister Maria reminded me of those nuns as she entered my office, dressed in her habit and wearing the traditional wimple and a veil over her head. A metal crucifix was hanging across her chest and she was wearing a ring on her right ring finger to signify that, indeed, she was a bride of Christ. She was accompanied by an English-speaking nun from the local church to interpret for us because, as it became apparent, Sister Maria spoke only French. After obtaining her history, I examined her and confirmed the Singida findings and noted more. The lump was ill defined, partly fixed and hard. There was one silver lining though, in the dark cloud. I could not feel any glands in the armpit, a good sign that it had not spread. "We will arrange a mammogram and a needle biopsy," I said.

"*Oui,*" said Maria in French, smiling broadly.

The mammogram and needle biopsy confirmed our clinical suspicion.

"I think we need to remove the breast, Sister," I said, looking at her expression as the sad tidings were translated by her companion.

"*Oui,*" Sister Maria replied and nodded vigorously to convey her acceptance. The fortitude and the patience on her face were a proof, if proof was ever needed, that she abided by the will of God. When we finished all the arrangements about her admission and operation, she said "God bless" as she got up. The effect of these first two English words she had spoken in front of me was profound. I felt like I had been blessed by the Virgin Mary herself.

The operation, on 7th March, 1995, was not easy. I did a mastectomy but as I came close to the lump, I found it stuck to the chest muscles. It needed sharp meticulous dissection to remove the lump along with the muscle sheath and a few muscle fibres to completely excise the cancerous tissues surrounding the lump. I explored the axilla even though I had clinically not felt any glands there. Sometimes the glands are too small to be felt with the fingers of even the most dexterous surgeon and yet they are found during operation. Sister Maria's post-operative course, her chemotherapy and radiotherapy which followed were all uneventful. During the few months she stayed in Nairobi to complete her treatment, Sister Maria used her time learning English and we could communicate much better before she left. I gently touched on her refugee status as mentioned in her doctor's letter. There was an expression of deep distress on her face and a polite reluctance to discuss the subject.

Soon, it was time for Sister Maria to leave. "The church has arranged for us to go to France because my beloved country, Rwanda, is still on fire with genocide," she explained. I bid her goodbye with a gurgle in my throat. On the face of this godly, gentle frail lady with, undoubtedly, a steely character were written the tragedy of Rwanda, mostly ignored by the world, sadness of her breast cancer and an unflinching faith in God. If I were to caption it, I would have used the words, 'suffering without bitterness'.

I thought that, like many others, her file would now go into my office archives, perhaps never to be resurrected. But surprise, surprise, at Christmas time, a greeting card arrived from Paris with a covering letter which said: *I wish you and your family a merry Christmas and Happy New Year, 1996. I do pray for all of you. I am happy here, getting better day by day. Thanks to God who makes marvels through men who help people. Hearty greetings to your secretary, who was very nice to me.* It ended with – *From your Sister whom you gave a new birth at Nairobi Hospital on March 7th, 1995. Sister Maria.*

I reciprocated her greetings by sending her a belated New Year's card. In December 1996, another Christmas card arrived, this time from Lourdes. *Dear Doctor and all the Family,* it said, *I wish you a merry Christmas and Happy New Year. May the Lord of Love fill you with His Grace as well as those whom God gives you to take care of. I am now in Lourdes and I am happy here. I go and see my doctor in Paris every six months. Thanks for all you did for me. I pray for you and do not forget you. Sister Maria.*

This time I wrote a reply. *Dear Sister Maria, I was delighted to receive your Christmas greeting and to know that you are well. I am so pleased to learn that you are happy in Lourdes. When my daughter was a student at Loreto Convent, Msongari and my son at St. Mary's School here, my wife and I took them on a tour of Italy. With their Roman Catholic schooling, they both expressed a desire to visit Lourdes* and see the world famous grotto. We found it a spiritually soothing place and I am sure you find it uplifting too. Please keep in touch as I would like to hear more from you.

This 'love affair' continued for over ten years with all the correspondence ending up in Sister Maria's file, until one fine day I saw her name on my office appointment list. "Are you sure?" I asked my secretary. "The nun who brought her here the first time rang me and made the appointment," replied Regina.

I could not hide my delight at seeing her in my office after so many years. Neither could she. Only her vows and my hesitation on the grounds of her vocation prevented us from being overwhelmed by raw human instincts. When we regained our poise, she spoke. "We are being repatriated to Rwanda because, at last, peace has returned there. I thought it was important to have a check up done before I go back home."

I was thrilled to see this woman of God, looking so well, both in mind and body. From then on, as per our usual protocol, she came for her follow up every six months. At her visit in January 2008, she said, "You must come and see my country. It's known as a country of 'a thousand hills' and is the only country where you can still see guerillas."

"Where do you live?" I asked her, "In Kigali?"

"No," she replied. "I live in Butare – the university town."

Before she left my office, she wrote on her file her phone number in Rwanda and also her contact in Nairobi. "See you in six months," I said bidding her goodbye.

Sister Maria must have prayed hard for me to see her beloved country. At the Council meeting of the College of Surgeons of East, Central and Southern Africa held in Livingstone, Zambia, in April that year, we received an application from Rwanda to join our College as a constituent country. Three eminent surgeons from there had come to plead their case. "We are now part of the East African family, a member of the Commonwealth and are in the process of changing from a French speaking country to an English speaking one. Our orientation is changing in favour of our East African neighbours and we cherish to be a part of this great College for training our surgeons and certifying them as fully qualified to carry out complex surgical procedures. We are very thin on the ground and the country is crying out loud for properly trained personnel. In your College, we see the possibility of our hopes being fulfilled."

Having made that touching speech, they invited the Council to Butare to see for ourselves the surgical and teaching facilities at the university medical school and assess their suitability of becoming an integral part of our College. The date of the meeting in Rwanda was 1st of August. On return from Livingstone, I asked my secretary to get in touch with Sister Maria's local contact, which she had given us at her last visit. "There is no need for Sister Maria to travel all the way here to see me in August. I'm going there for a meeting and will see her there." I said to the nun on the phone. She was the same one who had translated for us on Sister Maria's first visit. The College Council had booked us to stay at the le Prince Petit Hotel in Butare and I told her to tell Sister Maria to contact me there.

Six surgeons from Kenya flew together on a Kenya Airways flight. After landing in Kigali, we toured the capital with our surgical colleagues there before being driven to Butare, a distance of 135 kms. In Kigali, we were shown Malkolin Hotel, where the film – *Hotel Rwanda* – was filmed, our own Nakumatt, newly opened in the city centre and, finally, the Genocide Memorial. There, we saw a mass grave in which 256,000 victims were buried. That is roughly a quarter of the total number killed in cold blood in the ethnic cleansing.

Inside the building, there are films and photographs, which run continuously, depicting Rwanda – pre-genocide, genocide and post-genocide. As we went round, one Kenyan surgeon eerily remarked, "You can see how close we came to something like this after our 2007 elections." At the university in Butare, there is also a Genocide Memorial in the form of a mass grave. Apparently, five hundred students were called from their halls of residence on the pretext that classes were being held there. When they arrived, they were all brutally slayed.

Sister Maria contacted me at the Le Prince Petit Hotel. I gave her the usual check-up and a clean bill of health. We talked for a while and I told her of the two genocide memorials I had seen. "There is another one in Murambi, thirty miles from here and I want to take you there," she said. Without giving it a second thought, I agreed and she took me there the next day.

The memorial was gorier than the one in Kigali. Our guide noted that there were in fact body parts and bones preserved "for posterity to see that it never happens again anywhere in the world". Pointing to a games pitch, our guide said, "foreign troops – supposed to be peace keepers – were playing volley ball there while the genocide was actually taking place here." I had taken a wreath and, seeing a spot reserved for them, I placed mine there.

At this point, Sister Maria spoke about her ordeal for the first time. I suppose the gravity of the location provoked her to lighten the burden of silence she had carried for so many years. "Here are the remains of my ancestors," she said. "My whole family was butchered here in front of my very eyes before I was gang raped. I only survived because I appeared dead. I walked for seven days and seven nights before I found refuge in a church. They fed me for I was hungry and clothed me as I was in tatters. Later, they sent me to Singida for my safety."

As I felt the poignancy in Sister Maria's account, I was not sure who was more tearful between the two of us – she or me. Her last words, however, made me cry openly. "I carried the bitterness in my heart for a long time but soon realised that it was not doing any good. So, I eventually forgave the perpetrators of all the heinous crimes in my beloved Rwanda. While in Paris, I went to the cathedral of Notre Dame. I stood in front of Christ on the Cross and said, "Forgive them, Oh Lord, for they know not what they do."

18

Taming a testosterone-charged engine

We doctors take credit for women's liberation in a funny way. This is because we believe, with some justification, that women's empowerment came as a result of medical research, more specifically, the experimental study carried out by gynaecologists to find a contraceptive for women. After all, women felt truly liberated when they were able to control their own pregnancy and this was made possible by the advent of the pill and the coil. Until then, women were truly dependent on men to prevent pregnancy and if they did not bother, which was often the case, the poor woman bore the brunt of an unwanted pregnancy and all the misery that followed in its wake. Female contraception put an end to this gross biological disparity and inequity.

This single development, coupled with opening of new careers for women which made them financially independent, changed the social fabric of our society. From prim, proper, and prude Victorian housewives, women went on to encroach on what was considered an exclusive male preserve and reached the pinnacle of power as prime-ministers and even presidents. They attained equal status and often beat us at our own game and on our own turf.

Taming a testosterone-charged engine

During the transition period, the inequality of women was a hot topic of discussion. My take on the subject, albeit a little facetiously, was that women were different but certainly not unequal. I would then add my punch line: Thank God women are anatomically and physiologically different from us, because if they were not, we men would have a problem with them in the bedroom!

It is in connection with the 'Pill', and a woman's ingenious use of it, that I recall the case of Sarah. The story started in the nursery of the hospital where Sarah delivered her twins and continued with her visits to my office for a follow up on one of her twins.

"Maybe I'm talking to the wrong person but perhaps you might be able to help," Sarah said hesitatingly when I finished checking her twin son, Lawrence.

I had operated on Lawrence a couple of weeks earlier, when Dr. Were, my former student, now a newly arrived neonatologist had rung me about him. A neonatologist is a super-specialist who is trained to look after neonates and also those born prematurely. Paediatrics is a well recognised branch of medicine and was devised to look after the peculiar needs of children. However, it soon became apparent that newborn and premature babies have special problems and neonatology soon developed into a specialty of its own. Dr. Were saw the glaring gap in this highly specialised new branch and the rapid rise in demand for it and went abroad to train in it. In recent times, in centres of excellence, neonatologists are required to be present in the labour room and take charge of the baby as soon as it is born.

Dr. Were was called by Sarah's obstetrician when she was delivering her twins and, after examining and observing Lawrence for a couple of days, Dr. Were had called me on the phone. It was when I went to the hospital, at his request, that I first met Sarah and both her twins.

"Our mutual friend and colleague, Dr. Said, delivered twins three days ago," Dr. Were said when he rang me. "I was in attendance in the labour ward to check the newborn babies. Josephat, the senior twin, was fine but, Lawrence, the junior one, had a lump in the right groin."

Since the term senior and junior in relation to twins was new to me, I interrupted Dr. Were. "How do you define a senior and a junior twin?"

"Oh," replied Dr. Were. "Josephat was born first and Lawrence arrived five minutes later. According to our nomenclature, Josephat is senior by five minutes." Then, to educate me further, he added. "The terminology has legal implications." As I clutched the receiver tightly, out of curiosity, he added. "For example the elder son would most likely be the father's heir and, in the case of royalty, the crown would pass to the senior twin."

"Gosh," I expressed my amazement. "I had never looked at twins from that point of view. I must say you paediatricians are clever people."

"Good to know you think so," Dr. Were replied in the same vein, "because some people believe that child specialists have the brain of a child." As I laughed at his funny comment, Dr. Were reverted to the matter we were discussing. "As I mentioned, I noticed this lump in the groin of the younger twin, Lawrence, at birth and provisionally diagnosed it as a congenital hernia. I have been observing the baby in the nursery and have now discovered that the testis is also missing from the scrotum on the right side. Today, the boy has started vomiting and the clinical picture is clearer. I think that we are dealing with an obstructed hernia associated with an undescended testis."

"An undescended testis in a newborn baby is often accompanied by a hernia but the hernia getting obstructed soon after birth is a rare phenomenon. However, rare things do happen, though rarely, and it is possible that your little patient is vomiting because he has developed an obstruction in his hernia." I paused for a while and then asked. "I suppose you want me to see the little one?"

"Please."

I saw Lawrence, confirmed Dr. Were's unusual diagnosis of a mildly obstructed hernia associated with an absent testis in the right scrotum. Because of the obstruction, the baby needed an urgent operation. The decision to operate, however, had to be conveyed to the mother and her consent was required before I could do so. That is when I first met Sarah. Talking to her, it quickly became obvious to me that she was a highly educated and sophisticated woman. As if to counteract these very sober qualities, there was innocent mischief in her expressive eyes. She asked me some pithy questions before signing the consent form. One of them was about the urgency to operate. "Can't we wait till the baby has grown a little older and stronger? He seems so vulnerable, having to undergo surgery so soon after he has set foot in this world," she said.

"If the hernia was not obstructed and if he was not vomiting, we could have waited. But in the case, it seems that the hernia is blocked and that forces our hand. When we find a hernia and an undescended testis in a baby at birth, we usually wait until the infant is at least a year old before we operate. The tissues at that age are not as weak as they are at birth. But in this case, we have no choice. We have to release the gut caught in his hernia."

She talked to her husband on her mobile in front of Dr. Were and me and apprised him of her decision, based on my advice. He readily gave his approval and Sarah signed the consent form.

Surgery on Lawrence's hernia went off very well. My one year training at Queen Mary's Hospital for Children in Carshalton, soon after I obtained my fellowship in surgery, stood me in good stead. It enabled me to do considerable amount of intricate surgery on children and newborns until our locally trained paediatric surgeons came on the scene.

"While we are here, we might as well bring his testis down," I said to Dr. Masinde who was assisting me at the operation. I had released the herniated gut, which was the emergency part of the operation, and was now embarking on the elective segment. "Saves us going back into the area after a year," I added. That, too, proved relatively easy. I had no difficulty in lengthening the spermatic cord at the end of which the testis hung. I released the cord from all its attachments, preserving the blood supply to the testis and the vas deferens, the tube that would conduct the sperms when the boy was old enough to produce them. The testis sat very comfortably in the scrotum, its rightful abode and, at the end of the operation, I was quite pleased with the result. Post-operatively, the vomiting stopped and three days later, Lawrence, his twin brother and the delighted mother went home.

Sarah had now come a fortnight later with her son for a routine check. Lawrence's surgical wound had healed nicely and the right testis was comfortably settled in its new but traditional home. It was at the end of this very satisfactory meeting that Sarah gingerly introduced a new element. "Maybe I'm talking to the wrong person but perhaps you might be able to help."

"Ask me the question," I said lightly. "And you will soon know."

"Well," she said bashfully looking at the carpet in my consulting room. "I'm married to a testosterone charged fire engine and I don't know how to cope with him." As I sat silent, letting her talk, she continued. "I'm on the go all day with the twins and look forward to some sleep at night. As far as Sam is concerned, twins or no twins, life has not changed one bit. He still needs his regular night cap which happens to be me!" I was getting interested in Sarah's twitter and let her go on. "As he says, I'm already in a debit account. What with the last two months of twin pregnancy and then the confinement in the hospital he says that he's starving. He thinks I should clear the backlog and then revert back to normal service."

"And what's that?" I inquired.

"Normally he finishes work in the office at about six in the evening and goes to the bar. He has a few beers with his friends and then comes home where I serve him a nice dinner. Naturally, he is bursting with energy when we get into bed." She then became vividly descriptive. "He then behaves like a determined, aggressive, goal-orientated bull!"

"But surely you can say no. Can't you?" Seeing the intelligent amusement on her face I was emboldened to add. "You know when the the pill got onto the market we doctors had two running jokes about oral contraceptives. One was to tell our female patients that there was another oral contraceptive available to them, which cost nothing. This was just to say no. The other joke was the contraceptive pill for men. Instead of swallowing, they put in their shoe and it made them limp!'

"Not in our culture," replied Sarah, now looking serious. "Our men simply don't take no for an answer. Some men have framed their marriage certificate and hung it in a place where the wives can see it when they are in bed together! Any reluctance on her part and her attention is drawn to the vital document!"

"But you know we have now recognised rape in marriage and you can remind him of that clause," I argued. "What happened to your 'women's lib' and empowerment?"

Taming a testosterone-charged engine

"It's alright in theory," Sarah replied, "but doesn't work in practice. What is there to stop Sam from finding a locum or even a permanent replacement? After all, he is allowed more than one wife."

"Oh, well," I gave up. "I wish I could help you but this is not a strictly medical problem. As you yourself have implied, there are cultural, ethnic and traditional factors and I'm afraid I cannot resolve them all. Anyway," I reverted to my sphere of activity and concluded, "I need to see Lawrence in three months' time for a final check up. I just want to make sure that the testis stays in the scrotum and does not slide up as it sometimes does."

Three months later Sarah was in my office with her son. His scar was hardly visible and the testis was lying comfortably in its correct anatomical position. It was also growing in size as it always does when brought down. As they were leaving, I remarked on how fresh Sarah looked. "Last time, you really looked tired and worn out. Today you seem to be in the bloom of health. I doubt you would look like that if you had too many sleepless nights. So did you find a solution?"

"Oh yes, I almost forgot to mention it," Sarah replied. "As they say, local problems need local solutions. So I found one. You know when I was carrying the twins I had difficulty in sleeping so Dr. Said prescribed some mild sleeping pills. They were excellent. No taste, no hangover and no oversleep. The other day when clearing my cupboard, I came across some that were left over. Knowing that the twins would soon be old enough to ransack the house, I thought it was unsafe to keep them and decided to throw them in the bin." There was a strange wicked expression on her face as she went on. "Suddenly an idea struck me and I tried it that evening. I carefully crushed one tablet and put it in Sam's *ugali*. His beer in the bar with his friends and my little tablet worked wonders. By 10pm, Sam could hardly keep his eyes open. By the time, I checked on the twins and joined him in bed, he was snoring. Next morning, he woke up as bright as a button and so did I." As my eyes were popping out at the daring ingenuity of this elf-like lady, she continued. "Since then, whenever I need a good night's sleep, I give him my 'special treat' in the dining room. He then does not demand his 'special treat' in bed!" She then looked at me tenderly with that 'won't hurt a fly' expression on her pretty face and, with some guilt lurking in her big, black eyes, added. "When the twins grow up, I will make it up to him."

"How did you think of this brilliant conspiracy?" I asked.

With a sly smile on her face she explained. "You remember you told me two running jokes about oral contraceptives. One was merely saying 'no'. That as I told you is not practical in our culture. The other was a similar pill for men which they wear in their shoes and which makes them limp! I used that idea but just changed the route of administration. Instead of placing it in Sam's shoe, I laced his food with it – with the same remarkable result!"

19

The daughter or the wife ?

"As you sow, so you reap," said the professor, not hiding his indignation. "She has made her bed and she must sleep on it," he added as my gynaecologist colleague, Dr. Nderitu, the psychiatrist, Dr. Okonji and I looked at each other with grim faces. "She must carry the cross which she chose to bear," he added with finality. We realised that we had lost the battle.

"It was a momentary lapse, perhaps a foolish mistake," I argued, "and I don't think that she should be made to pay such a heavy price for it."

The professor was a man of great rectitude and I knew that he would not be a party to the termination of his daughter's pregnancy. He had made it clear to Dr. Nderitu earlier that his daughter must not be allowed to get away with her promiscuity. The doctor had then enlisted the help of the professor's newly-wed wife and she was the one who told him to invoke my assistance. "They are both buddies and I know that my husband listens to him. He is the only one who can change my husband's mind" she advised.

My friendship with the professor went back a long way. We met when we were studying in England; I was studying surgery at Guy's Hospital and he was studying philosophy at Oxford. On our return here, we went neck and neck, me climbing the surgical ladder and he creeping up the academic vine. He soon

The daughter or the wife?

occupied the chair in philosophy at one of the local universities and made a name for himself in the academic world. His research papers were avidly read by students at various universities abroad. He once told me that his role model was Bertrand Russell, the famous British philosopher, whose voluminous work filled the shelves in his study. However, he was a very private person and cherished his family. Unfortunately, he was not blessed with much happiness at home.

Firstly, his wife presented him with three daughters, one after the other. The arrival of the first baby was a very joyous occasion. At subsequent deliveries, however, I knew that he was yearning for a son. Like most of us do, I suppose, he believed that his son would carry his name and, perhaps, his exceptionally brilliant genes. When his second child turned out to be a girl, I could see the disappointment on his face. The arrival of the third daughter saddened him and, as a result, it was a very low key affair in the context of our culture. To add insult to injury, fate played a nasty trick on him. His fourth child although a boy, was stillborn and, to deepen the tragedy, his wife died at childbirth from post-partum haemorrhage. On this last tragic occasion, I was present at the scene of action. As a surgeon, I could not take part in the management of the case but remained at the side of the obstetrician who fought valiantly to save the mother's life.

This double tragedy left the professor bereft and lonely and he sought out Marie's and my comforting company. Whenever he was at a loose end, we either invited him home or took him out. While in England, his favourite dish was roast beef and Yorkshire pudding. I suppose it was the closest he could get to *nyama choma* and Marie often prepared that menu when he came home. He immersed himself in his academic activity with superhuman vigour to drown his sorrows. One adverse effect of this isolation was that his three daughters were left on their own with no parent to guide them.

The daughter or the wife?

Angela, fourteen, and the eldest, bore the greatest brunt. In addition to the loss of her mother and missing her father, the care of her two younger sisters fell on her shoulders. To aggravate the situation, Angela was undergoing an awkward stage in her life. She was entering womanhood and was going through her puberty without a mother's guiding hand. Everything proved puzzling to her. The pimples on her face, her budding breasts and other disconcerting signs of puberty bewildered and tortured her juvenile psyche. To top it all, something happened in her dad's life which proved very traumatic. Strangely, what was going to bring happiness to the professor's lonely and desolate life caused a psychological trauma to his daughter.

It was almost two years after the professor had lost his wife. He walked into my office one evening when I was just about to leave after a heavy consultative session. He looked hesitant and unsure. I thought it was because he had barged into my office without prior notice, something he had never done before. "I think my days as a hermit might be coming to an end," he announced with some embarrassment.

"Wonderful news! Who is the lucky lady?" I asked.

"She is a research worker in my department," he answered. "Initially, the relationship was academic and platonic. Lately it has changed." He paused and then added, "We have been seeing a lot of each other recently and it seems that there is some chemistry developing between the two of us." He paused again then continued, "I have one problem though: she is rather young."

"Since when has being young become a problem with women?" I laughed folding my stethoscope and replacing it in its leather pouch. "In my experience, women like to remain perpetually young."

"You know what I mean," he was now more forthcoming. "I'm pushing fifty and she is only thirty three. And then, I don't know how my daughters will take it, especially Angela. She has become very difficult. She took the loss of her mother very badly and time has not been a healer. It has deepened her grief further."

"This is an age of counselling," I replied. "Counselling before a man loses his leg or a woman loses her breast. And so, Angela will need to be counselled. If she and her two sisters are brought into confidence and prepared gently and gradually, in time, they will accept their new mother. Mind you, there will be initial resentment, which is only natural. And this lady who has won your heart – what's her name?'

"Her name is Pamela," the professor jerked at my unexpected question. "I call her Pam," he added with a blush on his face.

"Yes, if Pamela goes about it the right way, with tact and understanding, I'm sure she will win them over," I advised.

We left my office together and, though I was tired and yearning to get home, I could not let this happy announcement pass over without some celebration. I took him to the pool bar in the hotel near the hospital and we drank a toast to his wife-to-be and their future happiness.

When I met Pamela after the wedding, I discovered that she had many winsome ways. She was charming and easy to talk to.

Her personality was in sharp contrast to the professor but, like opposite poles which attract, they were complimentary to each other. She was bright, breezy, bouncing and carefree, but in a happy and lively manner. I was quite sure that she would light the tunnel which had remained dark and dreary since the professor's bereavement.

As expected, Angela and her two younger sisters considered Pamela an intruder but, within a few months, Pamela had them all in the palm of her hand. Unfortunately, in the brief period of resentment, Angela went and did something stupid. She got

The daughter or the wife?

herself pregnant. Ironically, when the pregnancy was confirmed and the huff with the stepmother subsided, Angela shared her secret with Pam. Poor Pamela had just come in the family and confronted with this teenage misdemeanour and knowing the close friendship between her husband and me, she turned to me. "Why do you think she did it?" she kept on asking.

"My psychiatric colleagues would call it an act driven by pique. It's like cutting your nose to spite your face," I explained. "Her late mother was on a pedestal and you were trying to step into her shoes. Angela deeply resented the intrusion and decided to cause her father pain for bringing you into the family. This is her way of paying him back in the same coin."

I rang Dr. Nderitu who saw Angela and, in turn, consulted Dr. Okonji, the psychiatrist. Between them, they decided that there were enough medical grounds to terminate Angela's pregnancy. It was the professor, who proved intransigent and that is why I was called in.

I saw the professor in their company. It was then that he talked about one having to reap where one sowed. Out of respect for me he mellowed a little. "Let her get married to the boy. I'm prepared to forgive them and, as a proof, will even pay to make it a lavish wedding. That way, we all will be happy and not feel guilty about snuffing an unborn baby."

The psychiatrist argued the case very ably. "I have interviewed your daughter and the boy. He is a university student and once he gets his degree he is going to the U.S. to study electrical engineering and settle there. He already has a green card. They both say it was a one night stand and marriage is out of the question."

"Then Angela will have to bring her child up, as a single mother – won't she?" The professor asked with finality.
And then a strange and extraordinary development took place.

The daughter or the wife?

Pamela rang me one early morning. "I wanted to catch you before you leave. I need to see you urgently," she said.

"What about?" I asked.

"Tell you when I see you," she answered.

"Okay," I said. "I have a full day at the hospital, so let's meet for a snack in the hospital cafeteria. Can I greet the professor?" I asked before I put the receiver down.

"He has already left," replied Pamela brusquely. Her strange reply deepened the mystery.

As I was driving to the hospital that morning, I wondered what Pamela wanted to talk to me about. Perhaps she could have prevailed upon the professor to change his mind about Angela. When she told me what it was, I discovered that they had done much more than that in their intimacy!

"I'm pregnant," Pamela said before we even sat down in the canteen.

"Marvellous," I hugged her. "What are you doing having these miserable sandwiches with me?" I asked. "Shouldn't you be celebrating with your husband over a bottle of champagne?"

"Go easy," Pamela cautioned. "He made me agree before marriage that we will not have children. I therefore had a coil but then I soon realised what an intellectual he is. I decided that I would deprive the world of another genius if I did not bear him a child. So I had the coil taken out." She looked coyly at me. "I'm going to announce the good news to him tonight when we are locked tight in bed. Will you see him tomorrow and change his mind if he is still resistant to the idea of me bearing him a child?"

When I met the professor next day, he sounded appalled. "I'm pushing fifty plus and past waking up at night, changing nappies, carrying cots and pushing prams. I had taken a solemn promise from Pam and now she has gone back on her word."

"So what's the way forward?" I asked.

The daughter or the wife?

"Abortion," replied the professor without flinching.

I now had the opening I wanted. "In your case, abortion would really mean love's labour lost. But worse than that, it would be double standard on your part. You will not allow abortion in the case of your own daughter and yet you order it in the case of your wife."

"There is no comparison," the professor argued. "They both have done wrong and must pay the price, one by continuing her pregnancy, the other by terminating it."

We had reached an impasse on both issues but, happily, a mere machine – inexpensive at that – delivered us out of this human dilemma and resolved the thorny issue to everyone's satisfaction.

Third month into Angela's pregnancy, ultrasound imaging showed that the foetus was developing hydrocephalus – water on the brain – and a lump in the back, both signifying the potential of a mentally and physically challenged child. There was now a genetic factor added to the abortion issue. All medical opinions agreed that abortion was not only indicated but was almost obligatory. If Angela was allowed to continue with her pregnancy, she would inevitably deliver a grossly deformed and defective child. "You have brought the wrath of God to put pressure on me and I have to abide by His will," the professor said in a broken voice when I put the medical evidence and opinion in front of him. "My decision to continue Angela's pregnancy has to be revised. What else can I do?" he asked.

"As the saying goes, there is a silver lining in every cloud," I tried to pacify him. "The same ultrasound machine tells us that the baby Pamela is carrying. .".I could not finish my sentence.

"No, no, no," the professor interjected heatedly. "You will not change my mind on that matter as well. A promise is a promise and if she broke it she must pay for it."

The daughter or the wife?

"Hear me out", I entreated gleefully enjoying the secret I held. "The same machine tells us that the baby Pamela is carrying is a boy."

"What?!" He shot out of his chair. "Did you say that your damn machine can see my son inside Pamela?" The professor asked with happy anticipation written all over his face.

"That's what I said. But because of your mutual understanding not to have a family, I arranged for Pamela to see Dr Nderitu regarding termination of her pregnancy," I threw in my tail twister.

"You must be raving mad," the professor chuckled. "How can she do that when she is carrying my son for whom I have waited 20 years?"

I wanted to remind the good professor about the disturbed nights, the nappy changes, the broken promises and carrying the cross. I thought I better keep quiet. Instead I rang the gynaecologist and said. "There is a switch of patients. You are to operate on Angela, not Pamela."

"Tell the good professor to make up his flipping mind," Dr. Nderitu retorted. "Is it his wife or his daughter?"

20

Paying for her sins

It was Tuesday, the day in the week when I am on call for surgical emergencies at the hospital. This means that any surgical emergency that arrives in the Accident and Emergency Department on that particular day is admitted under my care. Though there are doctors available in that department round the clock, they are mostly post-graduate students working as trainees to obtain experience in emergency work. By and large, they can manage minor problems but when it comes to something major, or if the patient needs admission, they invoke the help of the specialist on call.

Hospitals of repute, therefore, have a roster for consultants from each major specialty on call.

To make myself easily accessible, I also have a regular operating list on Tuesdays. With this arrangement, I can be reached quickly within the hospital. As a matter of routine, the last thing I do on Tuesday evenings before leaving the hospital is to pop in the department to make sure that there are no emergencies.

Just as well that I followed this regime on that particular Tuesday because I found Dr. Ombati on the phone asking the hospital operator to find me. "Ah, there you are, Sir," he said putting the receiver down. "I was looking for you."

"Doctors and Sisters in this department have a habit of calling me to attend to an emergency as soon as I arrive home. To forestall them, I always check before I leave here," I said in a light vein.

"Thank you," Dr. Ombito got straight to business. "I have an air hostess here with what looks like acute appendicitis," he added, leading me to the couch on which Rachael was lying. As I glanced at Dr. Ombito's notes in Rachael's file, I could see from the corner of my eye that the patient was in great pain. I, therefore, kept my history taking to the minimum.

"I was just leaving my flat for the airport to catch my flight to Dubai when I was seized with this terrible pain here," she said pointing to her right lower abdomen. "I felt faint and sick and so I called a colleague and asked her to bring me here," Rachael spoke in snatches. I asked a few more pertinent questions and started examining her. There was no doubt that she was very tender in the appendix area. But what puzzled me was the paleness of her face, nails and tongue. "When was your last period?" I asked.

"Should have started last week."

"So is it delayed?" I wanted to be sure.

"Yes."

"Is that usual?"

"Not really," replied Rachael.

The combination of slightly delayed period, paleness and fainting in a young woman with one-sided lower abdominal pain makes a surgeon think of diagnoses other than acute appendicitis. "She could be a case of ruptured tubal pregnancy," I whispered in Dr. Ombito's ear. As I was wondering if I should refer Rachael to a gynaecologist or order an urgent ultrasound to throw more light on the actual diagnosis, I suddenly caught her writhing in pain. Dr. Ombito who had briefly left me now returned. "I had ordered a blood test and when you mentioned tubal pregnancy, I thought I should check the result. I phoned the laboratory and they tell me that her haemoglobin is seven grams."

"Let's take her to the theatre now," I said to my junior colleague and then proceeded to explain to Rachael. "Your blood level is fifty percent of normal. I think you are bleeding inside your pelvis, very likely from a burst ectopic pregnancy in your tube. This is a dire surgical emergency and we must go in and arrest that haemorrhage without any further delay."

Rachael nodded in assent and I asked the Sister to get the consent form signed and send her straight to the operating theatre. "We will send her to the ward after I have finished operating on her," I added.

During operation, we found a ruptured tubal pregnancy which had caused a massive haemorrhage inside her tummy and was still actively bleeding. "Just as well you came to check before you left. We are fortunate not to have waited for a gynaecologist or ordered an ultrasound." Dr. Ombito who was assisting me remarked. "We could have lost her from internal bleeding while we were waiting."

Next day when I went to see Rachael she was a different person. She was sitting out of bed enjoying her breakfast. The glamour of an air hostess had returned on her face with her make-up and an attractive wig on. "You look ten years younger," I complimented her.

"That makes me sweet sixteen." Rachael sounded cheeky. She had a speedy post-operative recovery and was home a couple of days later with a certificate from me recommending three weeks off duty. I gave her one check-up in my office before I discharged her.

The next time I saw Rachael was when I was flying to London. She was one of the air hostesses on that flight and gave me VIP treatment. She even informed the captain who announced that a certain notable surgeon-writer was on board and extended me a special welcome. Because of my frequent flights in connection with Rotary and surgery, I enjoyed this privilege very often, thanks to Rachael.

On her outpatient postoperative visit to see me, she saw the 'Breast Clinic' signboard outside my office and booked herself for a check-up. All was well and I gave her my self-breast examination leaflet and, as per our protocol, asked her to see me once a year. She religiously kept her annual appointments and every time she came to see me, she brought a duty free item for me as a gift. In turn, I waived my consultation fees.

Then she disappeared out of my clinic and my life altogether. I saw her neither in my office nor on my regular flights. Because of the long association, her abrupt and sudden disappearance and disconnection did not go unnoticed. I often thought of inquiring about Rachael from the flight crew when I flew but for some reason, I never did. The mystery was, however, unravelled a couple of years later and it happened in a strange way and in a stranger place!

To the many projects my Rotary Club launched over the years to help the local community, the lady members of my club added an innovative one. They asked the members of the Club to bring old books and journals, women's clothes, soap, toiletries, talcum powder, cosmetics and shampoo to a central collection point. The idea was to donate all the items to the inmates of the Langata Women's prison. They successfully approached the prison warden to allow a deputation of Rotarians to go and present these badly needed items to the inmates.

Now, going to prison was not a new experience for me. Having said that let me clarify the matter in case my readers misunderstand me for a jailbird under the guise of a surgeon! I visited a prison before because the fictional hero of my latest novel, *Eye of the Storm*, ends up in Kamiti prison. To give some authenticity to my description of his prison life, I decided to visit Kamiti Maximum Security Prison. A friend made the arrangements with the prison commissioner for me.

The iron gates at the entrance of the prison looked forbidding. Getting out – as one would expect - was well nigh impossible but, judging by the security checks I had to undergo, getting in was equally difficult. A guard house was located inside the first iron gate where a lot of paper work was done related to my visit. All this time, armed guards were hovering round me, some surreptitiously side-glancing, others unashamedly gawking and a few giving me a passing look. Judging by their stealthy looks, I was obviously the subject of intense speculation and had to be thoroughly vetted before being let in. When all the slow formalities were over, and with a heavy grating of rusted metal, the second gate opened just wide enough to let me in. Once I was through, I saw large grounds, sprawling open fields with many tall trees and shrubs. Far in the distance I could see the prison house, walled and fortified. On the parapet above the internal gate, which led into the actual prison, I saw armed sentries and search lights.

Inside the prison, I saw prisoners dressed in their black and white striped uniforms exercising in the quadrangular compound. I could see all the blocks from A to G. The last one was reserved for those on the death row. "Though these men are condemned to death, the sentence has not been carried out for many years," the wardens whispered in my ear. I also saw the library, the sick bay, the TV room and the chapel. As I was watching the prisoners learning various skills in the workshop, the warden informed me, "The number plate on your car probably came from here!"

After this chastening experience a year earlier, I was a bit reluctant to visit Langata Women's Prison. Once again, the lady Rotarians in my club prevailed upon me. Just as well,

Paying for her sins

because the treatment at the prison entrance was much kinder, but more so because the puzzle about Rachael's disappearance was solved at last.

The lady prisoners were very pleased and grateful for the gifts we took to them and gave us a treat. The prison officer – a lady – gave them special permission to do a presentation in the form of dance and songs. As I sat there fascinated by their cheerfulness in the face of such adversity, mesmerised by their verve and vitality, their rhythm and their oomph, I suddenly saw a familiar face. It took some time for me to really recognise the person because I never expected her to be there. To see my glamorous air hostess without any make-up, minus her fashionable wig, wearing a shabby prison uniform and rubber chappals was a shock to my system. At the end of the programme, the prison authorities had laid a tea for us and we had an opportunity to talk to the prisoners individually. Rachael made a beeline to come over to me. She stood mute in front of me as I saw sadness and embarrassment written all over her face. I, too, didn't know what would be an appropriate opening remark under such drastically changed circumstances. "I wish you had let me know," I said tentatively, shaking her nervous, limp hand.

"It was all in the papers," Rachael replied, "and I thought you must have read it. The media had a field day and, to my utter shame and disgrace, they dwelt on my case with the most sordid details."

"As you know, I travel a lot and probably missed it because I was out of Nairobi," I said and waited for her to tell me how and why she ended up there.

"It was all a result of greed on my part, an attempt to make a quick buck and big money," Rachael explained as she sat on a rickety bench in the verandah where we were having our tea. "I got involved in the underworld of crime." I let her talk. "Somebody earmarked me because of my job. I became a courier to carry drugs from another country into Kenya. On the face of it, it sounded very easy. I would deliver money to a faceless person in the city to which I flew and she – clad in a buibui – would give me a parcel. It could be a toy in which the drug was stuffed or the consignment could be concealed in many other ingenious ways. As an air hostess, they thought I would have an easy passage and be above suspicion. I was paid good money for my services. But, in the end, the special squad at Jomo Kenyatta International Airport caught up with me. Perhaps they were tipped because as soon as I landed on that fateful night, my luggage was checked by sniffer dogs and I was thoroughly searched. The evidence was there and it was no use pleading not guilty."

"So what lies ahead?" I asked with pitiful uncertainty in my voice.

"Though I am now paying for my sins, in the end, I intend to come out on top," replied the intrepid girl. "I am using the prison library a lot and I'm studying for a degree in Human Resources. I'm also doing a lot of social work to help my fellow prisoners. Who knows, I might be let out on parole and my sentence might be commuted for good conduct. I can then start my life afresh."

"I hope so," I said. "I really do. In the meantime, if there is anything I can do, please let me know."

"I will," Rachael said, lowering her eyes.

It was time for us to go. The lady prisoners broke into a chorus and followed us all the way to the exit. As the iron gates closed behind us, I looked back at that forlorn girl and wondered. What will prison do to this wretched girl? Will she come out a hardened criminal or a reformed character?

21

Angels with dirty faces

Having studied in a convent school when I was a little boy, and having had my university education in a Jesuit College, I always visualised a nun in a habit, with her face framed in a wimple, and a Catholic priest robed in a cassock with a rosary round his neck. Naturally, therefore, I was not prepared to meet Father Holt who, apart from a clerical collar ,did not wear any other vestments of his ministry. He had been referred to me from Kisumu by Dr. Shaba, who had worked as an intern on my surgical unit at the teaching hospital. After qualifying as a doctor, Dr. Shaba worked in various district and provincial hospitals in the country, including Kisumu where he finally settled in private practice.

"Yes Father, tell me what your problem is," I said after making the above observations. Though Dr. Shaba had given me some information on the phone, I wanted to hear from the horse's mouth.

"Do you mind if I smoke?" he asked, further confounding the image I had of the clergy. It was in the days when smoking did not carry the same stigma as it does now and in deference to his ecclesiastical rank, I acquiesced. To my horror, he lighted a pipe and replied. "Blood in the urine."

"What?" I asked through the maze of smoke floating towards me and, suddenly, realising that he was now answering my question.

"It's like this," he elaborated. "One fine morning I found my urine red. Ho, ho, ho, I said to myself, this can't be normal. So next time I went to the loo, I took a bottle with me. Same again, more blood than urine so I carefully aimed at the bottle, filled it and took it to Dr. Shaba." He then shed the seriousness on his face, winked with mischief and went on. "Shaba laughed his head off. He thought I had picked up something, probably an infection." As I raised my eyebrows trying to comprehend what Father Holt was implying, he added. "As you probably know, he is a great cynic and doesn't think that people can honestly practise abstinence. He reckons that celibacy amongst nuns and priests is an antiquated notion."

"And is it?" I quickly sneaked the question which has always baffled me.

Shrewdly, Father Holt fobbed me off and avoided answering directly. "As always, this will remain a matter strictly between Christ, His ministers and His brides!"

"Any pain?" I changed my line of inquiry.

"None at all. Completely painless."

By now, I had heard Father Holt long enough to conclude that he had a Scottish accent. I also had some time to study the man's physical features. He was short and squatty with a big paunch. He wore thick, old-fashioned, horn-rimmed glasses and his head was bald and smooth. I knew I had encountered an unusual man, a refreshing change from the run of the mill. "You don't look a bit like a Roman Catholic Father," I remarked.

"The visible instruments of our vocation are now out of fashion. Even Rome has relaxed its injunction in the matter and does not insist on it when we are off duty. After all, Jesus did not go round wearing a uniform!"

I thought I had wandered enough from my own assignment and embarked on taking his full medical history. I then proceeded to examine Father Holt and, as I had expected, I did not find anything abnormal. I arranged a urine examination, special X-rays of his urinary tract and ultrasound of the kidneys. When all the reports arrived on my desk I had the answer I was looking for. Unfortunately, they all collectively proved that Father Holt had a cancerous growth in his left kidney. When he came to see me, I started with the benign report on his urine. "It only shows blood," I said. "Dr. Shaba was quite wrong when he thought you have picked up an infection," I added to humour him and then to mollify him further, and prepare him for the bad news, I had in store, I asked him. "How long have you been here, Father?"

"More years than I care to remember," he replied taking Balkan Sobranie tobacco from the tin and stuffing it into the bowl of his meerschaum pipe. He did a quick mental calculation as he lit it, holding the stem tight between his teeth and puffing hard at it. "It will be thirty years this Christmas."

Looking at the age on his file, I remarked. "So you were twenty-nine when you arrived in Kenya."

"Yes," replied the priest. "Did my degree in Theology in Glasgow and then joined a seminary outside Perth where I took my vows. I stayed in Scotland for a couple of years, to be matured as they called it, and was first shipped off to Mbale in Uganda. From there I was transferred to Kakamega, Kitale, Nyeri and now Kisumu where I have become a part of the furniture and fixtures!"

By now, the worldy-wise man of God had caught on to the fact that I was using delaying tactics. "What about the kidney X-rays and ultrasound?" he asked nonchalantly.

As I took my time choosing the right words to soften the blow, he nervously sucked at his pipe. God's chosen people are also scared to meet their Maker, I thought. "That kidney needs to come out," I said.

"And then?"

"You might need deep X-ray therapy and, perhaps, chemotherapy too."

I half expected him to ask why his kidney had to come out. Instead he said. "I have no earthly encumbrances to dispose off but the headquarters in Edinburgh and Rome would want to know..." The next few words hung on his tongue for a while and then he completed the sentence, "when to send someone to take over my job." As I quietly admired the charming euphemism he had used, he added. "Let's not forget. We are all in transit in this world and need to keep our travelling shoes on." He then changed the direction of his questioning. "Is the end painful?"

I knew I had come out of one corner and was being pushed into another. This time I had no recourse. "Depends," I said with a little gurgle in my throat, "on where it spreads. If it goes to the lungs, it may cause blood in the cough, but hardly any pain. If it goes in the bones, it can cause a lot of bone pains. But nowadays, pain is not a problem. We can control it adequately with drugs."

"You have still not answered my first question," Father Holt reminded me. "When must I ask for a relief?"

"I thought that as a clergyman you would know better," I turned his question round. "You would be conferring divine power on me if you expect me to know the answer to your question."

The operation to remove Father Holt's cancerous kidney was straightforward. So was his post-operative recovery. In consultation with my radiotherapy colleague, we decided to give him deep X-ray treatment. It meant his coming everyday to the hospital for half an hour, for about six weeks. This necessitated his staying in Nairobi, seeing me once a week. "This treatment leaves me a lot of time to do God's work," he once said to me.

"Like what?"

"I visit Kibera, Mathare and Korogocho. You must come with me and see these places," he suggested. 'It's a world where many of us don't want to go and yet which needs us most. What the eye does not see the heart does not grieve. But you have to go there to see the open sewers, flying toilets and the squalid conditions in which people live. There you find the drug peddlers, *changaa* brewers, petty thieves and violent robbers. You see wizened men who have lost all hope, children with pot bellies and withered legs, women who have nothing left to sell except themselves. I go there, sit with them, talk to them and try to comfort them. I put time with the children who did not choose to be born there. The more I see these kids, the more I'm convinced that they are angels with dirty faces." He then took a brief pause. "And as if that was not enough, there is the scourge of HIV and AIDS, constantly hovering above them. How would you react, or, indeed the country react, if two jumbo jets crashed in Kenya everyday? That is the toll this disease is claiming. Seven hundred people die of AIDS everyday in this country."

"But Father," I gently protested, "you have undergone a massive surgery. With one kidney lost you are running on two cylinders instead of four and you are undergoing debilitating radiotherapy. You should be resting or at least wait till you retire."

"Ah, good thing you mentioned retirement!" Father Holt exclaimed. "We never retire and if we do retire from the Church, we never stop serving God and His creation. That only ceases when we die." With a smile that never left his face, he continued. "That's one way of ensuring a seamless passage to paradise. As you know very well, I don't have long to live. Now, in my understanding, the shorter the lease, the longer the hours one must work to make up. For poverty is a luxury we cannot afford." He then looked at me with those cool blue eyes. "In going there, you know I'm also looking after your interests."

"How come?"

"If a country does not help its poor, it will not be able to protect its rich," he said. "The majority of people who live in Muthaiga have never been inside Mathare Valley and yet, only a roundabout separates these two vastly different worlds. Similarly, people in Karen and Ngong Road hardly ever venture into Kibera. It is in their interest to do so because until this gap is bridged, there will be no peace on God's earth and no guaranteed security for them either."

At the end of his treatment, I sent a full report to Dr. Shaba and told him to keep me posted. At his last appointment before leaving, Father Holt said, "this illness has opened my eyes to something I would never have seen otherwise. There is a purpose in everything that God destines for His people."

I bade him an emotional goodbye because, in my own heart, I knew that I was unlikely to see him again. But fate willed otherwise.

Dr. Shaba rang me a few months later. "I have a patient who has more money than sense," he said in his cynical manner. "He has a goitre and needs an operation on his thyroid. He runs a very lucrative private nursing home and would like the operation done here – but by you." As I was reflecting on this rather strange request, Dr. Shaba continued, "Money is no object. Name your fee." I remained silent. "You could do the operation on a Friday and then enjoy the weekend here. The chap has a beautiful house by the lake and is inviting you to stay there. He has also offered to arrange a trip to take you to Rusinga Island and visit Tom Mboya's historical resting place." Dr. Shaba's offer was getting more enticing by the minute. Lurking inside me, however, was the desire to see Father Holt and collect some more gems from this wise, old prelate.

The thyroid operation on the rich man went off very well but I couldn't wait to see the richer man – Father Holt - richer in heart, mind, ideas, altruism, sense of service to God and His creation. Dr. Shaba had informed him and he invited us for tea at his rectory. I was appalled to see the deterioration in his physical condition. One thing however, stood out – his indomitable spirit and his indefatigable energy. After tea, he took Shaba and I out for a walk. We were on a hill from where we could see the beautiful lake and sprawling town.

He identified the various landmarks through the blazing colours of a glorious sunset. We were halfway down the slope when he said, "I want to complete a project which I started before I fell ill," he said pointing at a church.

It was an unusual circular building with stained glass windows and heavy, wooden doors. He took us inside the church. "I want you to see the paintings inside, done by a local lad, a budding artist then but now a celebrity." As we walked along the circular wall, I saw magnificent frescoes. "There is John the Baptist," Father pointed out. "Here is Virgin Mary next to the manger with infant Jesus and Joseph."

"Ah," I said, "I can see Moses parting the sea," I added.

"And there is Noah's ark," Father Holt said, looking pleased and proud at the excitement on my face at seeing the nativity scenes in such vivid colours. Suddenly, I noticed a serious omission in the Ark.

"Where is the window?" I asked.

Father Holt was taken aback, looked at the painting again, confirmed the missing window and, with his acute presence of mind replied, "You can't see it because it's on the other side!" Suddenly, changing the subject he went on, "And here we have the school for adults to promote numeracy and literacy amongst them, but more than that, to give them vocational training so that the lost men and women will learn to earn their livelihood, become self-sustaining and regain their dignity. We are soon going to build a house for the street children, where they will be offered shelter, food, clothing and, again, vocational education so that when they leave here they will earn an honest living and not return to glue sniffing and foraging in dustbins. I also have plans to open a rehabilitation centre for prostitutes." The ubiquitous pipe came out of Father's breast pocket. He filled it with his favourite tobacco and lit it. As he puffed away at it, he added. "No woman goes to the street by choice. It's a life forced on her and our mission is to give her another opportunity to forsake the street of sin and provide her with an enabling environment to lead a clean life under God's shadow. No one has fallen too far to be uplifted by God. Once again, we intend to train them on tailoring, hairdressing and beauty treatment. We even have plans to run a micro finance programme to help them start small businesses of their own. That way, they will never earn a living by flesh peddling or fall in the evil hands of touts and 'Madams' who run houses of ill repute."

I realised that this was Father Holt's last testimony, a priest's final confession. For this time, when I bade Father Holt goodbye, I knew that it was final. The curtain was due to fall and pretty soon. It did, but before it happened, I added my tiny drop to the oceans of service which he had created. Dr. Shaba rang me a month after I flew back to Nairobi. "Our mutual patient came to see me the other day for a repeat prescription of his blood pressure tablets and, in conversation, he mentioned to me that he has not received your fee note for his thyroid operation."

"There is a reason for the delay," I said. "Please tell him to write a fat cheque in the name of Father Holt to fund his magnificent project. I don't want to see the figure but let it be commensurate with the size of the project and the enormity of Father Holt's life long service which will undoubtedly live long after him."

22

Time to prescribe tender, loving care

I first visited South Africa in 1975 when the country was under apartheid rule. I went there to satisfy two cravings: to appease the travel bug in me and to see, first hand, the workings of the apartheid system. With our mixed marriage, as a result of which, our daughter takes after Marie and our son after me, it was bound to be an interesting experience. And indeed it was. It started the moment we arrived at what was then called Jan Smuts Airport in Johannesburg. We were soon put in our places! Marie and Jenny were led into a queue for 'whites only' and Jan and I were herded into the 'non-white' category. Our son was too young to understand it all and he found it quite amusing. To the chagrin of the stern-faced immigration officials, he started waving to his sister across the racial divide! Our queue was moving slowly, because of the paucity of immigration officials assigned to the non-white channel. This emphasised the point I always made then, which was that apartheid implied not only a separate society but an unequal one too. When Jan got bored with the wait, he violated the sanctity of the abhorrent and inhuman system by going over to talk to his sister!

Inside the country, there were some strange arrangements. For example, in Durban, there were beaches reserved for whites and non-whites, next to each other, sharing the same sea, sun and sand! Taxis displaying 'whites only' sign ignored me when I hailed them but stopped when Marie flagged them down. The litany of 'whites only' and 'non-whites' was littered all over restaurants, clubs, hospitals and schools. Strangely enough, the shopping malls were open to all. I suppose black money was as precious as white!

There was one glaring exception though. All hotels, including the 5-star category, were open to even non-whites provided they were not South African nationals, making it the only country which discriminated against its own citizens. So with a non South African passport we could stay in any hotel. Within a week, the apartheid system was so entrenched in our psyche that when we saw two swimming pools at the Elangeni Hotel in Durban, we naturally thought that one was for whites and the other was for non-whites. However, the Boer general manager gave us a pleasant surprise. "Sir," he explained, "the pool on the east side of the hotel is to catch the morning sun and the one on the west side is to trap the afternoon sun!"

My most recent visit to the post apartheid South Africa was last year, as the newly-elected president of PAAS - Pan African Association of Surgeons. Like the African Union, trying to unite the countries of Africa under one umbrella, PAAS is a conglomerate of the surgical bodies in different parts of Africa. It is a fusion of West African College of Surgeons, South African Association of Surgeons and our own Association of Surgeons of East Africa, thus taking care of the three corners of our continent. The north, more Arab than African, is integrated both culturally and historically with France, its former colonial master. We select the presidents of PAAS in rotation from the three constituent segments. In 2006, it was the turn of East Africa and I was duly nominated and elected to that prestigious position. As president of PAAS, I was invited to the World Congress of Surgeons held for the first time on African soil,

Time to prescribe tender, loving care

in Durban, South Africa. As usual, we wanted to mix business with pleasure and, at the end of the conference, Marie and I decided to take a holiday in the Cape. We stayed at the beautiful Water Front Hotel and visited the famous Table Mountain. We also took a boat from the waterfront to Robben Island – made famous by Nelson Mandela's imprisonment there. It was on the boat that we first met the British family of three.

They were a part of our tourist group which was being taken round to see the island. We saw the postage-stamp sized prison cell where Mandela was confined. We saw the famous bucket which served as his toilet and, of course, the stone quarry where he worked under the scorching African sun in a common prisoner's uniform.

On the boat trip back to Cape Town, we found ourselves opposite the trio and as often happens with tourists, the lady introduced herself and her two male companions. "I'm Carol Rawlings," she said stretching out her hand, "and this is my husband, Nick," she said turning to her right. "This is our son in-law, Frank," she added gesturing towards the man on her left.

We introduced ourselves as a surgeon and nurse from Kenya. We politely shook hands all round and chatted as the speed boat bounced on the sea which had turned stormy until we reached our destination. We bid the trio goodbye, never for a moment thinking that we would meet them again. We then travelled along the famous Garden Route where all the vineyards of the country are located and their world class wine made. En route, we stayed in some of the best hotels on their coast. Finally, we went to Cape of Good Hope and, from there, decided to spend a couple of nights at a hotel overlooking the southern tip of Africa where the Atlantic and Indian Oceans meet. To our pleasant surprise, we bumped again into Carol, Nick, and Frank.

Time to prescribe tender, loving care

"Long time no see," said Carol greeting us like long lost friends. Soon we developed an affinity with this trio and often sat together on the beach and shared a table in the dining room. Perhaps it was my profession which impelled Carol to tell me something one morning, when we found ourselves alone, sitting by the beach, reading. Her story reiterated my contention that truth is stranger than fiction.

It was all triggered off by a question which I asked as a matter of routine. "Are you enjoying your holiday?"

"Yes and no," replied Carol and then elaborated. "First of all, it is not purely a holiday. Secondly, we three are here to get over a terrible family tragedy. Finally, our main reason of coming to this particular spot is to fulfill our daughter's dying wish. She wanted her ashes to be scattered over the sea at this confluence of waters."

Naturally, these series of bombshells made me sit bolt upright. I closed my book and was all ears. "Since you are a surgeon, you will find this story interesting," said Carol and then seemed poised to tell the whole saga. As expected, the story was narrated in snatches, with an interrupted rhythm and in a jolting manner but, to save my readers a roller-coaster effect, I will paraphrase what Carol told me, but still retain her poignant version.

"My husband and I live just outside Liverpool. Our only daughter, Kathy, also settled in Liverpool after marrying Frank. I thought all four of us were destined to live happily ever after. But it was not to be because, within a year, Kathy was diagnosed as a case of multiple myeloma." Carol was referring to generalised bone cancer resulting in bone destruction. "It was discovered when she fell down and sustained a fracture of her arm bone. She went to the accident department at Liverpool Infirmary thinking that an X-ray would confirm the fracture and her arm would be put in a plaster cast. To her horror, the X-ray showed that the fracture was caused by weakening of the arm bone, which was extensively eroded by myeloma. This led the surgeon to do a full skeletal scan which, sadly, revealed that her bones were riddled with cancer." Carol poured some bottled water in a glass as she continued. "In time, the bone marrow was replaced by tumour tissue and Kathy got excruciating pain in her body and developed severe anaemia. Radiotherapy melted the tumour deposits in her bones but they recurred as quickly. Chemotherapy too controlled them for a while but then the tumour became drug resistant. She was just about trying to cope when one morning she found her body paralysed from waist downwards. A myeloma deposit in her spine caused the collapse of one of her vertebrae and damaged her spinal cord. She was now incontinent of urine and faeces and I decided to become her full time carer." There were tears glistening in Carol's eyes as she gulped a mouthful of water. "It was at this lowest point in her life that Kathy read about Dignitas, a Swiss group in Zurich which arranges legal euthanasia. Soon, she started corresponding with them." Carol took a long pause as if trying to recollect her facts. "The final crunch came when she developed a mild stroke. As soon as she recovered from it she said to me, "Mum, I'm ready to die. I can't risk another stroke. The next one might incapacitate me physically, mentally or both and then I might not be in a position to make the decision. While I'm capable of doing so, I have written a note to that effect." The next day, she told the same thing to her father and her husband.

As a practicing Christian, Kathy used to attend the church on Sundays. The Vicar knew of Kathy's plans to have an assisted suicide and, in spite of his private and the church's views on the matter, gave her communion at home on the Sunday before she flew to Zurich with me.

"I don't want Dad or Frank to come with me to Zurich. I just want my Mum," Kathy said. She went away to Jersey for three days with her husband and on her return she had a full day with her dad alone before we both flew to Zurich. That night, at the hotel in Zurich, my daughter and I had a meal together. "This is our last supper, Mum," Kathy said to me, "we might as well enjoy it." Next morning, before we left the hotel for the clinic, reality dawned on me and I shed a few tears. "Don't cry, Mum," Kathy comforted me. "Remember the words of Sydney Carton in Charles Dickens' novel *A Tale of Two Cities*, "It is a far, far better thing that I do, than I have ever done; It is a far, far better rest that I go to, than I have ever known."

In the room, at the Clinic, there was a potted plant and a candle. Chopin's soft music was playing in the background. I told Kathy that I loved her. We had a glass of wine together. Then she said, "I am ready now."

"Are you sure?" the nurse asked. "You can still change your mind."

"I am sure," said Kathy when I literally offered her the poisoned chalice, as previously agreed by us three. Kathy readily drank the killer draught. I later learnt that we were on CCTV and this whole conversation was recorded for legal purposes. She drank the cocktail and I put her favourite swiss chocolate in her mouth. After three minutes she slipped into a coma and it was as if she had gone to sleep with a smile on her face. She was holding my hand tight and when her grip loosened I knew that she was gone. "Bye bye darling," I said and then cried and cried.

"I returned to Liverpool with her ashes and the next day, two beautiful cards arrived in the post, one for me and Nick and the other for her husband Frank. In both, Kathy had written a touching message to say how much she loved us and apologised for the pain she had caused us. She had also arranged a set of plants to be delivered to thank me for the support I gave her in the final hours of her life. Then there was the final instruction which said. "I recall the happiest period of my life was when Frank and I went for our honeymoon to Cape Town all those 30 years ago. We stayed in a hotel at the southern tip of Africa. I was so happy there that I want to continue that joy until eternity. To ensure that, I want you to scatter my ashes in the confluence of the two great oceans of this world."

I recalled that sad story and wondered how Carol got away with what she did, when recently I read of two similar cases in the UK. They both ended differently and the case of Debbie Purdy brought this anomaly to the forefront. This 46 year old woman, bedridden, with her hearing and eyesight deteriorating from multiple sclerosis, went to court in Britain to make sure that her husband would not be persecuted if he helped her to die.

Initially, her calls for a clarification of the law were rejected but she refused to give up. As a result, a few months ago the highest court in Britain agreed that the law on assisted suicide was unclear. That explains why the court's decisions in the following two recently reported cases in the British press were vastly different.

The first one was the case of a 31-year-old woman, Lynn, who, from the age of 14, was bedridden, having been struck by a muscle disease which left her paralysed from the waist down. Her throat muscles were also affected and she could neither speak nor swallow. She had to be fed through a tube and needed full time care. She had even attempted suicide, made a living will and directed that a 'do not resuscitate' notice be put on her file while she was in the hospital.

One cold morning in December, at home, her mother passed a syringe containing a fatal dose of morphine. Lynn injected the drug herself and died a few hours later. The prosecution brought a charge against the mother but the jury brought in a non guilty verdict. The special circumstances of Lynn's case, her attempted suicide and her living will proved the saving grace for her mother.

In the case of Tom, a 22 year-old boy who sustained serious head injuries, the verdict was the opposite. Tom was seriously brain damaged but in his doctor's opinion, there was a possibility of recovery. His mother, however, thought otherwise. She bought heroine on the street and injected Tom while he was in the hospital. He survived and the mother was charged for attempted murder and banned from seeing him. Driven by the desire to relieve her son, the mother did not give up. While still on bail, she tricked her way into her son's hospital room, super-glued the door and, to be doubly sure, injected heroine into both his thighs and arms. With the quadruple injection and perhaps four times the fatal dose, she succeeded but was hauled up in court on a charge of murder. In defence, she said, "I held Tom and told him everything would be alright. I did it with love in my heart." Notwithstanding this touching plea, she was convicted and sentenced to nine years in prison.

If there is a thin line between genius and lunacy, apparently in law, there is a thinner line between murder and assisted death.

I'm relating these sad stories because we surgeons face the same dilemma on a regular basis. One of the hardest tasks a surgeon faces is to tell a patient that the end is nigh.

A surgeon's next dilemma is, how to deal with terminally ill patients, who suffer from unrelenting pain, loss of dignity from incontinence of urine and stool and lack of memory. Active euthanasia is illegal in many parts of the world and so very few doctors would dare practise it. In contrast, passive euthanasia is informally prescribed everywhere.

Time to prescribe tender, loving care

This means that after taking a couple of second opinions to make sure that the case is terminal, in consultation with family members, a priest, a lawyer, sometimes with connivance of the patient, a note is put on the patient's file. It simply says TLC – Tender Loving Care. It implies that no over-enthusiastic measures to prolong life are to be taken.

To bring this dismal dissertation to an end, let me introduce a light note for my readers. To do so, I must turn from the sublime to the ridiculous. All that I have written above is a far cry from the time when I was a junior trainee surgeon in London. The sister-in-charge of the surgical ward in that hospital filled her syringe with what she called 'The Elixir'. It contained a hefty dose of heroin laced with gin. Once the case was authentically diagnosed as hopeless, she administered that injection. Looking back, I wonder how many of her 'elixir' cases were in fact assisted suicide, mercy killing or murder. Once, when I sheepishly tackled her on the subject, she put me in my place. "It happens at Buckingham Palace," she said to me. "Apparently, the doctor of King George the 5th gave him something similar in 1936 before issuing a medical bulletin which announced – The King's life is moving peacefully towards its close. Then with a wicked wink of her blue eyes, she added. "What's good for His Majesty the King Emperor is good enough for my patients!"

23

Good riddance to bad rubbish

"Can we revisit the issue of gastric band surgery?" Lucy asked.

"What more do you want to know than what I have already told you?" I inquired.

"Success rate, dietary restrictions after surgery, complications, ..." Lucy rattled the list.

"Indeed there are dietary dos and don'ts and if you religiously observe them after surgery, the results are very good," I replied. "As for complications, every operation has certain hazards. In recent times, however, a band can be put round the stomach without opening the abdomen. It's now a laparoscopic procedure that makes it simpler and safer," I concluded Lucy's visit and her inquiry about this innovative procedure, known as 'obesity surgery' was not entirely unexpected.

I had first met Lucy when she was referred to me by Dr. Matano, the school doctor. She was in Form Four and had developed pain in her tummy, while at school. "I think she has appendicitis," Dr. Matano told me on the phone. "The pain started round the umbilicus and, within a few hours, settled in the right lower quadrant," Dr. Matano continued. "She vomited once during recess and reported to the school nurse who called me. I have seen her and she is very tender in the appendix area.

I'm, therefore, sending her to the hospital and will be glad if you would please take over."

When called to see Lucy after she arrived, I found a petite girl who gave a clear history of her illness. "Tell me if you feel any pain," I said as I systematically examined her abdomen, starting the palpation furthest from the site of suspected pathology. As I have always taught my students, this approach is to prepare the patient to feel the increasing pain gradually rather than feel the full blast at the very first touch of the surgeon's hand. This very unfriendly act shocks the patient into agony and shatters the patient's confidence.

"You are getting close," she warned as I approached the appendix region. "Ouch," she let out a stifled yell as I gently touched between her navel and the right hip bone. Her abdominal muscles went rigid as I felt deeper.

"Dr. Matano is right," I said to Lucy's parents, who having been rung by the school, had just arrived on the scene. "There is no doubt about the diagnosis and the sooner we take Lucy's appendix out, the better." Turning to Lucy, I asked. "When did you last have anything to eat or drink?"

My anaesthetist likes a gap of at least four hours between any oral intake and administration of anaesthesia to obviate the danger of vomiting and inhalation of food in the lungs.

"I had breakfast at seven," replied Lucy as I saw the mother nod in agreement.

I looked at my watch. "We are alright," I said. Let me organise the theatre."

Everything was arranged and, within an hour, Lucy lost her appendix.

When she saw me in my office after her discharge from the hospital, Lucy made a special request. "The SSLC exam is due next week," she said referring to the secondary school leaving certificate examination.

"I need a medical certificate to sit the exam."

"Do you think you are fit?" I asked.

"If I miss it, my planned university admission will be delayed. In any case, I am fully charged. I doubt if I will ever be this ready again," she replied.

I readily gave her the certificate and she sat the exam. She came out with flying colours and, soon after the results were announced, she came to thank me for the certificate. "What career do you intend to pursue?" I asked after congratulating her.

"Environmental Studies," replied Lucy. "I have got admission at the university."

"Can't go wrong," I remarked. "It's a hot topic, especially with global warming and green house gases." We both laughed at my inappropriate use of the term 'hot'.

I did not see Lucy for ten years until she came to deliver her first baby, who was born with an umbilical hernia. "The baby is fine,'"her obstetrician, Dr. Kayonga said to her, "but he has an abnormal bulge in the navel."

"What does that mean?" Lucy asked.

"It's a type of hernia where the intestines protrude under the belly button from inside the abdomen."

"And what do we do about it?"

"I think we need to consult a surgeon," replied Dr. Kayonga. "Is there anybody special you would like me to call or would you leave it to me?"

Lucy gave my name. "He took my appendix out a few years ago," she said, "and I can't even see the scar now."

"That's fine," Dr. Kayonga agreed. "He would have been my choice too."

After seeing the baby in the nursery, I was taken to see the mother in the maternity ward by the Sister. There, for the first time, I also met Chris, Lucy's husband. What surprised me was

Good riddance to bad rubbish

Lucy's weight gain. The slim, shapely girl from a decade ago was now a big girl in all respects. Her girlish appearance had disappeared and motherhood seemed to have given her a mature expression. What did not escape my notice was her overall size. I remembered the thin layer of fat inside her abdominal wall which enabled me to remove her appendix in fifteen minutes, skin to skin. But that was a decade ago when she was only seventeen. I gave her the benefit of doubt and attributed it to her recent pregnancy.

"Congratulations," I said. "You have a lovely baby there."

"Thanks but Dr. Kayonga tells me that he has an umbilical hernia."

"Nothing to worry about," I reassured Lucy. "Lots of children are born with it and quite a few of these hernias close spontaneously."

"You mean he doesn't need an operation?"

"We usually watch these kids for about a year during which time we give them a chance to cure themselves. If they don't, we operate."

Under observation for a year, the child behaved very well and obviated the necessity to go under my scalpel. Unfortunately, the mother did not! She continued to put on weight and was now grossly obese. "Your little boy does not need any follow up. He has cured himself," I said. Then, looking at Lucy, I hesitatingly offered my unsolicited advice. "You, on the other hand certainly need medical help in connection with your weight."

Instead of resenting my comment, Lucy opened up. 'It's not for lack of trying," she said. "It all started with my pregnancy. I ate for two and put on several pounds. But I took comfort from the assumption that once I delivered I would go back to my original weight but nothing doing," she lamented. "I continued to put on weight. I reached the stage where I only had to look at food and my weight would go up. I saw my physician, who put me on different diets. Nothing seemed to work. He checked my thyroid and sent me for some tests to the lab. My thyroid gland was okay – I was told. I went to Dr. Kayonga who delivered Jeremy. He ordered more tests to see if there was a hormonal basis. Again we came across a blank wall." She then looked at herself with despair and concluded. "I don't like this body of mine, five feet, six inches frame, carrying a weight of 20 stones and wearing size 22 clothes."

I felt sorry for Lucy but was glad that the woman was not in denial. She was fully aware and conscious of her problem, trying hard to resolve it and, in fact, asking for help.

Just to complicate matters, a few months later, her husband, Chris, came to see me – alone. After first asking me what could be done to help his wife, he suddenly changed his tune. "She is no longer the woman I married," he said in a turn of voice which worried me about the continuation of their marriage.

At her next visit to see me, Lucy confirmed my fears and suspicions. 'I'm really worried. I see Chris looking at other women with longing eyes – especially those with hourglass figures. He keeps on taunting me about my body and does not hide the fact that he finds me unattractive." Then, staring at me with that shy, uncertain look, she added. "We have no sex life any more. Knowing that it's a need for a man, I reckon that Chris must get it from other sources. You will agree he's a good looking chap and there can't be a shortage of women in Nairobi throwing themselves at him."

"There are now surgical measures to control obesity," I informed Lucy, desperately keen to help her.

"You mean there are operations to make fat people become thin?" Lucy asked with an incredible look. "The surgeon will have to pluck a lot of fat from my body to do it." I laughed. "Our weight is like our bank balance. If you keep on taking out of your account what you put in, you maintain the same balance. The same applies to putting calories in the body and spending them. If you put more calories than you burn, you get a fat body." I could see that Lucy was taking my simile very seriously. "Therefore, all weight losing measures are directed towards putting fewer calories in and expending more. The former is achieved by dieting and the latter is the common aim of exercises, gym and sports."

"I have done it all," Lucy replied, "without much success."

"For people like you, we surgeons have come out with an innovative procedure. We shrink the stomach by surgery so that a person feels full after a small intake of food. As a result, after the operation, both inches and pounds fall off. This is popularly called gastric band surgery."

"Can you do it?" Lucy asked eagerly.

"It has become a specialty and I am afraid there is nobody locally who has the necessary know-how and experience. So if you decide to undergo this surgery, we can send you to South Africa, India or the UK."

It was with reference to this prior conversation that Lucy had come to ask me to revisit the issue of gastric band surgery. After I gave her all the answers, she came out with it. "I have corresponded with an obesity clinic in London and they are prepared to do it after checking me up."

"Well done," I said. "Is Chris coming with you?"

"No," she said. There was something in her clipped reply which indicated to me that there was more to it than met the eye. "He will stay here and look after Jeremy." I recalled – it was the name of their son who had narrowly escaped my knife!

It was another five years before I saw Lucy again. I had difficulty in recognising her when she walked into my office. She looked more like Lucy whose appendix I had removed rather than Lucy whose child I had seen with umbilical hernia.

At a rough guess, her weight could be no more than nine stones. She had all the curves in the right places. Silently, I felt sorry for Chris for he must be busy warding off all the male admirers hovering round his wife like bees to a honey pot.

"How is your husband?" I asked Lucy. "I forget his name."

"Good thing too," replied Lucy. "His name was Chris. It's Daniel now."

"How come?"

"It's like this," replied Lucy. "I liked England and so after my successful surgery, I started looking round and found a lot of openings for one qualified in environmental science. I found a plum job and decided to stay there. The fall out benefit of the gastric band was that I regained my self-esteem and confidence. I loved my new figure and so did the men! For the first time in my life, I noticed men looking at me and I was flattered. It was in contrast to me watching Chris looking at women longingly when I was overweight. In time, I met Daniel – another Kenyan who worked with me and we fell in love. I was honest enough to inform Chris about my new relationship and we settled on an amicable divorce. He even agreed to give me custody of our son. Daniel and I are back now here with Jeremy." As I was grappling with these earth shattering disclosures, with venom in her eyes, typical of a woman slighted and scorned, she added. "After all, Chris once told me that, I was no longer the woman he married. He had forgotten that he had also ceased to be the husband I had wedded!"

24

Expect me when you see me

Many years ago I filled a form in which I had to list my hobbies. Without any prior thinking, and just to complete the task I was assigned, I mentioned reading, writing, golf and travelling. As they say, many a thing said in jest comes true. This is one of them because all four have matured into more than mere hobbies.

Reading takes a large part of a surgeon's life if he wants to keep abreast of his specialty. When I joined medical school, the American dean, in his orientation address, told us that before we became doctors, some of what we learnt during our five years in the institution might become obsolete. The only way to prevent the obsolescence was to constantly read surgical journals, research online and also take part in continuing professional development activities. The same applies to Rotary. It has been said that a well informed Rotarian is a good Rotarian. The information is derived from reading the plethora of literature sent from the headquarters and by going online and scanning the Rotary website.

As for writing, it has become a second string to my bow. With ten books on the booksellers' rack, one to be imminently published, one more in my computer, one in my head wanting to burst out into print and, finally, the 'Surgeon's Diary' in its

33rd year – creative writing is now a natural thing to me. In fact, it is more like the tail wagging the dog! It has turned into a full fledged occupation.

With the above two 'hobbies' operating at an indoor cerebral level, I had to find a physical outdoor dimension and this is how golf entered my life. By the very nature of the game, golf has, in my case, converted itself from a hobby to a mistress – torrid, unpredictable, at once frustrating and uplifting. After many years of competitive golf, during which time I secured a hole in one and also became chairman of the medical golfing society, I am now a lone ranger, by choice, playing a couple of rounds of nine holes a week, on my own. I usually play early in the morning when the course is quiet and, as a result, I don't have to suffer the humiliation of having to give way to groups of two, three and four golfers. I thoroughly enjoy the fresh smell of the wet soil, the twittering of the birds, sweet fragrance of the flowers and the solitude of my own company.

That brings us to travelling. Though considerable part of it is related to surgery and Rotary, thus converting it into a working holiday, a term I greatly cherish, I count it as a genuine hobby because Marie and I derive great pleasure from it. Like a schoolboy who collects toy sports cars and a philatelist who preserves stamps in an album, I keep a list of all the countries Marie and I have visited and, at the last count, the tally stood at 105. When Adam and Eve were released into the wide wicked world, they were reportedly told to 'go forth and multiply'. When I was let loose, I presume, I was instructed to 'go forth, travel and enjoy the beauty of your world!'

While planning our last holiday, Marie and I decided to go off the beaten track and our latest 'conquest' was Montenegro. It was on a day trip in this Balkan country when my surgical skills were suddenly and spontaneously called into action. No rest for the wicked as they say.

Let me dwell on my travelogue before I change gear. Montenegro is part of old Yugoslavia which was held together with other neighbouring countries like Serbia and Croatia by Marshall Tito. In collaboration with like-minded statesmen, like Colonel Nasser of Egypt and Jawaharlal Nehru of India, he founded the block of non aligned countries, when the world was neatly divided and suffered from tension generated by two super powers – the USA and USSR.

Unfortunately, after Tito's death, Yugoslavia was dismembered and, after one of the bloodiest ethnic conflicts in Europe in which thousands of young Muslim men were murdered in cold blood, the constituent countries became independent states, Montenegro was one of them. It is a country of beautiful landscapes, shares the sparkling Adriatic Coast and enjoys warm, sunny weather for six months in a year.

We booked with a tour company which arranged our flights hotel and excursions. We were in a group of 20 and were based at the Montenegro Hotel on the picturesque bay of Becici, with the charming city of Budva only two miles away.

Our first excursion was called Montenegro panorama, a scenic tour of the country. Our tour guide was Eva, a full six-foot sturdy woman. Her opening remark, appropriately, was, "As you can see, we Montenegrans are tall people. I'm the shortest in my family. All my brothers and sisters are two metres plus." This introductory remark reminded me of my own observation that the waitresses in the hotel were also tall. As they poured coffee in my cup at breakfast, it looked like it was being poured from a kettle poised on top of the Eiffel Tower in Paris or the Big Ben in London! "I might as well add," Eva continued, "that we Montenegrans are not very hard working people. Our national sport is sleeping. In my country, if you put ten workers on a construction job, they quickly devise a shift system whereby, at any one time, two are working and eight are resting." That self-depreciating, funny remark set the tone for a full day of happy sight-seeing, except for the serious surgical emergency which tarnished it.

"Good thing we are in Cetinye, in the mountains, today because, according to the weather forecast, the temperature in Becici will rise to 29 degrees Celsius. In the mountains it will be about 15 degrees." The comfortable tour van gently ambled out of the hotel parking as Eva continued her commentary. "That is the charm of my country. In the winter you can ski in the mountains and within half an hour descend to the plains to enjoy cappuccino in a seaside café and bask in warm sunshine!"

After negotiating 25 hair-raising bends on a single track road, requiring great dexterity on the part of the driver and equally great trust in him by us, we arrived in Cetinye. On the way, we passed a valley full of stones. "This is officially called sea of stones but the English poet, Lord Byron, described it better when he passed through these mountains. "It looks as if someone has magically transferred me from this world to the surface of the moon," he wrote in his diary, obviously aware that the moon's surface was rocky. The other was a stop at the oldest restaurant in the mountainous region, established in 1890 and known for its ham sandwiches. Eva took us to the special chamber where the ham was cured all winter and smoked by burning special beach wood collected from the nearby forest.

Our first stop in Cetinye was at King Nicholas palace and museum. "He was the last and most loved monarch of Montenegro before the monarchy was abolished in our country soon after the last world war," commented Eva. Inside the palace, we were shown his lounge, study and taken round the King's bedroom and the Queen's bedroom. "In spite of separate bedrooms, the royal couple produced 12 children," quipped Eva. "The king died in exile in Italy where, because of republican feelings at the time, he was denied a royal burial in the church next to the palace as he had wished,'"Eva went on. "But he was called people's monarch because of his popularity during his reign. About 30 years ago, when anti-monarchist feelings had settled down, his and his wife's bodies were exhumed and brought here to be buried there," she said, pointing at the church next door.

It was while we were walking to the church to see their graves that calamity struck a female member of our group. We were climbing the few steps from the garden to the church, walking behind a lady who was animatedly chatting to her two companions. Suddenly, I saw her stray too close to the edge of the step and slip. She did a complete somersault and, as she fell, her head caught the sharp rugged edge of the step causing a big gash on her scalp, stretching from the front to the back. As she landed on the ground, she hit her chest on the side of the steps and twisted her neck as well.

"Stay there," I shouted from behind her, "and don't move," I was worried that if she had fractured her neck, any movement might cause neurological damage and she could be paralysed from neck downwards.

"Where is the surgeon from Kenya?" someone from the group shouted behind me. Earlier in the tour, we had self introduced ourselves and since most members of the group, all *mzungus,* could not pronounce my name, I was dubbed the surgeon from Kenya.

"I'm here – with the patient," I shouted back.

The injured woman was lying on the ground, bleeding furiously from her split scalp. I took my handkerchief out of my pocket and pressed it on the wound. I borrowed Marie's scarf and tightly bandaged the woman's head to stop the bleeding.

Marie, in the meantime, alerted Eva who had gone ahead of us in the church, who phoned for an ambulance. The injured woman who, initially, looked as white as a sheet from the copious haemorrhage was now turning blue. "Do you recognise me?" I asked to ascertain that, in addition to the chest injury which explained her cyanosis, she had not also suffered brain injury.

"Who is me?" she asked looking blank. I was pleased – at least she was conscious.

"The surgeon from Kenya," I replied and saw a faint smile from the terrified face. I cradled her head on my lap as I saw my handkerchief and Marie's scarf soaked with blood. I was getting very worried when I heard the siren of the fast approaching ambulance and saw two smartly uniformed female paramedics jump out of it. It had taken precisely three minutes from the time Eva had called them on her mobile. One carried a metal drum carrying sterile dressings. She put on gloves and removed my improvised blood-soaked dressing and put gauze, large wads of cotton wool and wrapped a firm crepe bandage round the woman's head. The other paramedic was carrying a sterile cannula in one hand and a plastic bag containing normal saline in the other. She too donned gloves, put a rubber band around the patient's arm to distend the collapsed vein in the crook of her elbow, punctured it, saw blood flowing back, removed the stellate, safely secured it with adhesive plaster and connected the saline to combat the blood loss.

In the meantime, two porters who had also travelled in the ambulance brought the stretcher out and placed it by the side of the patient. They carried her on it, pumped it up to the level of the platform on the back of the ambulance, slid it down the rails and slotted it in place. Just before the door of the ambulance closed, the wounded lady spoke. "Can the surgeon from Kenya accompany me to wherever you are taking me?"

Expect me when you see me

There was silence and I understood the reason. I rushed to Eva. "I think there is a language problem. The paramedics don't seem to understand what the patient is saying." Eva quickly translated the patient's request. "Sure, sure," replied the senior paramedic with an East European accent. "Please jump in."

Marie, half expecting it, waved as she saw me climb in to the ambulance. "Bye Marie," I shouted. "Expect me when you see me." Married to a surgeon for over half a century, she accepted the brief interruption in our holiday most graciously.

At the hospital, a blood transfusion was started on the patient. A CT scan of the head, quickly done, showed no brain injury. X-rays of the chest showed a couple of cracked ribs explaining her transient cyanosis. Soon after, she was wheeled into the operating theatre for her scalp wound to be stitched. The young surgeon asked me if I would like to scrub. "Once a surgeon always a surgeon," he reminded me. I enjoyed reliving my days as an intern, cutting the stitches he inserted. I remembered the little line that Lord Milton wrote in his classic, Paradise Lost, which said, 'those also serve who stand and wait!'

The patient was pleased to see the 'surgeon from Kenya' by her bedside when she came round from anaesthesia. "Thank you," she said touching my hand tenderly. "It is nice to see a familiar face, a knowing smile when you are a patient in a strange land."

In consultation with me it was decided that the patient should rest in the hospital for a couple of days before returning to the hotel. "Bless you," she said to me. "You can now join your wife. Tell her that I'm sorry for having interrupted your holiday."

It was six in the evening when the young surgeon drove me into the Montenegro Hotel. Marie was in the lounge waiting anxiously and her first question. "How is the lady?"

"Doing well," I replied. As we walked to the restaurant for dinner, I whispered in Marie's ear in good homuor. "Remember our marriage vows, for better or for worse, in sickness and in health. Here, sadly, it was the tourist's sickness which tested the strength of our marriage vows."

"Never mind," she replied. "You love the term 'working holiday' and this certainly was one."

25

Please certify me HIV positive

"I have two favours to ask you." Mildred said as I comforted her immediately after the death of her husband. He had been admitted under my care in the hospital a week earlier.

"What are they?" I asked feeling sorry for this young widow.

"One, please don't mention in my husband's death certificate that he was HIV positive."

This request was not new and I had heard it often before. Considering the stigma still attached to the disease and occasional forfeiture of life insurance claim, it was understandable.

"And the other?" I asked.

"Please certify me HIV positive."

I was stunned. "I understand the first request but why the second?"

Mildred was hesitant to explain but once she started, I understood her initial reticence. The matter was touching on her traditions and customs and she was not prepared to discuss them with any one.

"My being HIV positive might deter my brothers-in-law from inheriting me," she concluded.

I looked at her late husband's file on which a blank death certificate was pinned for me to fill the cause of death and sign. Oloo had been admitted with multiple injuries following a road accident. "I was driving home on Waiyaki Way when a speeding truck came out from James Gichuru Road and rammed into my Toyota without stopping at the road junction." He had said when I went to see him in the Accident and Emergency Department. Dr. Macharia, the doctor in-charge of the casualty section had made a provisional diagnosis of ruptured liver and spleen. "I think I briefly passed out because the next thing I remember is being examined by the doctor here," Oloo added looking at Dr. Macharia, now standing beside me.

"Where else do you think you could have been injured?" I asked Oloo.

Road traffic accidents these days cause multiple injuries and it is important, at the very first assessment, to get a grip of the whole problem rather than discover them piece meal. Luckily, Oloo was *compos mentis* and could feel pain and relate his symptoms.

"I feel a lot of pain here," he said pointing at his upper abdomen.

"Alright," I said. "I'm gently going to feel your tummy. Please shout if I hurt you." Before I started on the local abdominal examination, I did a general examination. His pulse was fast and feeble and his nails pale. I pulled his lower eyelid down and his conjunctiva was white. All the signs indicated a massive blood loss. Since there was no visible external bleeding, I surmised that the man was bleeding internally. Palpation of his belly pointed at the liver and spleen as the sites of haemorrhage. Dr. Macharia was holding the abdominal ultrasound and it confirmed the clinical diagnosis.

"What about the head injury?" I asked Dr Macharia. "He gives history of brief unconsciousness."

"I thought we would do a CT scan of his head after we have treated this life-threatening haemorrhage in his abdomen."

That sounded like a very logical argument. Respiratory embarrassment and bleeding take priority over all other concomitant injuries because they can quickly kill the patient. We constantly tell our students that other injuries can wait.

Please certify me HIV positive

If we neglect breathing difficulties and blood loss in favour of tackling other injuries first, we might end up with the oft quoted paradoxical situation where the operation was successful but the patient died! Dr. Macharia, as my student, had often heard this exhortation from me and it was heartening to see him returning the compliment as it were.

We quickly took Oloo to the operating theatre. "Suck," I said to Dr. Macharia on seeing a large pool of blood on opening Oloo's abdomen. "Please keep sucking so that I can identify the source of this massive bleeding," I added, desperately wanting to close the 'tap'. We had ordered blood for transfusion and I saw my anaesthetist replacing saline with blood, connected to Oloo's vein on the back of his hand. After a few anxious moments, I could see the torn artery and vein of the spleen bleeding furiously. I clamped them both, tied them and removed the spleen. "That's one dragon slain," I said to Dr. Macharia and then turned my attention to the liver. It was torn in various places – all the tears pouring out bright red blood. I put coagulant gel foam to seal the bleeding points and sutured all the tears. Having closed all the gaping wounds in the liver, I asked my anaesthetist, "How is he?"

"Much improved," she replied. "The blood pressure has come up, the pulse has slowed, his oxygen saturation is good and his breathing is better."

Thus firmly reassured, I checked the rest of the abdomen to see that there were no other sources of bleeding. Finding none, I closed it.

It was while my anaesthetist was reversing and bringing Oloo out of anaethesia that she started suspecting something amiss. "He's not coming round," she lamented.

Oloo's history of brief unconsciousness now became very relevant and the need for an urgent CT scan of his head more acute. It was now 3 a.m and I felt guilty calling the CT specialist and my neurosurgical colleague. I stayed till they arrived.

"He has got a massive bleed in his brain." The two specialists concurred. "It's not the anaesthesia but clots around his brain which are keeping him unconscious," they added. The neurosurgeon carried out a craniotomy – opening of skull – and evacuated the blood clots. We felt gratified that all his injuries had been competently dealt with in one go. It was the dawn of a new morning when we finished.

I was hoping it was also the dawn of a new life for Oloo. But it was not to be. We all fought death for a week but in the end it had the better of us. It was in this phase that we received the result of the HIV Test. It was positive. With our policy that HIV status should not be discriminatory in the choice of treatment, and the urgency to treat Oloo's life threatening injuries, we had sent his blood for the test earlier on. We, therefore, did not wait for the result before instituting the urgent surgery required on him. The positive report, as expected, compounded his problems and, perhaps, put him in a disadvantageous position. I kept Mildred in touch with all the developments as we went along. I counselled her and asked her to undergo the test as well. She did and, to our relief, she was negative.

It was with reference to all the information that she had been provided that Mildred now made two requests. One was not to mention that her late husband was HIV positive. I had no difficulty in complying with that wish. "Your first request is easy to comply with," I said, "because your husband's HIV positive status might not have played any part in his death. His brain injury was enough to account for that."

It was her second request which puzzled me. "Why do you want me to give you a false certificate about your own status?" I asked.

Please certify me HIV positive

It was in reply to my naive question that she went into the details of the tribal practice of wife inheritance and then added. "It will save me from being forced into a cultural tradition which I find repugnant. Being a born again Christian, it is also against my religion."

I knew about the ills of wife inheritance from a medical perspective and could recount a common scenario which I often witnessed. A HIV positive surgical patient comes in the hospital. We check the wife, she is positive too. The man dies and the woman is inherited. She gives the disease to her brother-in-law who then passes it to his first wife thus widening the circle. As surgeons we understand how firmly entrenched this tradition is amongst our people. Our endeavour has always been to veer them gently from these retrogressive cultural practices. However, I had never come so close to an actual victim as I did with Mildred.

"Mildred," I said lacing my regret with all the sympathy I had for this unfortunate woman, "much as I feel sorry for you, I cannot bring myself to give you a medical certificate which is patently false. It's against my medical ethics. But more than that, I don't want to brand you HIV positive. The diagnosis of HIV and AIDS still carries a heavy stigma in our society and being branded positive might hurt you in many other ways." Looking at her crestfallen face, I added. "Don't write me off just because I have not been able to accede to your plea. Don't hesitate to ask for any other help. Anyway, please keep in touch."

This she did and, initially, it was to cry on my shoulder. The first time she came to see me, she informed me about her being locked out. "One day, not long after I lost my husband, I went home after work and found my house locked. My three bothers-in-law were seated outside. Previously, each one of them had come individually and had asked for my hand in the old traditional way.

My curiosity about this repugnant cultural tradition was aroused. "What is the traditional way?"

"First time he comes, he knocks on the door and asks if I need any help. Next time he brings a little present and makes very suggestive remarks in tribal parlance. I had politely declined these overtures. So now they had joined forces. Initially, they tried to overwhelm me with their genuine concern for a sister-in-law, widowed at such a young age. But I could also see their glee at inheriting such a youthful bride. Once they realised that I was not going to budge, they showed their true colours. They ordered me to leave home because I had now become a bad omen."

I was both fascinated and touched by her trials and tribulations.

"I went to the local chief to obtain help and he simply told me to cooperate. I went to the police and they said they had no petrol to drive to my house and confront my in laws. Neither did they have the authority to interfere in family matters. So I went to my church where my kind pastor put my life back on track. He had officiated at my wedding and knew that I had interrupted my university education to marry."

"Why don't you resume where you left off?" he asked.

"I have no money," I said and left.

At this point, I interrupted her because her resolve and focus had impressed me. "What university course were you enrolled in before your marriage interrupted it?"

"I was studying for a degree in journalism," replied Mildred, "and I would very much like to pursue the same. This way I can promote women's rights and stop them from succumbing to these outdated customs. Ostensibly, they are practised to take care of the widow and her children. But looking at the lustful eyes of my brothers–in–law, I realised that there was more to it than family ties. There was the element of lewd desire mixed up in this family concern. This became obvious when I did not comply with their demands. They simply took over and shared my late husband's property. I realised that if I had children, they would have nothing to inherit, simply because their mother had refused to be inherited. Anyway that sounds like a pipe dream now."

"Hold on and, not too fast," I said, "you have made a strong case. I happen to be connected to a foundation which gives scholarships to cases precisely like yours."

Mildred jumped off the chair with delight. "Just write an application stating your case, the course you want to pursue at the university, the amount of fees you need and the special circumstances which make you a deserving candidate," I advised.

Mildred did that and next day delivered her application to me. I took it to the next meeting of the trustees of Marie Rahima Dawood Foundation, which fortuitously was due to meet soon. I did not have to plead Mildred's case. Her application said it all. The trustees had never come across a case like this and were bowled over. At the interview, Mildred made a great impression and came out as a genuine and needy candidate. She had already done two years at the university before her education was rudely interrupted and the trustees granted her bursary for two successive years subject to satisfactory performance. This was an unprecedented decision because usually trustees approved one year at a time. In fact, it was made clear to the applicants that the Foundation was not bound to continue financial support beyond one year.

Thereafter, I saw Mildred briefly every year when she came to give me the satisfactory university report and take a cheque for the subsequent year. Our last and recent meeting was a source of mutual joy. "I have obtained my degree in journalism and I am already working as an intern with a media house," Mildred announced.

"Congratulations," I said with a gurgle in my throat. We parted after a short chat, during which she was the ardent speaker and I the intent listener. She then got up to go and shook my hands. "Good luck and keep in touch," I said, still feeling very emotional.

Before reaching the door, however, Mildred turned back. "And one more thing," she said, "thank you for refusing to label me HIV positive, when I asked you to do so." This time there was sheer joy written on her face. "I met another journalist on the course and we fell in love. In due course, he proposed to me and we intend to get married soon." Mildred then looked at me for a while. "I wonder if he would have done so if I had been certified HIV positive. In any case, trying to explain how and why I obtained it would have been an inauspicious start."

26
When chasing is more fun than the conquest

Though I knew Jay as a patient for some time, he was first introduced to me as a Rotarian after he was inducted into the Rotary Club of Nairobi, of which I have been a member for many years.

Traditionally, after formally introducing a new member at the induction ceremony, which is usually a dignified procedure, his or her sponsor is required to make sure that the newcomer informally meets each and every member of the Club. This is to facilitate his seamless integration into the Club and make him feel at home with his fellow Rotarians.

This also promotes fellowship, which is the cardinal principle of Rotary, on which the organisation was founded. Though Rotary is better known as a service organisation, it was really started in 1905 by Paul Harris, a lonely attorney, with the sole purpose of fostering friendship and fellowship. He had moved to the big, windy city of Chicago from a small town and, as he put it in his autobiography, there were a lot of people around but not a friend in sight! He, therefore, called three like-minded business and professional colleagues to his office on the 23rd of February, 1905 to try and see if they felt the same need as he did. Obviously, they did because the first

When chasing is more fun than the conquest

Rotary Club was born on that drizzly chilly evening. The name Rotary was agreed upon because at that historical meeting, the four founding fathers decided that they would subsequently meet every week in each others' office in rotation. The element of service was added later to make the organisation more enduring.

In pursuit of this objective, Jay's mentor, Rotarian Liz, made sure that her newly inducted candidate sat on different tables and mixed with different Rotarians at every weekly lunch meeting. Not long after, I found Liz and Jay seated on my table. "Meet PDG, who I'm sure joined this Club before you were born," Liz said to Jay, not knowing that Jay had consulted me on a professional matter a few years ago. Since these matters are usually confidential, neither Jay nor I tried to disillusion Liz. As a matter of fact, since Liz had used my official title in Rotary to introduce me, Jay took the cue from there.

"What does PDG stand for?" asked the new Rotarian.

"Past District Governor," Liz replied.

"It also stands for past dead and gone or permanent dinner guest, as some of us tend to become after we finish our mandatory one year term of service!" I added to make the nervous looking young novice relax.

A few months later, at a Rotary lunch meeting, Jay wanted to informally revisit a medical issue, which we had professionally discussed in my office some time ago. In a light vein, I recounted to him a previous occasion when a senior Rotarian consulted me on a medical matter soon after I myself was inducted.

He sat next to me and, rather sheepishly, started the conversation.

"Having been widowed for a few years, I have recently met a nice, young woman who has agreed to spend the rest of her life with me," he said.

When chasing is more fun than the conquest

Looking round the table to make sure that no one was listening, he added, "As you can see I'm getting on in years. I'm actually in my seventies and the lady who has won my heart is only 35! I wonder if as a doctor you have some advice for me."

Knowing that the man was taking advantage of our Rotary relationship and seeking for free advice on aphrodisiacs, I brushed him off and said. "I suggest you take a lodger."

A few months later, we happened to sit on the same table and, knowing that he had indeed married the young lass he talked to me about, I asked him. "How is the wife?"

"She is pregnant," he replied, not hiding his pride.

"And the lodger?" I asked.

"She is pregnant too!" he replied clicking his loose denture.

As we both laughed heartily at the virility of the old man, I related to Jay another story based on the same theme. I told him of the time I was lamenting to a fellow Rotarian, who was an advocate. "I'm a little tired of people trying to get free consultation out of me at sundowners and other such social functions," I said. "I 'm sure they do the same to you in your line of work and wonder if you have devised a magic trick to put them off."

"Easy," replied the lawyer. "I just send them a professional fee note the very next day and they never do it again."

"That's a brilliant idea," I said. "I will try it next time somebody tries to obtain free professional advice."

"Well, you can imagine my indignation," I said to Jay, "when two days later, I received a professional fee note from our learned friend for the advice I had obtained from him!"

There were gales of laughter once again as I added, "Now don't let me put you off. Let's discuss the matter which is on your mind."

When chasing is more fun than the conquest

"I take the point," Jay said smiling. "It's not a specific problem but a general matter on which I need a chat with you. Come to think of it, let's meet for lunch in a nice restaurant." He took no notice of my protest and we decided on a mutually convenient day, time and venue.

Jay had booked a table for two at a posh restaurant in town. He picked me up from my hospital office in a chauffeur-driven Mercedes 500. As we entered the restaurant, it became obvious that he was a valued patron of the establishment. He was greeted warmly by the manager and escorted from the entrance right to the table which was reserved for him. As we sat down, he pressed a five hundred shilling note in the palm of the waiter. "I believe in tipping my waiter before, and not after," he said as he looked at my puzzled expression. "That way the waiter is left in no doubt and you receive right royal treatment from the word go."

As we were perusing the menu, I gave my usual apology. "I'm a one dish man and I don't think I can do justice to this fine assortment."

"Pity," replied Jay, "because my guests rave about the smoked salmon and the sweet trolley here."

"I have an operating session this afternoon," I said, "and can't risk a full stomach and the drowsiness that follows."

"I wanted to talk to you again about surrogate mothers," Jay said as the waiter brought our food. "There are divergent views on the subject and my wife, Aarti, thought that I should talk to you. She realises that you are a surgeon and not a gynaecologist but surrogate is a topic that must interest all health workers as it does everybody else. She and I would, therefore, value your advice on using a surrogate mother."

"I think it all depends on how trustworthy the lady whom one has chosen to carry one's baby is." I was trifle surprised at the topic and gave my initial reaction in general terms exactly in the way the question was framed.

When chasing is more fun than the conquest

Jay soon went on the specifics. "As reliable as we will ever find," he replied. "Priya is a young widow whom Aarti has known for many years. Like Aarti, she is originally from Kenya and, like Aarti's family, her folks emigrated to the UK. They were at the university together in Leicester and she was also Aarti's bridesmaid. Priya married in the UK soon after Aarti and I were married. I brought Aarti back home to Kenya. Unfortunately, Priya lost her husband in a bomb blast in London."

"Are you sure Priya will not change her mind after carrying your baby for nine months?" I asked after taking a little time to absorb the volley of facts fired at me in quick succession.

"I don't think so, but that is a risk we have to take," Jay replied.

We were still discussing the matter when a very handsome couple approached us. "I'm Rajiv, Jay's kid brother, and this is Noleen," the man said putting his hand out and introducing his exquisite looking companion. He then turned to Jay. "Thanks for the lunch, Big Brother."

As I noticed the expectant expression on the two intruders' faces as they left, I was convinced of one thing; their plans for the afternoon were radically different from mine!

Soon the waiter arrived with two bills on the salver. I was intrigued and unashamedly craned my neck. One was a modest bill for what Jay and I had consumed. The other one had a long list of items and was much more expensive. "Your brother, Sir, is a connoisseur of food and enjoys it too," the waiter remarked.

"He has a rich elder brother and, I haven't," replied Jay and signed the bills.

As I was driving home that evening I recounted the details of Jay's case. He and Aarti had been married for ten years and had no children. I had examined Jay and found him normal in all respects. His semen analysis was normal too. I sent Aarti to Dr. Ogutu, my gynaecological colleague and he had diagnosed her with a rare condition. "She has an infantile uterus," Dr. Ogutu had told me when we met in the hospital corridor. "There is nothing wrong with her ovulation and since there is nothing wrong with her husband's sperms, there is no reason why they can't have children. The problem is Aarti's uterus, it is as big as a thimble and has no space for the pregnancy. It can be solved if we can borrow a womb for Aarti." Dr. Ogutu reminded me that his science had made tremendous progress to help childless couples as he added.

"We now have surrogate mothers who will lend their uterus to nurture somebody else's child."

He and I discussed the new development with Jay and Aarti. After a couple of years of intense investigations and search, the couple found a person who agreed to offer her services to them. The lunch in town was to take the plan to a more concrete level.

This was followed by another rendezvous at the casino to take the matter still further. This time, Jay brought Aarti with him and invited Marie to accompany me. The International Casino offered an exotic programme those days. Entrance entitled one to a sumptuous dinner, a stage performance and then complimentary admission into the gaming room. The Can-can dancers from Moulin Rouge in Paris, in their skimpy dresses, exposing long legs, were performing that night and the auditorium was packed. As we were strolling in the large gaming room after the show, I instantly recognised a face sitting at the roulette table. "Hi," he waved. "I didn't think surgeons frequent these dens of vice," Saying so, he put his hand round the slim waist of the lady sitting by his side. "Meet Rukhsana," he said. I noticed that Rukhsana was as beautiful as Noleen, who was with Rajiv on a previous occasion.

"Ah big brother," Rajiv said as he saw Jay standing behind me. "Always there when I need him." He quickly took Jay on one side and the brothers held a long conversation. I then saw a large wad of currency notes changing hands "The blighter has lost one hundred thousand shillings and thinks he can regain the loss if he could buy more chips," Jay said when he came back to us.

"And you gave him the money to buy them?" Aarti was visibly annoyed.

"What could I do?" Jay replied. "After all he is my kid brother."

Finally, Jay and Aarti announced that they were going to London after all medical arrangements and those pertaining to the prospective surrogate mother were already made. Before they flew to the U.K, Aarti and Jay gave us one more treat. This time it was Aarti who rang Marie. "Once the baby arrives, we will be grounded. So why don't we go to the races on Sunday? It's the Derby and I think we will enjoy it."

Ngong racecourse was a beehive of activity. Punters wearing twill sports jackets and trilby hats, binoculars hanging from their shoulders and sun glasses resting on their foreheads were strolling as their women, wearing flowery dresses, long gloves and broad hats socialised. Bookies were writing their bets on the small blackboard hanging at the entrance of their booths. For Marie and I, this was a whole new experience. Not surprisingly, Rajiv was very much a part of the scene. He was resting on his wicket stick, a beautiful carnation in his button hole, and true to character, a gorgeous bird perched by his side.

"Any tips?" I asked him. "Marie and I have set aside a princely sum of five thousand shillings. When that is exhausted, we retire as punters!"

Rajiv looked at his race card. "Put the lot on Thatcher," he said pointing to the name on the card. "She's running at two to one and is a safe bet.'

I did as directed and was delighted when the horse won and my money was instantly doubled. Seeing Rajiv talking to Jay, I went up to him. "You must have made a packet, considering that you don't gamble in small money," I said.

"Lost the bloody lot!" He sounded indignant. "Smart punters don't go for safe bets. I went in a big way for Scheherazade, an outsider who was running at 33 to 1. I knew he was in good form and was leading the pack up to the finishing line when something horrible happened and he did not even make the first three." He then looked at Jay. "I think I can recover the loss if I had some cash to put on the next race." This time it was Jay who took his kid brother on the side. Once again I saw a handful of notes change hands! Rajiv winked at me - his eyes bubbling with mischief.

Soon Aarti and Jay were on the flight to London. Before they left, I rang them to wish them good luck and asked them to keep in touch. They did. A month later, Jay rang me. "The in-vitro fertilization has been a success and soon the embryo will be implanted into Priya's uterus. Once that happens, I will return home."

Once again, I asked him about the surrogate mother. "She's fine. She and Aarti are like sisters and they both, in their own way, will enjoy the pregnancy!"

Then there was a silence for a couple of months and I was wondering what had happened until one day Rajiv rang me out of the blue. "I must see you urgently. I want an obstetrician to take care of my wife who is three months pregnant."

"Sure," I said. "Come right now." I had developed a liking for this young man who lived mainly on his wits and the wealth of his brother.

I was wondering if this pregnancy was an unintentional result of his multiple flings. "Anyway what's the news of Jay and Aarti?" I asked.

When chasing is more fun than the conquest

"I will tell you when I see you," he said. Within an hour he was in my office with yet another chick. "My wife Priya," he said introducing the ravishing beauty.

"First tell me about Jay and Aarti," I interjected him.

"Yes," Rajiv replied. "I did not want to tell you on the phone because I know it would have shocked you." As my heart took a somersault at what might be coming, he gave me the devastating news. "Two weeks after the successful implantation, Aarti and Jay died in a car crash on the M4. I received the news and had neither the time nor the mood to inform any of our friends. I flew to London and arranged the cremation. And there I met Priya."

This time, the name rang a bell. "Did you say Priya?" I asked.

"Yes, I did," replied Rajiv. "She's carrying Aarti's and Jay's child. Their child is my child and Priya's too so we both set about to know each other with an intention to get married. Needless to say, that this will be a case of love after marriage. I am calling her my wife but we can't get officially married until 100 days of mourning are over. But she certainly needs an obstetrician to take care of her right now."

"That's no problem. Dr. Ogutu was Aarti's gynaecologist and he can provide antenatal care to Priya too."

"Fine," Rajiv said. "You will be interested to know that Jay left everything to me in his will. At the time he wrote the will, I was his only blood relative."

"That's good news," I said. "You won't have to beg for money any more."

"I don't know." Rajiv replied. "As they say, chasing is more fun than the conquest. Same here. It was great fun asking big brother. Never once in so many years that I went with a begging bowl, did he refuse me. Bless his soul. I'll miss him!"

27

Forgive them for they know not what they do

I first visited Zimbabwe in June 1981. The country was emerging from the horrors of UDI – Unilateral Declaration of Independence – and had just discarded its colonial name, Rhodesia. The capital city was still Salisbury and it was some time before it became Harare. Other name changes had already occurred. For example, Rhobank had become Zimbank and the main streets of the capital had been renamed after Samora Machel of Mozambique and Julius Nyerere of Tanzania in recognition of the support the two leaders gave to the freedom fighters.

On my return, as I often did then, I wrote a feature article on my impressions of the country which was published on the editorial page of the Daily Nation. The photograph in the centre of the page was that of Ian Smith and Robert Mugabe, with an appropriate caption underneath which read, 'Learning to live together'. I had gone there to attend a surgeons' meeting in the company of five surgeons from Kenya and Uganda. As we approached Salisbury, a very efficient control tower guided us down from the clear African skies into what was then known as Charles Prince Airport, a small version of our Wilson airport. It was explained to us that the name was not a misprint; it had nothing to do with Prince Charles!

Forgive them for they not know what they do

I wrote in my article that Kenya and Zimbabwe had very much in common. Both had won their independence after a bitter guerilla war in the bush. At the end of it, whites in both countries had feared severe reprisals from the African governments. Their fears, however, were dispelled because of the wise leadership, which prevailed in both countries at the time of independence. Like the wise old man of Kenya, Mzee Jomo Kenyatta, the wise young man of Zimbabwe, Robert Mugabe preached the policy of 'forget and forgive'. While there, I had an opportunity to talk to people of different ethnic origins at all levels of society. It was interesting to note that the Europeans were even reluctant to use the word 'white'. They preferred to call themselves Caucasian. That too was reminiscent of post-*Uhuru* Kenya. I recall people here hesitant to say whether they wanted white coffee or black coffee. Instead they said - with or without!

On the dinner table there, one of the local surgeons told us. "You must hand it to us. We brought Smith down on his knees when the mighty British Empire behaved like a paper tiger."

After dinner, he showed us a video of the BBC Panorama current affairs programme, first screened on 15th of June that year to commemorate the fifth anniversary of the Soweto uprising. It was entitled 'To the Last Drop of Blood'. Peter Taylor, a reporter, set the tone by his opening ominous statement. "Millions of blacks inside South Africa are convinced that revolution will come, that they are now writing the epitaph on white South Africa's grave, that one day the land of South Africa will be theirs, stained with their blood if necessary." The programme which featured young South African blacks undergoing military training outside the Republic showed interviews with Oliver Tambo, Bishop Desmond Tutu, Mrs. Winnie Mandela and also the historical footage of Nelson Mandela. The mercurial South African foreign affairs minister,

"Pik" Botha was also given the floor. Unfortunately for him, he lost his temper when asked if there would be a one man one vote in his country. "There isn't one man one vote anywhere in Africa," he replied. "So why insist on it in my country? I cannot see it happening in my lifetime!"

My impression of Robert Mugabe, with whom I personally talked when he opened the Surgeons' Conference, was that he was indeed the young Kenyatta of Southern Africa. Perhaps it was a wrong assessment on my part, or maybe as his supporters claim, under provocation of broken promises by the colonial masters, the man snapped.

To resume the story of Zimbabwe, I entered what was then known as Rhodesia from the back door in June 1980. I went to Livingstone for a meeting and while there, walked over the bridge on the Zambezi River. The 650 feet long bridge connects the town of Livingstone in Zambia to Victoria Falls town in Rhodesia. That was the first time I saw the spectacular Victoria Falls. I also learnt the local name of this awesome sight, *Mosi-oa-tunya,* which means the smoke that thunders. It is very descriptive because the mist that ascends from the Falls looks like smoke and its roar heard, for up to 10 miles, sounds like thunder. The contrast between the two neighbouring countries was tremendous. Zambia was going through severe economic hardship as a result of having nationalised its copper mines and having invoked the wrath of the Western world. Rhodesia, on the other hand, having been officially liberated from Smith's UDI – Unilateral Declaration of Independence – on 18th of April of that year, was booming. I was so impressed that I decided to make a special visit to Rhodesia at a future date.

That opportunity arose in June 1981 when, in a bid to join the Association of Surgeons of East Africa, the surgeons in what is now Zimbabwe hosted the Council meeting of the Association. Since then, I have regularly visited that country

Forgive them for they not know what they do

and witnessed both its rise and fall. Tourism dried up more or less completely. The Harare Club, very much of the standard of our Muthaiga Club in the good old days, started looking derelict and grossly neglected. The historical pictures in the lounge lay askew on the walls which were yearning for a coat of paint and naked bulbs were hanging from the ceilings.

I found it at its lowest ebb when I went there in 2009. Amongst other things, it was pathetic to see 50 trillion dollar currency notes in circulation, not worth the paper they were printed on! This in stark contrast to my first visit in 1981, when one Zimbabwean dollar was worth two US dollars! I bought one currency note, not for its monetary value but as a collector's piece, a stark reminder of how things could go wrong and as a sad memento of the country's utter degradation.

After seeing it at its nadir, I was delighted to see a new dawn there when I visited it again in April 2010. Once again, I saw at least one similarity between Kenya and Zimbabwe. Like us, it was governed by an uneasy coalition. Notwithstanding that, the President and Prime Minister seemed to have put their country on the road to recovery.

This time, I noticed the difference while attending the surgeons' conference in the town of Victoria Falls. Tourism was very much in evidence with plane loads of foreign tourists arriving at the tiny airport of this quaint little place. Restaurants, cafes, guest houses and hotels were packed with visitors. The Victoria Falls was overflowing with water as if to keep pace with the peace and prosperity in the country, its "smoke" billowing high and its thunder heard for miles around. I could not help recollect how David Livingstone described them when he first set eyes on them. 'Scenes so lovely, it must have been gazed by angels in their flight,' he wrote in his diary.

One unusual trip we took there this time was called 'Walking with the Lions', in which we actually walked with

Forgive them for they not know what they do

three cubs. This is a wonderful project to save young lions from their predators. Here, adult lions are mated and baby cubs are reared in the game park, under very scientific conditions and exposed to the company of human beings before they are let loose to fend for themselves. It is while they are at this stage that tourists are allowed to walk with them. Once they are two or three years old, the cubs are released into the wild and gradually taught how to defend themselves against their killers – humans and hyenas – who seem to be mainly responsible for the depletion of their population there. It is the best way to increase their numbers and save them from extinction as we were told.

To compensate my readers for this rather long introduction, I am going to relate two surgical episodes. One is related to a Zimbabwean in Nairobi and the other is concerning the dilemma of a surgeon operating in a hospital in Harare.

I met the former while conducting my weekly outpatient clinic at our teaching hospital. He was escorted by a prison officer, a steel strap clasping their wrists together. The officer was wearing a starched khaki uniform while his prisoner wore striped knee length trousers and half sleeved, square collared shirt, made of coarse cotton. The policeman punctiliously handed me a letter. It was from the prison doctor and read. *Mr. Mauchaza has been complaining of upper abdominal pain for a few weeks. I diagnosed hyperacidity and put him on antacids which temporarily helped him. The pain is back and I think he needs further investigations and an expert opinion.*

"Good morning Mr. Mauchaza," I greeted the foreigner. "Where do you feel pain?"

"It is here," Mauchaza said pointing to the pit of his stomach.

"How long have you had it?"

"Since I was put in remand."

Forgive them for they not know what they do

"Ever had pain like this before?" I asked.

"Yes, two years ago when I lived in Bulawayo. It was a bad attack and diagnosed as exacerbation of a duodenal ulcer."

I examined the patient, ordered a barium meal on him to see if he had an ulcer and asked Sister to make an appointment for him to see me when the investigations were through.

At the weekend I met the prison doctor, Dr. Leile, at a medical symposium. "Thank you for seeing Mauchaza," he said. "He's coming to see you again on Monday."

"What's he in for?" I asked.

"Drug trafficking," replied Dr. Leile. "He, his wife and two year-old child were travelling from Dubai. The dogs at the airport sniffed his luggage and led to the discovery of Mandrax tablets which, as you know, is now a banned drug."

"Why travel with the whole family while carrying drugs?" I asked.

"That is a ruse. Drug peddlers assume that airport police might not suspect families indulging in that sort of crime, but police dogs don't discriminate. He has been accused of smuggling drugs and his wife is charged for being an accomplice. One more interesting point," added Dr. Leile. "He's a clinical officer and knows quite a bit about medicinal drugs."

On Monday Mauchaza came to see me and Sister handed me his X-rays. "Your X-rays show that you have a large ulcer in your stomach. I am putting you on a course of triple therapy, which is the latest treatment and will see you in a month. One important precaution," I added, "being a clinical officer, you must know that you must never touch aspirin because, in your case, it can cause a nasty haemorrhage." Looking at him pointedly, I added, "sometimes fatal."

I never saw Mauchaza again. It was a year later when I met Dr. Leile, again at a sundowner arranged by a pharmaceutical company to launch a new drug.

The last word

"What happened to our friend, Mauchaza?" I asked Dr. Leile.

"Died," replied the doctor without any emotion.

"What?"

"Yes," Dr. Leile elaborated. "Died of haemorrhage from his ulcer. Bled to death."

"What caused the haemorrhage?" I asked.

"He took an overdose of aspirin. No one knows how he got hold of it but you know there is a lot of this going on in prison. Cigarettes, drugs and mobiles are constantly smuggled in," Dr. Leile explained.

"But I had warned him never to touch the stuff," I said.

"Probably that's why he took it," Dr. Leile said. "He was very upset that his wife was in as an accomplice and their little baby was suffering too. If he killed himself the case would collapse and, as a result, his wife and daughter would be released."

"And were they?" I asked.

"Oh yes, there were not enough grounds to hold them once the main culprit died," Dr. Leile explained. "I suppose he died to spare his wife and baby further pain of prison life." As I looked aghast, he added. "The moral of the story is there is honour amongst thieves."

Now to my surgeon friend in Harare. All my visits to Zimbabwe were related to surgery, first in connection with the Association of Surgeons of East Africa and later to attend the Council meetings of the College of Surgeons of East, Central and Southern Africa. All these meetings usually began at eight in the morning and ended at about the same time in the evening. Though we worked hard, we enjoyed harder! There was a social function that always ended with a barbecue.

It was at one of these happy evenings around the fire that surgeons let their hair down on their unique surgical experiences. There was a lot of bonhomie, fun, fellowship and bantering.

Many episodes were related but the one that is etched in my memory is the one narrated by a local surgeon. I will write it the way it was recounted:

"One night I was operating on an emergency case at the Harare General Hospital which in those days was the only hospital Africans could go to. It was a case of a stab wound in the chest and the man was bleeding furiously. I opened the chest, sucked out a couple of pints of blood which had leaked out of the injured lung and repaired the lung. I asked my assistant, a trainee surgeon, to close the chest," As he bit into the roasted goat rib, he continued. "As I was changing in the surgeon's room, I received a phone call from the Emergency Department. "There is a patient here brought in by the police. He has been shot in the leg and the bullet has made a hole in his femoral artery. He needs to come to the theatre immediately to save both his limb and life." I could understand the doctor's concern. He could tie the main artery and stop the bleeding, but that would lead to gangrene of the leg and eventually an amputation. The only way to save both life and limb was to immediately repair the artery which only I could do."

We the visitors were watching the stars in a clear African sky as the surgeon continued. "The operating theatre was mobilized within 15 minutes during which time we quickly pushed a pint of blood into the patient's vein. Once he was on the table, I cut his skin, went through his muscles and exposed the bleeding femoral artery in his thigh. The bullet had exited but had left a gaping hole in the blood vessel. I put special clamps on each side of the pipe-like artery to stop the bleeding and started repairing it with fine nylon sutures. It was a delicate and crucial part of the operation demanding intense concentration on my part, when, suddenly, I felt a gentle tap on my shoulder. "Excuse me sir. I'm sorry to interrupt you," I heard a female voice and as I looked up, I saw the familiar face of the night sister. "Your wife has just rung to say that there has been an armed robbery at your house. The police arrived at the house in time and chased the thugs. They shot one of them in the leg and, according to the news on the radio, he has been rushed to Harare Hospital. She has rung just to inform you that she and the children are all safe, so that you don't worry about them."

"Well, well, well, that was a real apocalypse," the surgeon exclaimed. "I was repairing the artery of a man who had robbed my house."

As we all stopped chewing on our barbecued chicken legs, he continued. "My first instinct was to remove the clamps on each side of the gaping hole in the artery and let the man bleed to death, which he would have done within a few minutes, under my very eyes. But then I remembered the Ten Commandments. 'Thou shall not kill' said one of them. I also remembered my Hippocratic oath. "I will use my power to help the sick to the best of my ability and judgment. I will abstain from harming or wronging any man by it."

"It all came back to me. I had taken that oath when I graduated. I took a deep breath closed my eyes and prayed for divine guidance. It came and guided my hands to leave the clamps on and continue repairing the artery. At the end of the operation I checked the limb carefully. It had good colour, it was warm and I could feel the pulse in his foot. Indeed, both the limb and the life of the man had been saved. I left the rest to my assistant and rushed home. My wife and children were still recovering from their terrible experience. I hugged them all and held them close. They gave their own version of their ghastly ordeal. "There is an interesting follow-up," I said to them when they finished. "As you know, the police brought the man to Harare Hospital. I was in the operating theatre when he arrived and was asked to deal with his cut artery. I have just finished repairing it and have saved him and also his leg."

"There was an inordinate silence and then my wife reminded me of what Jesus had said, 'Forgive them for they know not what they do.'"

28

A surgeon dies a thousand deaths

"I can't feel her pulse," the anaesthetist, Mrs. Naidu, announced in a charged voice, as my boss Mr. Anderson and I were draping the patient with green sterile towels, in preparation for surgery on her thyroid gland. We both raised our heads and instinctively looked at the console of the cardiac monitor, attached to the patient. True enough the spiky tracings of the normal heart had flattened to an ominous plateau. It became obvious to both of us that the patient had developed what is known in surgical jargon as cardiac arrest – sudden stoppage of the heart.

The theatre Sister who had scrubbed to assist us, pulled her gloves off her hands and pressed the button to summon the cardiac arrest team. Mrs. Naidu instantly stopped the anaesthetic gases running into the patient's lungs and flooded them with pure oxygen and the theatre staff put all appropriate and regularly drilled measures into action. Mr. Anderson started an external cardiac massage to stimulate the patient's heart back to life. He pressed the heel of his palm on the patient's chest, rhythmically doing so roughly once every second. This was to mimic the heart's action to pump blood in and out of its chambers. Under the direction of Mrs. Naidu, I was busy injecting various drugs into the intravenous drip which I had set up on the patient, Mrs. Olawale, before the operation. All the time, our eyes were rivetted to the cardiac monitor to see if the heart was responding. All our efforts were directed to flogging her heart to beat again within a minute or two. Any delay beyond that critical period would stop the patient's respiration and take her to a point of no return or at best would starve her brain of oxygen long enough to save her life but render her a 'vegetable'.

All the time I had my fingers on the patient's pulse and after an agonising ninety seconds, I suddenly felt a flicker. In a wave of wishful thinking, one often mistakes one's finger pulsation for the welcome return of the patient's pulse. To avoid falsely raising everyone's hopes, and to ascertain that it was the real thing, I looked up at the cardiac monitor. "I think the pulse is coming back though it is very faint," I said as I saw the flat line on the screen coming back to life, ever so slightly. The stressful emergency had lasted precisely a minute and a half but it felt like eternity. The boss continued with his cardiac massage till the electrocardiogram tracing on the screen built to a normal pattern. "The tension and volume of the pulse are improving," I added as I saw beads of perspiration on Mr. Anderson's forehead. This was something I had never seen before in all the time I was working as a trainee surgeon under him in a London hospital preparing for my final fellowship examination in surgery.

Suddenly, the tracings went wild and irregular and they were reflected on my index and middle fingers, still on the patient's wrist. "The woman is fibrillating," Mrs. Naidu whispered loud enough for all to hear. The cardiac arrest team had just arrived and saw the console which was recording the patient's fibrillations.

On seeing them arrive, Mr. Anderson moved out of the way and let them take over. One of them put the defibrillator on and, as it was priming, brought the electrodes out of the drawer. He connected them to the patient's chest, adjusted the jowls on the machine and shouted, "Please move away, I am giving the patient an electric shock." As we all stepped back from the operating table, we saw the patient convulse as a result of the electrical stimulation given to her heart, a recognised method to bring it back to normal rhythm. The tracing on the screen did not change significantly and so, in quiet consultation with his colleague, he delivered another electric shock, which almost threw the patient off the table. We all rushed to hold the patient and prevent her from falling off when we heard the team member's welcome remark. "The heart's rate and rhythm are coming back to normal. It seems to be behaving." He then quickly injected a drug into the patient's system through the intravenous drip. From my recent reading for my examination, I surmised that it was a cocaine derivative used to calm the heart. The deadly emergency was now under control and we could all heave a sigh of relief. Once again, I looked at my boss, whose face had turned ashen gray from the terrible experience. The most dreaded fear of every surgeon is to lose a patient on the operating table from any cause and he had just escaped that stigma by the skin of his teeth. Though, in this particular case, it was very likely to be an anaesthetic mishap, in the public perception, any death occurring inside the operating theatre is attributed to the surgeon because it is considered to be his sole sanctuary!

"The heart seems to have reverted back to normal and so have all her parameters." Mrs. Naidu announced after observing the patient for a few more minutes after the cardiac arrest team had departed. "Do you wish to continue with the operation?"

Mr. Anderson continued staring alternately at the patient's face and the cardiac monitor. In the turmoil of the last few minutes, he had removed the mask from his face. He seemed to be in a haze and the uncertainty on his distressed face was visible. He had suddenly aged.

"I don't know," he replied. "Perhaps it may be better to keep her under medical observation for a couple of days before taking the risk again." The anguish in his voice was patent. I remembered what had been drummed into me when I was choosing surgery as my career. To be a surgeon, one must have the eye of an eagle, the fingers of a lady and the heart of a lion. Looking at Mr. Anderson's sombre expression, I could see that the lion's heart was bleeding.

We kept Mrs. Olawale in the recovery room adjacent to the theatre until she came round from anaesthesia. We also wanted to make sure that she was not left with any permanent adverse effects as a result of her terrible ordeal. Following the axiom that the show must go on, we soldiered on with the rest of the list until lunch time. In between, my boss and the anaesthetist certified Mrs. Olawale fit to return to the ward after making sure that she was fully conscious and all her observations were normal.

"I think we better see Mrs. Olawale and explain to her what happened, before we start on the outpatient clinic," Mr. Anderson said as we munched sandwiches in the Sister's office during our lunch break.

It was a Friday, a day when Mr. Anderson had an operating list in the morning and an outpatient clinic in the afternoon. He had made a name for himself as a great teacher, both in clinical and operative surgery, amongst the postgraduate students like me. Those of us who went to the UK for the purpose of training in our chosen specialty and passing the FRCS examination earmarked people like Mr. Anderson. A few months' spell under him would polish us, both to face the examiners, and our patients after successfully passing the examination. As I was looking for my final six months' posting in an accredited hospital, my compatriot, Dr. Saleh, who was then working under Mr. Anderson, whispered in my ear. "I'm due to finish in a month's time and I suggest you grab the post. He is a brilliant surgeon and a brilliant teacher too." Dr. Saleh added. "You might earn the distinction of being his last surgical registrar, because he is reaching the age of 65, which will be soon."

I applied, was called for an interview and was selected. I soon realised how lucky I was to have landed the job. Postgraduate students who were preparing for their final FRCS examinations thronged his outpatient clinics, ward rounds and operating sessions.

A month earlier, Mrs. Olawale, a recent immigrant from Nigeria, had come with a referral letter from her GP. As Mr. Anderson's assistant, it was my job to take her history. As she gave it to me, her diagnosis stared me in the face. "I have had this lump in my neck for a month," she said. "Recently, my husband noticed that my eyes are bulging. I'm also sweating a lot and losing weight," she added. I took quite a detailed history and presented the case to my boss. As usual, postgraduate students from the Commonwealth and Middle-East countries, who all came to the UK for training to obtain the highly respected post-graduate surgical qualification, were circling the couch. Having heard my history and staring at the patient's neck, Mr. Anderson asked them. "What do you think it is?"

"Thyroid goitre," replied the Egyptian.

"What sort of thyroid goitre?"

"Toxic goiter," an Indian gentleman spoke.

"Why do you say so?"

"The bulging eyes, fast irregular pulse, sweating palms, finger tremors." It was the turn of the Ghanaian.

The teaching session went on for half an hour and then Mr. Anderson and I talked to Mrs. Olawale alone. "As you heard from the young surgeons, we need to cool this hot thyroid with anti-thyroid drugs. That would take a couple of weeks. Once that happens we operate and remove your thyroid."

Mrs. Olawale was very impressed. She felt proud that her case was important enough to be put up for discussion by the coterie of potential international surgeons.

Having suppressed her thyroid actively to a manageable level by outpatient medication, she had been admitted the previous day – Thursday – for operation on Friday. But now, in the face of the most stressful and rare complication of cardiac arrest, we had to abandon surgery. We were now on the way to explain to Mrs. Olawale what had happened. Paradoxically, in the drama in the operating theatre where we almost lost her on the table, she had remained utterly oblivious to it all. As Mr. Anderson told her of the happening in the theatre, she seemed to be wondering what all the fuss was about. "I think we should let you get over this unpleasant episode this weekend and operate on you early next week,' Mr. Anderson concluded.

"Oh no," Mrs. Olawale lamented. "I will die of anxiety. With the drugs you gave me to cool my thyroid, my sweating has stopped, my pulse is stable, my shakes have gone. Now I can feel them all coming back. I don't think I will survive the weekend. In fact, I have continued to starve so that I'm ready for anaesthesia." Mr. Anderson's quandary was obvious on his troubled face. The rare possibility of a rebound phenomenon, which would bring all her thyroid symptoms back, perhaps with a vengeance, were clearly weighing on his mind.

"Alright," he turned to me. "Dr. Naidu was quite happy to proceed even at the time. Let us ask Dr. Newton, our cardiologist, to check Mrs. Olawale. If they both consider her fit for surgery, we might as well get on with it later this afternoon."

It was five in the evening when we put Mrs. Olawale on the operating table again. As Mrs. Naidu injected pentothal to induce her, Mr. Anderson and I stayed around. We had decided to scrub only after establishing that the patient was safe and sound under anaesthesia. Dr. Newton was also there like a knight in shining armour. Made wiser by the events of the morning, Mrs. Naidu had assembled every drug in the pharmacopoeia on her trolley to tame Mrs. Olawale's prodigal heart, if the need arose. We had also asked the cardiac arrest team to be on stand by. Above the surgeon's mask, in the deep blue eyes of Mr. Anderson, I could see the anguish of a surgeon, still wondering if he had made the right decision and hoping that lightening would not strike again. But luck smiled on us. There was relief all round as we noticed no change in the heart's tracing as observed on the cardiac monitor and the reassuring smile on Dr. Newton's face as he held the patient's wrist and felt her pulse.

"Can you lower the head end of the table?" Mr. Anderson made the usual request when we had finished painting the patient's neck and draping her. This position is always assumed in operations on the thyroid to drain the blood away from the gland by gravity and cut down the bleeding. Dr. Naidu complied and adjusted the position of the table by lowering it at her end. Mr. Anderson made the usual 'collar' incision on the neck and then the melodious commentary started.

The students had kept in touch with the developments during the day and had all come back to the hospital in the evening to watch the delayed operation. Seeing them all back, Mr. Anderson seemed to have regained his theatre sprint and elaborately described every step of the operation to the motley of students. Amongst them, he was known as a wizard in operative surgery but thyroid surgery was considered his masterpiece. The setback in the morning had somehow spurred him on to improve his performance – if that was possible. There was a strange mixture of relief and disappointment when we put the last stitch on the patient's neck, relief because, in contrast to the morning, the evening had gone off uneventfully and disappointment on the part of the students because Anderson's symphony of surgery had ended so soon!

"She better go to Intensive Care Unit for the night," Dr. Newton advised as she was being wheeled out of the theatre. "Just as a precaution," he added to allay our anxiety at his suggestion.

I was dog tired and flopped in my bed at the end of a hard day, hoping to enjoy an undisturbed night's sleep. But it was not to be. At about four in the morning, my phone rang, "Dr. Newton here," the husky voice said at the other end. "Can you rush to the ICU?"

I hurriedly put my shirt and trousers on top of my pyjamas and ran all the way to the ward. Poor Dr. Newton, I thought. Mrs. Olawale was doing to him at night what she had done to us in day time. I found Dr. Newton in the Sister's office, his face a deathly pale. "I wonder if we did the right thing in operating on her," I remarked. "Perhaps we should have held our ground. It would have been better if we had insisted on her resting over the weekend," I added.

Dr. Newton ignored my remark and walked out of the office. I followed him and, on the way, I passed Mrs. Olawale's bed. She was fast asleep – snoring. The focus of activity was the bed diagonally opposite her. Doctors and nurses were struggling round the patient, attached to various bleeping and twinkling gadgets. I could not clearly see the patient yet.

Dr. Newton looked at my puzzled and creased face. "It's Mr. Anderson," he whispered. "He was brought in by his wife in an ambulance an hour ago with severe chest pain. Seems like a massive coronary."

Dr. Newton and the team of ICU doctors worked hard to revive this surgical icon, hitherto a mentor and teacher to many of them, a man whose reputation went far beyond the borders

A surgeon dies a thousand deaths

of his own country and whose protégées worked in various parts of the world, having learnt their skill from this unsung hero. Mrs. Anderson sat by his side, visibly praying. Two hours later as dawn was breaking on Bethnal Green in the city of London, one of its most distinguished surgeons breathed his last.

"The mishaps in the theatre that a surgeon encounters all his professional life must leave silent clogs inside his coronaries," Dr. Newton remarked. "A surgeon must die a thousand times as he fights to save his patients from death. Mrs. Olawale suffered a spurious attack in the form of a cardiac arrest and recovered but, in the process, gave her surgeon a genuine, fatal heart attack."

29

Getting both the girl and the money

"At this rate, we will soon have one eye specialist operating on the right eye and another one on the left." I said, lacing my sarcasm with some wit. We were young trainee doctors, having our dinner in the doctors' dining room at the Maidenhead General Hospital.

Maidenhead is a small town in Berkshire, not far from London, with stunning view of the River Thames. Being a small hospital with 100 beds, some of its blocks built during the last war, still standing on stilts, it had established a tradition where resident doctors assembled for dinner every evening at 7pm. An exception was only made if a resident was dealing with a dire emergency. Breakfast was invariably staggered, depending on how busy the resident was in the wards the previous night and his or her clinical commitments during the day. Lunch, especially on weekdays, was invariably a formal affair because the visiting consultants from Slough, Windsor and Heatherwood Hospital joined us for lunch. They came to conduct outpatient clinics and do an operating list. Those who came in the morning had lunch before they left and those who came for the afternoon lunched with us before they started their session. Our dining room was, therefore, honoured by the presence of renowned specialists from the neighbouring larger medical centres and even from the London teaching hospitals. Under the prevailing hierarchy of guru and chela, we the junior staff were expected to be on our best behaviour! It was, therefore, only at dinner time that we had a chance let our hair down.

There were four of us working in our respective specialties, manning the four main departments of the tiny district hospital in Maidenhead. We also formed a miniature United Nations – all hailing from different countries and cultural backgrounds. Dr. Tahir was from Egypt and worked on the medical side. The paediatric house physician, Dr. Okudetzo, was a Ghanaian. Working on the surgical side and preparing for my fellowship in surgery examination, I had initially come from India, but was destined to, eventually, settle in Kenya. Jim Bishop, my opposite number in obstetrics and gynaecology, was the only Englishman. Tahir and Okudetzo were housemen while Jim Bishop and I were Registrars, a middle grade of trainee category, which allowed us greater responsibility in the management of patients. This included independently operating on them too.

This was typical of hospital staffing in the years after the inauguration of the National Health Service in the UK. There were not enough "natives" and though consultant positions were tenaciously held by local talent, most hospitals were heavily staffed at the junior level by doctors coming for training from Britain's crumbling colonial empire. I often wondered if Aneurin Bevan, the architect of Britain's post war free health services, a brilliant Welshman who had risen from labour ranks to the position of health secretary, had envisaged this when he passionately steered the new scheme through.

I could clearly remember Bevan, having seen and heard him at the Grant Medical College, when I was a final year student there, where he delivered a speech to the medical students on his visit to India. His reputation had preceded him and the lecture hall was full to the brim. Loud speakers had been placed in the grounds of the college so that he could be heard by the large number of students who could not get inside the hall. For those of us, who were on the way to become doctors and who knew how many people died in our country because they could not afford to pay for medical services, a politician who abolished the need to pay before provision of medical care was an idol. He was also a great orator and turned his slight stammer to his advantage by using it to emphasise a point. The ravages of war were very fresh in the minds of people and his clarion call for a permanent peace was topical. "The only war we are now allowed to wage is a war against poverty, ignorance and disease," he declared in his booming voice, pushing back the shock of silvery gray hair from his forehead.

My last memory of this outstanding British statesman was quite sad. It was a photograph I saw of him on the front page of one of the British broad sheet newspapers. He was standing at the door of his house in Wales with his wife, a Labour politician in her own right. With the couple were Jawaharlal Nehru, the Indian Prime Minister, and his sister, Vijyalaxmi Pandit, the Indian High Commissioner to Britain. According to press reports, Bevan had been diagnosed with an inoperable case of stomach cancer at a national health hospital in London and had been sent home. Nehru, while on a state visit to the UK, had been told about it and had found time from his busy schedule to visit his hero at home. The front page picture showed Bevan, grossly wasted from his disease, standing outside his house with his wife, bidding goodbye to his hero, Nehru, and his sister. There was mutual admiration in their eyes and a forlorn expression on their faces, confirming their fear that they were not going to see each other again.

At the dinner table, the topic of discussion was our day's experience and, if there was nothing dramatic to report, we always found a subject on which we could hotly debate and give a vent to our contrary views. That particular evening, when I cuttingly remarked about a one–eye specialist for the right eye and another for the left, we were discussing the eternal question of specialization in medicine and surgery. All branches of medicine were developing fast and the terms, sub-specialists and super-specialists were fast coming into vogue. Jim Bishop looked at the issue from the perspective of his own country, where there was a surfeit of surgeons and specialisation was not only feasible but also desirable. We three from developing countries were arguing from different points of view. We did not have adequate number of surgeons, certainly not enough to staff our rural district hospitals and, therefore, needed general surgeons who knew something of everything. They were designed to be Jacks of all trades who could open chests, abdomens and skulls, mend fractures and even perform Caesarean sections in emergencies. Naturally, poor Jim Bishop was outvoted - three to one. "This is yet another drawback of an English hospital being mostly manned by foreigners," he lamented. "I find myself in a minority in my own country!"

In pursuit of my aim to become a general surgeon in its broadest interpretation and learn all the skills I would need when I returned home, I, wisely, did not leave the matter at an academic and discussion level. I decided to put into practice what I preached and, in my free time, went to the maternity and gynaecology wards to gain some experience. Jim Bishop drew a line there and though he did not put it in as many words, I could sense that he disliked my presence in his unit. To make matters worse for him, his boss, Mr. Tait, the consultant obstetrician and gynaecologist, seeing my interest in his line of work, took me under his wing. Whenever Jim Bishop was busy with emergencies or off duty, he asked me to assist him at surgery

Getting both the girl and the money

and sometimes let me carry out straight forward obstetric and gynaecological procedures, including some operations.

On that particular afternoon, Mr. Tait was removing a womb full of fibroids and Jim Bishop was assisting him. I was off for the afternoon from my surgical unit and was watching the operation as a learner. Just at a very crucial stage of the operation, when Mr. Tait was tying the uterine artery – a large blood vessel which nourishes the womb – Jim Bishop felt a tap on his shoulder. Standing behind him, I could hear the message given to him by the nurse. "It's the labour ward on the phone. Mrs. Howell's cord has prolapsed and the foetal heart rate is becoming slow and irregular." Mr. Tait overheard the message and raised his head. Obviously, it was a dire emergency. The umbilical cord of a woman in labour had been caught between her unborn baby's head and her pelvis and, as a result, the blood supply to the baby was severely compromised. The woman needed an immediate Caesarean section to save the baby, but Mr. Tait could not release Jim Bishop at that critical moment. "He has done a few Caesarean sections with me," he said, looking at me. 'Surely he can do one in the next theatre and call one of us if he encounters a problem.'

I was delighted with the challenge and carried out my first Caesarean section with aplomb. I was getting the experience I was craving for; after all, I had nothing to fear. Help was literally next door.

That night at dinner, I found Jim Bishop looking a bit peeved. He obviously resented being sidelined by his boss and me grazing on his exclusive turf! He made it very clear that he did not think it right that a general surgeon like me should dabble in obstetrics and gynaecology – certainly not in England. As it happened, this professional rankling was aggravated by the fact that he and I were trying to date a pretty nurse who had just joined the operation theatre team. With a male chauvinistic attitude very much normal at the time, Jim Bishop and I had laid a bait that whoever took the lass out first would win a "fiver" from the other.

Jim Bishop left soon after dinner, still in a sulky mood. The rest of us continued to watch T.V. in the lounge. We were in the middle of an exciting series when the phone rang. "Dr. Ponce-Paz here," it was the Bolivian casualty officer. "We have a woman aged 27 here complaining of pain in the right abdomen and we think it is acute appendicitis. Could you please come and see her?" "He spoke in his faltering English.

"I will, but who do you mean when you say 'we'?" I asked. "It is only Her Majesty the Queen who says 'we' when she means 'I'." With my characteristic humour, I tried to give him a lesson in the English language. It was not out of place because he had made it abundantly clear that he was not there to learn surgery but to learn the local language!

"Well," Dr. Ponce-Paz explained, "when I first saw the lady I thought that there were some features of ruptured tubal pregnancy. That being a gynaecological emergency, I called Dr. Bishop to see her. He saw her and ruled out my diagnosis. He was sure it is acute appendicitis and asked me to call you. That is why I was using the royal terminology and when I said 'we', I was including Dr. Bishop's opinion."

"Ah," I humoured him, "at this rate you will take home with you the very exclusive Queen's English!"

I went and saw the patient, Mrs. Hopkirk, in the company of Dr. Ponce-Paz. After examining her, and as we came out of the cubicle, I said to him, "Looks more like a ruptured bleeding tubal pregnancy. That would also explain her paleness."

"Dr. Bishop went over her thoroughly and is equally convinced that it is not tubal pregnancy," the Bolivian replied.

"Let me discuss the case with him," I said. "I know he does not like general surgeons to deal with gynaecological emergencies and I am pretty sure that this is not acute appendicitis but ruptured tubal pregnancy."

"Ok," replied Dr. Ponce-Paz. "I will ask the operator to get him."

A couple of minutes later, Ponce-Paz was back. "The operator tells me that there is no reply from his room. He has left a message to say that he is out for the rest of the evening and should not be disturbed."

"Oh, well," I said. "In that case we have no choice and he cannot blame us if we open a gynaecological emergency. In fact, he has pushed us into it."

My hands were a little unsteady as I made an incision on Mrs. Hopkirk's abdomen. More than a matter of diagnostic acumen, it had become an issue of personal honour. As I cut the last layer to enter the abdominal cavity, my hands began to shake. Underneath the shiny lining of the belly, I should see blood if my diagnosis of tubal pregnancy was correct. If Jim Bishop was right and it was acute appendicitis, I should encounter pus. My vision was blurred out of nervousness and I could not decide what I was seeing. "Sucker ready?" I asked the theatre Sister who was assisting me. I would need the sucker in either case. I took the plunge and made a cautious, hesitant cut in the lining with my scalpel. To my utter delight, red blood and black clots gushed out. I felt like a prospector who had hit both oil and gold! I extended the incision, located the tube in which the pregnancy had erroneously lodged itself, clamped it, removed it and arrested the haemorrhage. I took a breather, both with a sense of relief and triumph; relief at saving the woman's life, and triumph at correctly overriding the diagnosis of a gynaecologist on a gynaecological emergency.

I slept like a log that night but woke up early. I couldn't wait to see Jim Bishop at the breakfast table. Before I arrived there, he had obviously heard of the happenings of the previous night

Getting both the girl and the money

from Drs. Tahir and Okudetzo who wallowed in the reflected glory of their colleague.

"Now you see the advisability of a general surgeon being general in the truest sense of the term," I got on my high horse. "Last night I dealt with a gynaecological emergency by default but in our countries, I might be the only surgeon around and would have to deal with such cases deliberately – and be exposed to such cases all the time."

Dr. Tahir and Dr. Okudetzo did not spare poor Jim either. Having mauled him savagely, they left. Jim Bishop and I were left alone. I was tucking into my full English breakfast and relishing the kipper, my favourite, which happened to be on the menu that morning. Jim Bishop was slowly sipping his tea. I could see that he had something on his mind and was trying to find the right words.

There was an embarrassing silence which he finally broke. "Congratulations on a brilliant diagnosis," he said. "Now can I have the 'fiver'?" he added, stretching his hand out. I soon realised that he had done so not to shake my hand to felicitate me on my accurate diagnosis but to collect his lolly.

"What do you mean?" I asked.

"Well," replied Jim. "Why do you think you couldn't find me last night when you wanted me?"

"Why?" I asked and was completely disarmed when I heard his reply.

"I had taken that chick out."

"What chick?"

"The new theatre nurse on whom we had placed a bet of five pounds." All the wind went out of my sails as with a glint in his eye, he added. "While you were struggling with that bloody burst tube, I was having a good time with that lassie."

He quickly relieved me of five precious British pounds. Worse still, he left me with a funny feeling. To this day I am

Getting both the girl and the money

not sure if Jim Bishop had really made an erroneous diagnosis. I have a grudging suspicion that he had come to the same diagnosis as I had done. But he did not want to take the patient to the theatre and operate on her, because he had already made a date with the pretty, newly arrived theatre nurse. By giving me the satisfaction of winning the argument, he had thoroughly enjoyed a carefully planned delightful evening with the pretty doll and had also won five pounds in the bargain!

30
A bull in season

"Asking me to undergo a semen analysis is tantamount to doubting both, my fertility and my potency," Simeon sounded indignant.

"Nothing of the sort," I tried to placate him. "Infertility is now considered a joint problem. Therefore, to investigate the condition, we have to do tests on both parties. The battery of investigations we need to do in a woman is elaborate, expensive and even invasive. As for the man, there is only one test required and that is a semen analysis."

"I agree," Simeon replied. "But why don't you take my word for it? Women that I have consorted with have invariably commented on how well endowed I am," he bragged unashamedly. "This was of course before I met my wife." He added the precautionary rider after noticing that his wife was seated beside him and listening to him intently. "And to this day I am like a testosterone-fuelled engine in bed," he continued, still looking at his wife, as if beseeching her for an endorsement.

"You are absolutely right," I explained. 'But in men, potency and fertility are two separate faculties, controlled by two different systems. Fertility is based on the quantity and quality of sperms which are produced in the testes, conducted through a fine tube and finally discharged at ejaculation. Potency, on the other hand, is more complex. It is a combination of various sensory stimuli and motor reactions. Therefore, a man can be super-potent and still be sub-fertile. Let me assure you that semen analysis only measures fertility. It is not meant to verify your potency, for which there is no laboratory test. Even if there was, I wouldn't order it because I don't doubt your word," I reassured him.

Simeon sat thinking for a while and I thought he was relenting. "I still can't bring myself to undergo a semen analysis. It would hurt my pride," Simeon was adamant.

"Very well," I said. "In that case I have no choice but refer your wife to my gynaecological colleague, Prof. Ogendo and see if he will agree to put Dorothy through all the tests without clearing you first."

A couple of days later I rang Prof. Ogendo who is both a friend and a professional colleague. Prof. Ogendo had a fantastic sense of humour. He always claimed that he was one of the few lucky ones whose business was his pleasure. He had just finished his term as the president of the local obstetrics and gynaecological society and his experience, which he related with relish in his valedictory address, still reverberated in my mind. "When I was a trainee in midwifery," he once told his distinguished audience, "I had to go out of the delivery room in between the process to talk to 'pregnant' husbands, who were anxiously waiting outside and also to inform them about the sex of their newborn child. There, I overheard this conversation!" Prof. Ogendo paused to create the right amount of expectancy. "It was between a veteran, whose wife was delivering for the seventh time and a novice whose wife was delivering her first baby. The novice turned to the veteran and inquired. 'You seem to be a very seasoned father and I wonder if I can ask you a question?' The old man nodded with a serious demeanour and so the young man posed the question which was obviously troubling him. 'How soon can a couple resume marital relations after the wife has delivered their baby?' The older man took a little time to ponder and then replied with all seriousness. 'It depends on whether your wife is in a private room or in the general ward!'"

Still grinning under the mouthpiece, I rang Prof. Ogendo and explained to him the dilemma I was in. "In my experience, when a situation like this arises, you can bet your last shilling that the man is guilty. Anyway, I will talk to the couple and see if I can change the husband's mind," he replied. "If he remains obstinate, my only option will be to explain the position to the wife. If she agrees to undergo the tests without her husband providing a semen sample, then we are legally and morally covered."

Obviously, Simeon did not soften his stance but Dorothy had more sense than her husband and she agreed to undergo all the elaborate tests. Perhaps she wanted to prove to her husband, and indeed to his immediate and extended family, that she was not responsible for their childlessness. In our culture, infertility is still solely attributed to the woman and carries a greater stigma than in other societies. Also, it provides grounds for the man to marry another wife.

Dorothy, obviously, wanted to acquit herself of all these allegations and clear her name, as it were. So she subjected herself to extensive investigations. She underwent a salpingogram to check the patency of her tubes. This meant pushing a radio-opaque dye up her vagina and uterus to see if it flowed freely through the tubes into her belly. The test, usually done under general anaesthesia, showed that both her tubes were patent. Various biochemical tests were carried out to prove that she produced an egg every month at the right time in her monthly cycle. She underwent a D & C, another procedure carried out under anaesthesia to scrape the lining of her womb and put it under the microscope. It confirmed that the lining of her womb was healthy and receptive. In short, all her tests were negative. Her clean slate created a sort of a stalemate and Prof. Ogendo and I decided to talk to the couple. "Simeon needs to give semen for analysis so that we can establish if he has enough healthy sperms to impregnate a woman. If he has not, there could be two reasons for it. Either his testes are not producing any or enough sperms in which case we could give him drugs to stimulate them. The other possibility is that the vas, the tube which conducts his semen to the outside, is blocked and needs surgery to unblock it." Simeon remained mute while Dorothy looked at him expectantly but there was no shift in his position. "In that case," Prof. Ogendo broke the ice, "the only advice we can give you is to live in ignorance, continue trying for a baby and hope for the best."

When the couple left, Prof. Ogendo let his steam off. "With the husband being so cussed, I felt like telling the couple to try with different partners and it will soon become obvious where the fault lies!"

Strangely, a few days later, Simeon came to see me alone. I thought that he had a guilty conscience and wanted to get it off his chest.

But it was the reverse. I gathered from his conversation that he had come to justify his obduracy and do so by blowing his trumpet and talk about his sexual prowess and his conquests. "I'm not being difficult," he bragged. "I constantly feel like a bull in season and cannot understand anybody wanting to check either my ability or my capacity." He then brought out a newspaper cutting from the British paper, *Mail on Sunday* and laid it open on my desk. "You see there, Simon Covell, the chap who sits as a judge on the "X Factor" in the UK and "America has got Talents" in the US, boasting about his virility. He says that as a rough guess, he thinks he has bedded between 70 and

100 women. The chap is making a big issue about it and I feel like writing to him that, compared to some of us in Kenya, his score is very modest and he has a long way to go before he catches up with us!"

I was getting a bit tired of this chap and his inability to grasp the difference between potency and fertility. So, in my usual gentle tone, I dropped the crucial question. "How many have you impregnated?"

"None," replied Simeon.

"So?" I asked, feeling smug.

"This is because I was taking precautions!" He disarmed me with his reply. "I am no fool!"

Once again I went over the matter with him. "Simeon," I said. "As I have repeatedly told you, you could be a casanova but firing empty bullets. The semen analysis will give us an answer and we can then take the necessary measures to correct the situation." I knew I had made no mark on the man.

A few months later, I ran into Dorothy in a rather unusual spot. One early morning, as I often do, I went to play nine holes, on my own, at the Muthaiga Golf Club, within walking distance of where I live. That day, I saw a solitary female ahead of me. She was painfully slow and delaying me at every hole. I wanted to finish my round quickly and get to the hospital. At some point, the stranger remembered the etiquette of golf and decided to give way. So when I arrived at the next tee, she was waiting to let me through. In spite of us both being in our golf attire, there was an instant mutual recognition.

"Gosh," she apologised. "I didn't realise that I was slowing down my own surgeon."

"Nice to see you, Dorothy, outside of my consulting rooms." I greeted her warmly. "How are you?"

"Recently, I decided to take up golf and took a few lessons from the club pro. Just last week, I got my handicap and I'm playing my first round without the L-plate this afternoon. I thought I will do a practice round on my own this morning so that I don't torture my companions in the afternoon. Do you mind if I join you?" she asked.

"You obviously have no compunction about tormenting your surgeon!" I laughed.

After the usual polite exchanges, our conversation naturally veered to professional matters. "So how is it going?" I asked.

"Not well at all," Dorothy replied. "As it is common in our community, the blame for a childless marriage lies at the door of the woman, even if all the tests have proved that there is nothing wrong with her. My mother-in-law comes home and says. 'No daughter – no bride price.' Simeon's sister comes and laments. 'No son to carry the family name.' I think they are all brainwashing Simeon and soon you will hear of a divorce."

"Have you told them that their dear Simeon refuses to undergo a test which will determine his fertility status?" I asked.

"What's the point? They don't want to ever imagine that anything can be wrong with a man. Certainly not with their son and brother Simeon."

Dorothy's prediction came true earlier than she reckoned. Within a year, Simeon was divorced and remarried. But Dorothy was not going to take it lying down either. Lo and behold, a year later, she married the club pro. He had obviously given her lessons in matters other than golf! When she came to see me soon after the wedding, I asked her. "This time, did you check your man out?"

"Of course," she replied. "He has two children from his previous marriage. He also checked me out."

"What do you mean?" I asked.

"I'm two months pregnant," Dorothy replied proudly.

A bull in season

Two years later, Simeon came to see me with his second wife. "Different wife, same problem," he lamented.

"Same set of investigations and in the same order," I replied.

This time he complied without a murmur. In spite of the problems he had given Prof. Ogendo, his ex-wife Dorothy and me, I felt sorry for him when his semen report arrived on my desk. It read 'azoospermia' – no sperms.' I talked to Prof. Ogendo and he did not see the point of putting Patricia, Simeon's second wife, through any investigations. We left the couple to decide whether they would like to go for artificial insemination by a donor or adoption and are awaiting their decision.

In the meantime, Prof. Ogendo with his wicked sense of humour reminded me, when we met in the newly opened doctors' lounge at the hospital, of something he had said to me earlier. "You remember the time when we told Simeon and Dorothy to continue trying and hope for the best. Do you remember what I told you after they left?" As I was raking my brain, the good professor reminded me. "I told you then that we might be able to identify the guilty party if they tried with other partners. Well they have done it now and we have the answer. If they had taken my advice, Dorothy would have become pregnant with another man, it would have been an unconventional insemination by a donor, Simeon would have been none the wiser and he and Dorothy would still be married!"

31

The saving grace

"Is there a history of breast cancer in the family?" I asked Christine.

"Loads," replied Christine. "My aunt, from my mother's side, died from it a few years ago. My mother also had the dreaded disease but, mercifully, it was caught pretty early and she survived thirty years after it was diagnosed and treated. In fact, she died of cancer of the ovary, which I was told was not related to her breast cancer. Finally, my sister is currently under treatment for the same."

"Anyone on your father's side?" I spread the net a little further.

"Not that I know of," Christine replied.

Christine had come to see me in my 'Breast Clinic' for a second opinion. It was October, traditionally known as breast cancer awareness month, and she had been to one of the hospitals in Nairobi which conducted free breast check-up to observe the special occasion.

Now Breast Clinics, observing breast cancer month with the rest of the world in October to promote breast awareness and running free breast clinics during the month, are welcome recent developments in our country. For a long time, breast cancer was considered a rare disease in Kenya. The commonest malignancy was cancer of the cervix. This was related to lack of personal hygiene and early sex with multiple partners. However, with the discovery that this cancer is caused by the human papilloma virus, for which there is effective vaccination, and in the wake of public health measures taken to educate our women, the incidences of this now highly preventable disease have been steadily falling. Breast cancer, on the other hand, has shown both an apparent and real increase in its incidence. In fact, recent statistics released by KEMRI – Kenya Medical Research Institute – show that 20 percent of female cancer deaths in Kenya are caused by breast cancer. Cervical cancer has been relegated to second position with 19 percent of female deaths caused by it. The apparent rise in breast cancer is accounted for by the fact that women neglect painless lumps in their breasts, the commonest mode of presentation in breast cancer in its early stage. Lack of breast cancer awareness, lack of transport facilities and shortage of investigative and therapeutic facilities in government hospitals has, per force, caused low reporting. There is also a real rise in its incidence because of our changing lifestyle. The risk factors connected with this disease are, early menarche, late menopause, fewer children, no breastfeeding, late first pregnancy, use of high hormone pills and hormone replacement therapy to avert menopausal symptoms. We are more exposed to these dangers as our socio-economic status improves.

Reverting to Christine's story, she went on. "The doctor at the clinic thought he felt a lump in my breast but was not sure. I think he was a relatively junior doctor and ordered lots of special X-rays and ultrasound imaging. It was a mass screening exercise and there was very little time for one-on-one dialogue. So I thought I will see you before I go for all these elaborate investigations." Christine added, placing the request forms for the various tests on my desk.

"I don't want to be influenced or prejudiced by the investigations suggested. Let me take my own history and examine you first."

It was in the course of normal history taking that I asked the relevant questions on family history of breast cancer. The information she gave me horrified me but I proceeded with the rest of my routine questioning without alarming her and then went on to examine her. "Have you noted anything abnormal in your breasts yourself?" I asked her as I felt a vague lump in her right armpit.

"Not recently," replied Christine. "My breasts have always been lumpy and I stopped worrying about them except when they became painful before my periods. That is when they drew my attention."

"You don't still get your periods, do you?" I asked looking at her age on the file which was recorded as 58.

"They stopped five years ago," Christine replied.

"That was rather late," I remarked as I now felt an equally vague lump in her right breast. With such a strong family history, it was imperative that Christine underwent at least three investigations – mammogram, ultrasound scan and a needle biopsy of both lumps, one in her right breast and the other in the right armpit. I told her so.

"You have not mentioned an MRI," replied Christine. 'The other doctor wanted that and two more tests done in addition to what you have suggested," she added.

"I did not do so for two reasons," I explained. 'Firstly, the three essential tests will give us an answer and adding an MRI without seeing their results first would be an over-kill. Furthermore, an MRI is a new modality of investigation for breast cancer and we in Nairobi do not have enough experience in reading breast MRIs. The reports can, therefore, be misleading."

The saving grace

"Thank God," Christine heaved a sigh of relief. "The cost of an MRI was going to make a big hole in my budget."

"Let me clarify, however, why the young doctor who saw you at the breast screening center was not sure," I explained. "Yours is a difficult case but I think the investigations will soon give us an answer."

And they did. In doing so they confirmed my worst fears. When Christine came to see me a couple of days later I said to her. "We have the diagnosis now."

"And what is it?" Christine asked, her voice tremulous.

"I'm afraid you have caught the family disease."

After a few emotional outbursts she touched on the scientific aspect of the case and asked. "Is this a familial disease?"

"There are various risk factors associated with this disease and one of them is heredity. In your case, you have a strong family history so it is more likely to be so."

Christine took a long pause and then asked. "Can I give it to my daughter?"

"You can but you told me that you have no children, so the question does not arise," I said as I quickly referred to her file to confirm that this was what she had told me earlier.

There was another mysterious and inordinate pause. "How can you be so sure?" Christine seemed relentless in her search.

"We have now identified specific genes and if a woman inherits breast cancer genes, she very likely will suffer from the disease."

"Can you do this genetic test on me?"

"Yes," I replied. "We have no laboratory facilities to do the test here but a local pathologist has connections with a South African laboratory."

"I would like to undergo that test." Christine replied.

"Shall we do it after we finish surgery on you so that we don't waste valuable time?" I asked.

"I would like to undergo that test before surgery, if you don't mind." Christine replied decisively.

The test was done and she was positive for BRCA 1 genes – the special genetic element which predisposes to breast cancer.

"Shall we now schedule surgery?" I asked knowing that she was carrying a bomb in her bosom which could go off any time and spread to the rest of her body, converting a supremely curable case into an advanced one.

"Sorry," replied Christine. "I need some more time." I was a bit puzzled at the dilatory tactics of an intelligent woman on such an urgent matter. "I have an important matter to settle," she added.

"How much time do you need?" I asked in desperation. Usually one does not see such an early case of breast cancer in our setting, diagnosis arrived at by mammography and subsequently confirmed by cytology, even before a proper lump is felt in the breast. Here was one, which with immediate treatment could lead to a guaranteed cure.

"Difficult to say - at least three months," she replied, looking visibly uncertain about both – the time and wisdom of her decision.

I was sorry to see Christine go but could see that her mind was made up and it was no use trying to change it. Neither did I think it was my place to ask her what it was that she wanted to settle.

Three months later, she duly turned up in my office – as promised. "I'm ready for an operation now." She gave me the carte blanche.

"Am I now allowed to ask you why you delayed it by full three months?"

"Suffice to say, I'm at peace with myself now and it will undoubtedly hasten my recovery. The rest will have to wait till after surgery."

The saving grace

Christine's surgery went off very well and she did not keep me in suspense for long either. As soon as her post-operative condition allowed, she came out with the most amazing confession.

"As they say, nobody can change their past – not even God Almighty." Christine said when I went to see her alone, as requested by her, through a message left with the ward Sister. "I have a past which has always haunted me and this gene related breast cancer brought it to a head," she continued. "I was only 18, when I went to the UK for my university education. Having attended a convent school here for girls only and then being suddenly thrown into a British university, where students' lifestyle was very different to what I was used to, I was utterly lost. I couldn't cope with the persistent demands for sex and fell prey to a student in my first year. I knew that all my lady friends were on the pill but I could not bring myself to use them and soon found myself pregnant. Coming from a strict Roman Catholic family, I did not have the courage to inform my parents. The university counselling service was very helpful and found a hospital where I could secretly deliver my baby. They even approached an adoption society who arranged the adoption of my daughter immediately after she was born. I was only allowed to see my baby once after birth and then she was taken away. I cried for weeks but finally came to terms with myself." She gulped some water from a glass on her side table. "It was all done correctly and legally and I thought the matter had closed for good. It was all in the past until you announced that my cancer was genetic. I decided to find my daughter and warn her." As I looked at her, admiring her strong maternal instincts, she continued. "I went to the UK and got in touch with the office which deals with Registration of Births and Deaths. When I told them I wanted to get in touch with my biological daughter to warn her that she might have inherited a gene that puts her at high risk of developing breast cancer, they put my case on the fast track and traced her within weeks." There was a weary look on her face as she continued. "I had two worries. If she already got it, she would never forgive me and neither would I. Secondly, how would she accept a mother who had abandoned her soon after birth?"

I sat there in awe at the courage and filial affection of this waif-like woman as Christine went on. "Evelyn – that was her name – seemed aloof initially but her adoptive parents were very helpful. She was naturally upset that I gave her up for adoption but when I explained my situation, she understood."

"I hope you knew that you were letting the cancer grow in your breast while you were doing all this," I reminded her.

"Actually that was the saving grace," replied Christine. "When Evelyn realised that I had put my own life on the line for her, she was won over. Anyway, we put her immediately under the care of a breast clinic which specialises in genetic breast cancer. Luckily, they found nothing in her breasts but she will remain under close surveillance. She will also be fully investigated for the genetic factor. That way, if she ever develops anything, she will be immediately picked up, diagnosed and treated. For that, I'm sure she will think better of me and forgive me. But that is not all." For the first time there was a glow on Christine's face as she added. "We are reunited. Mastectomy was a price worth paying because in losing a breast, I have found my long lost daughter."

32

Like the customer, the patient is always right

It has often been said, in medical circles, that pain drives a lay person to alcohol and a health worker to drugs. This is so because doctors and nurses have an easy access to drugs. Many years ago I wrote about a nurse, I knew, who was driven to drugs – by doctors! I was a member of the medical team and, however junior and voiceless I was, I must bear some responsibility for it. I was just an intern tagging on to the end of the teaching round, which turned into a long procession, when Sir Osmond Clarke, the famous orthopaedic surgeon from The London Hospital, came to visit us in Blacknotley, a backwater in Essex.

The nurse in question was Liz Clarke, a staff nurse who worked in the male surgical ward. She was about 30, wore old fashioned thick glasses and walked with a wide waddle. She was, by no stretch of imagination, an oil painting! Her most endearing quality, however, was her total dedication to her vocation, for which the patients adored her. She led a very private life and it must have been in one of her unguarded moments when she let me peep into her family details. She told me that her entire family consisted of an ailing mother at home who needed constant nursing. Her father had died when she was very young and her only brother had emigrated to Australia. They never heard from him. I suppose she was implying that she was never off duty from nursing. If she was not doing it in the hospital, she was busy doing it at home.

Like the customer, the patient is always right

I was in the third month of my term there and while Mr. Dunn and I were conducting an outpatient clinic, Liz was brought in with sudden excruciating pain in her lower back.

"I was lifting this rather heavy patient who was on traction for fractured hip when I heard my back snap," Liz said to Mr. Dunn, when he asked her how and when the pain started.

"Have you had any problem with your back before?" Mr. Dunn asked.

"None whatsoever," Liz replied.

After the usual history taking, Mr. Dunn asked Sister to put Liz in a cubicle and he followed them. As a gesture of courtesy to a nursing colleague with whom I had worked closely and whom I knew very well, I stayed out. "Perhaps a disc," Mr. Dunn said when he came out of the cubicle. "Let's have an X-ray done," he added. Then, addressing Liz's escort, he added. "Ring me when the X-rays are ready and tell Dr. Kelly that I want to see the films with him."

X-rays revealed a condition which I had not seen before. Though I had read details of the disease in preparation for my fellowship examination, to be rattled out if a question was asked about it, I had never actually seen a case. I was mightily pleased because the diagnosis with the difficult name of spondylolisthesis was now added to my small repertoire of orthopaedic cases. "It is a condition that a person is born with." Mr. Dunn gave me an instant tutorial. "The two adjacent lumbar vertebrae have a false joint but the problem does not become manifest until the person has grown up and suddenly and quite accidentally the back is subjected to a severe strain as happened in the case of Miss Clarke. The false joint then gives in, the upper vertebra slides over the one below causing pressure on the adjacent nerves resulting in severe pain."

"And the treatment?" I asked.

Like the customer, the patient is always right

"Fuse the two vertebrae with a bone graft," Mr. Dunn continued in his didactic tone. "Of course it is advisable to try medical treatment before resorting to surgery. It consists of bed rest, use of corset, physiotherapy and anti-inflammatory drugs."

Liz was given a full course of conservative treatment without success. Finally, she underwent the operation and everything was fine until she was mobilised. Worse still, when she started working, the pain came back with a vengeance and she had to be confined to bed again. For the pain, she now needed increasing doses of morphine every night. Being a nurse herself, she regularly asked for it and this aroused suspicion if she was becoming addicted to it. "Try distilled water injection," Mr. Dunn advised me. "It might work as well." Junior as I was, I had a feeling that my boss subconsciously resented what he considered his failed surgery. That night, I saw Liz suffer pain as I had never seen before. At 3 am, out of compassion, I gave her the usual dose of morphine and she slept soundly.

"There could be a psychological basis," the physician whom we consulted, advised. "I have done some homework. Miss Clarke has a bedridden mother who she nurses at home. Also you can see that she is not the most attractive girl in Essex and matrimony is out of the question. She is condemned to being permanently tied to the apron strings of an ailing mum. Fertile ground for psychiatric pathology. Don't you think?"

When I went to see Liz, after the psychiatrist's visit, there was a hurt expression on her face. She was a bit sulky and after considerable humouring on my part, she came out with it. "You all seem to think I'm going nuts. So would you if you had as much pain as I do," she lamented.

Soon it was time for the orthopaedic guru from London to come to Blacknotley with his team. We the junior resident medical staff looked forward to these monthly visits. They

Like the customer, the patient is always right

were like a breath of fresh academic air and a waft of city sophistication to our dry and drab rural existence in Essex. "You think we could ask Sir Osmond to see Liz?" I hesitantly suggested to my boss.

"If you so wish," he said, without showing much enthusiasm for the idea.

As Miss Clarke described her pain to Sir Osmond, she broke down and burst out crying. He listened to Liz's story carefully and gave her a thorough examination, which lasted for half an hour, I had an opportunity to watch him and he reminded me of an Edwardian monarch. To complete the image, he even had a well trimmed full beard which, according to the hospital gossip, he had grown in readiness to kneel before the Queen, to receive his knighthood which had been announced in the Queen's honours list. "Do we have a good radiologist around?" he asked at the end of his very meticulous examination.

"Yes, indeed," replied Mr. Dunn. "Dr. Kelly is very competent and experienced."

"Let's have two X-rays done on Miss Clarke, one with her back straight and the other with it flexed," Sir Osmond advised.

In deference to the visiting oracle, Dr. Kelly himself came with the X-rays. Holding the films on the viewing box, he announced. 'I'm afraid the bone graft is moving when Miss Clarke moves."

"Let's transfer her to my unit at the London Hospital," Sir Osmond said after carefully looking at the films on the viewing box and confirming in his own mind what Dr. Kelly had discovered. "I will re-graft her back and you both can assist me." Looking at Mr. Dunn sideways, he added. "This young surgeon should know how to fuse spines before he returns home."

Like the customer, the patient is always right

Six months later, Liz Clarke was back at work. Needless to add, she had a dig at me. "I want to consign the lot of you to a loony-bin!"

In contrast to Liz's story where I was part of the problem, I now want to relate a similar case, which I saw recently and where I proved to be the solution. In fact, the patient was so grateful and thrilled with the result that I could be labeled her salvation! This lady, Rebecca, created instant affection in my heart for her, because it is the name of my favourite novel, a Gothic classic written by Daphne-du–Maurier. Our Rebecca's story started six years ago. "I get this pain in the left side of my tummy, right down," she said pointing at her groin. "It comes when I travel and stand for long or walk long distances. It also appears when I am in the supermarket, usually when I am picking up the fifth item on my shopping list." The story sounded strange and even aroused my suspicion about its credibility when she added. "I have already seen 15 doctors for this problem. Sometimes it starts in my back and even goes to my chest, then I sweat, vomit, my vision goes hazy and I pass out. I sometimes even drop objects which I am holding."

"Do you see a lump in your groin?" I asked, as the most likely diagnosis of hernia came to mind, if I denuded her story of all the frills and the extraneous symptoms. "Something like a bulge?"

"Yes," replied Rebecca. "Very painful and I can push it back. I also have difficulty in passing urine when it appears. My gynaecologist thought it could be connected with my coil and removed it. No good."

"Has anybody else, other than you, seen the bulge?" I asked.

"I have," the very understanding and sympathetic husband who had accompanied Rebecca to see me replied.

"So has my daughter," Rebecca added.

"Cough," I said as I wanted to see if the hernia in her groin would descend as it should. Alas, no visible lump, not even an impulse suggestive of hernia.

I saw Rebecca a few times, in search of the elusive hernia. Not once did she oblige! 'Your story, if the symptoms like fainting, chest pain, backache and sweating are eschewed, sounds like a hernia but I have seen no clinical evidence of it on repeated examinations. I can't bring myself to explore the groin without the slightest proof. Can you come and see me when you see the bulge?'

"It never stays for that long," Rebecca replied.

In view of her persistent complaint, which sounded genuine by its repetition, I referred her to an eminent neurologist to see if there was a neurological reason for her pain. He went over her with a tooth comb – as neurologists do. Out of clinical curiosity, I was with him when he examined Rebecca. He placed on her skin test tubes containing hot water and cold water to assess her temperature sensation, he touched her tibia with a tuning fork, he pricked her skin with a pin to see if she felt pain and touched it with a blunt object to check her touch sensation. He too drew a blank and suggested various investigations. In the meantime, Rebecca continued to see me, with the same refrain making me wonder if there was a psychological basis for her clinical syndrome. I almost earmarked a psychiatrist but then remembered Liz Clarke and the hurt expression on her face after she had been seen by a psychiatrist at our bidding. To my pleasant surprise and deep gratification, help came from an unexpected quarter.

"Rebecca wants to see you urgently," one fine morning my secretary announced. This time Rebecca came fully fortified, with her husband, her daughter and clutching a letter. "I developed the pain while I was shopping at Sarit Centre yesterday afternoon and saw the bulge. I didn't think it would

Like the customer, the patient is always right

stay till I came to see you. So I consulted a doctor at Sarit Centre and she gave me this letter."

The young lady doctor was clear, detailed, explicit and specific. What she had seen, she affirmed, was undoubtedly an obstructed hernia.

"I now have grounds to operate though I myself have not seen your hernia," I said to Rebecca and her accompanying family.

Now, I have operated on hundreds of hernias in my time, but none with so much trepidation as this one. A couple of hours after I finished my operation list, Rebecca's husband was on the phone enquiring. "Open a bottle of champagne and don't forget to include the surgeon in the celebration," I told him. "We found the dragon and slayed it!"

As I drove home that evening I recalled the advice I often give my students. I remind them of the English proverb which says that the wearer of the shoe knows where it pinches. I then end my exhortation by adding, "Remember that, like the customer, the patient is always right."

33

Rescuing a social butterfly

Brian was a permanent patient and seemed to enjoy hospitals and operations. In fact, he looked bored, if the period of good health between two illnesses was protracted! Luckily for him, his vast business interests provided him with an opportunity to travel out of the country often and satisfy his predilection to consult eminent specialists, making him an international patient and a medical tourist!

He was also a social butterfly. The few diplomatic sundowners and company receptions I was invited to, he was invariably there. After he became my patient, I heard interesting details of the social functions he had attended. I also formed an impression that he was pretty upset if he was not invited to one.

"Any past illness?" I asked him, the first time he came to see me – with piles.

"Many," he replied. "Sir Robert, who has his office in Harley Street, was the first to diagnose my diabetes. Then, when I was in Berlin, the surgeon to Schroeder, the German Chancellor, lanced a boil on my bottom." As I was fast jotting down the names of renowned world authorities in medicine, he went on. "For my piles, I must have consulted at least ten surgeons. I saw

Dr. Gates at the Mayo Clinic and then Dr. Brooks at the Lahey Clinic, both in the U.S.A. While I was in Rome, I consulted Prof. Valdoni and as I was passing through London, I managed to get a quick appointment to see Sir Sean Hughes who looks after the British Royal Family for their colonic problems. Finally, last year, I had to attend a conference in Delhi and saw Prof. Mukerjee at the All India Institute.

"And what did they all say?" I was trying hard to keep a straight face.

"They all agreed that I was suffering from piles and advised surgery," he replied.

"So why didn't you have it done?" I asked.

"Because I know how painful this damn operation is," he replied with the facial expression of a child, scared of needles and syringes. "So when I came home, I touted round and zeroed on you. I was told that your operations are both painless and scarless."

I was flattered and did not tell him something that was on the tip of my tongue. In the case of piles, scars did not matter except perhaps in a very special class of people! "Yes, I have devised a method of injecting long acting anaesthetic in the anal sphincter before operating on piles and this does make surgery relatively painless," I said.

Luckily for me, the special injection did its job admirably and Brian was very pleased. He was one of the few patients who inflated my professional fees by twenty five percent instead of asking for a discount of that value.

I did not see him for a couple of years until we met up at a sundowner. He looked very fit and trim, a young 64, I thought and said so to him.

"Went to a health farm in Kerala," he explained. "These are places where you pay exorbitant fees to be starved," he smiled. "Lost 10 pounds in four weeks and three inches round the waist. They have wonderful facilities," he went on. "Full medical check up carried out as if you are on a conveyor belt. X-rays, lab tests, CT scans, MRI, tread mill, echo, all done one after the other. Then exercises, aerobics, keep-fit classes, well-regulated life, early to bed and early to rise, strict diet and calories measured in decimals!" As I looked at him, amused, he went on. "Met there members of the royal family from Bahrein. As usual, they were flaunting their petro-dollars."

His last visit to see me professionally was two years ago. As soon as he entered my office, I could see that the spring in his step was missing. His face was drawn and he had lost his usual cheery mood.

"I have noticed this lump in my tummy," he said pointing at the pit of his stomach.

By now, with the catalogue of his illnesses, and the large wad of X-rays and scans he carried, I had concluded that the man was highly introspective if not a frank hypochondriac. I could imagine him subjecting himself to frequent self examinations, sitting in the bath, prodding at various parts of his anatomy and seeing the contours of his body in the mirror. I went over his history and examined him in great detail. Just as I well, I did so and was not carried away by my prejudices. "It looks as if you have something in your colon," I said.

"What do we do next?" he looked terrified.

"Let's do a few investigations like a Barium enema and a colonoscopy," I replied.

Through a colonoscope, a tumour was clearly visible in his transverse colon and a piece was taken for biopsy. Put under the microscope, it proved to be cancerous. For the first time, I saw Brian looking down and out. The veneer of sophistication suddenly vanished under the onslaught of a genuine calamity.

"What are my chances?" he asked when I suggested surgery.

Rescuing a social butterfly

Knowing his penchant for big names, I thought I could impress him with a true surgical story. "Sir Gordon Gordon Taylor, the eminent British colonic surgeon suffered from the type of tumour you have. He was operated upon by one his own protege – another big name in the specialty. Twenty years later, Sir Gordon was knocked down by a car while crossing the road near Lord's where he had gone to watch a cricket match between Australia and England. He died on the spot. At postmortem, no evidence of his twenty year old colonic cancer was found. He had died of ruptured liver and spleen!

Brian seemed duly impressed. "Can you do it here?" he asked.

"Indeed," I said. "Standard, routine surgery."

"Fine," he said. "I have an important business trip lined up in London for a week. Let me finish that, then I will be literally in your hands."

I knew he was going there to consult all the big wigs in colonic surgery, barons, lords and the proctologist to the royal household, but kept my cool.

Ten days later, he was in my office, loaded with large envelopes carrying X-rays, laboratory reports, ECGS, ultrasounds – every conceivable investigation under the sun. "I am ready for surgery now," Brian said valiantly. "When will I be out of the hospital and fit for travel?" he asked. Before I replied, he explained. "Lord and Lady Lindsay's only daughter is getting married in London in three weeks and though I have not yet received an invitation I'm sure that one is in the post. I will have to fly out."

I did not mention that I had already received my invitation. "I know them," I said. "When they came on a safari here last year, Lady Lindsay's ingrowing toe nail became very painful and I had to remove it as an emergency. They were very grateful and told me about the family wedding and promised to send me a card too."

Once again, the operation on Brian went off successfully. The tumour was small, early and I expected an uneventful recovery. However, after three days of normal progress, Brian started going downhill. His secretary came daily and delivered the post, which he looked at eagerly and then lapsed into lassitude and lethargy. I called in all my specialist colleagues and no one could pinpoint the problem. Then I had a brain wave and made a phone call. Two days later, something was delivered to Brian by DHL. Next day, Brian handed me a gold rimmed envelope. Inside was a card which read – Lord and Lady Lindsay request the pleasure of the company of ...

From then on, he did not look back and soon went out of the hospital in bouncing health.

I met him at the wedding in London and he was in his element. He was like a man invited to have tea with the Queen at Buckingham Palace.

I went up to Lady Lindsay when I saw her alone. "Thank you for sending that invitation card at my request. It brought him back to life."

"I was determined not to send him a card," replied the lady. "Until you rang me and said that it was a matter of life and death." Then, not hiding her annoyance, she added. "I didn't mind him dropping names, but when he started telling people that he was having an affair with me, I thought he took his hobby a bit too far!"

34

When things accidentally spill over

As my favourite author, Somerset Maugham, said – we must accept people as they are, not as they should be. In the case of Shashi, much as I tried, it was difficult to abide by Maugham's ediction. Quite unlike me, I took an instant dislike to the man, though I did not have any reason.

Dr. Mwaniki, my gynaecologist colleague, and I were due to attend a conference on infertility in Mauritius. We both have done considerable work on the subject in Kenya, Dr. Mwaniki mainly on the female side, and I on the male aspects of the problem. Over the years, we have come a long way from the general belief that a woman is solely responsible for failure to conceive in a marriage. To amplify this view, this particular meeting invited experienced surgeons like me who mainly deal with male causes like absence of sperms and erectile dysfunction, and Dr. Mwaniki who treats women with blocked tubes, defective eggs and non receptive wombs. Having worked jointly on this subject for a few years, we had become good friends and when we found that a world cruise was offering the Mombasa – Mauritius segment at that time, we literally jumped on the ship.

On my first evening in the lounge, I ran into this gentleman who was talking to Dr. Mwaniki. "This is Shashi," Dr. Mwaniki introduced him. "His full name is very difficult to spell or pronounce and, therefore, everybody calls him Shashi."

"People call you by your nickname only if you are very popular," Shashi said as he shook my hand, almost pulverising it.

"What would you like to drink?" he asked.

I told him what I wanted. Shashi was busy talking to Dr. Mwaniki and, as I sipped my drink, I had ample time to study the man. He was short and fat. The big, smooth circle on his head was ringed by frizzy hair. As he held a large goblet with whisky and ice, I noticed his right hand had short stubby fingers like drum sticks. I was glad that he was not a surgeon because, with such clumsy looking club-like fingers, he would have raised a whole cemetery to his name.

"So where are you two off to?" Shashi asked.

"To Mauritius," Dr. Mwaniki replied.

"What a pity!" Shashi remarked. "On a ship like this you don't stay for less than a month." He brought out a pure leather pouch filled with large Havanas and held it in front of us. As we politely declined, he continued. "In fact, I would have signed up for the trip round the world but after a month I'm due in Düsseldorf to sign a machinery deal for our factory in Thika."

Dr. Mwaniki winked at me as Shashi went on. "Soon after, I fly to Zurich to negotiate a loan with Credit Suisse." He gulped his drink and put the glass down. "I then fly to San Francisco to attend a conference."

"Same again?" the bartender asked.

"Yes, all round," Shashi said and went on. "Since I have a meeting with Toyota whose agency we hold for our region, I thought I will cross the Pacific and fly to Japan that way."

"That's a tall order," I chipped in just to participate in the conversation.

"Well," the big man replied. "A rich entrepreneur's life is not a bed of roses. First class flights, five-star hotels, chauffeur-driven limos, business lunches, cocktail parties, company of rich important people – all great fun but hard work too."

Suddenly, I found the reason why I had not talked to the man. He was a braggart, a plain-unadulterated braggart – a quality I loath.

"We better get to the dining room and find our table." Dr. Mwaniki seemed as keen as I was to get away.

"Thank God, we don't have to do that." Shashi's bragging resumed unabated. "We are in the Queen's Grill. Ah! there she is," he added, looking at somebody across the bar.

"I see Natasha is with you," Dr. Mwaniki said as I almost fell off the bar stool. Natasha was an utter contrast – slim, delicate, seductively charming and graciously elegant. She wore a black low cut dress with a plunging neckline. A beautiful pearl necklace was occupying the bare territory in front. As she came closer, I could see her auburn hair, beautifully coiffeured. She gave a regal nod of acquaintance to Dr. Mwaniki as Shashi turned to me. "My wife," he said as if showing me his best pedigree puppy.

"Long time, no see,' Dr. Mwaniki said to Natasha. As his greeting vanished in her smile, Shashi responded on her behalf. "We like to see our doctors socially rather than professionally."

"Yes indeed," Dr. Mwaniki said and moved away. Knowing him as I did, I could see that there was more in his sudden departure than met the eye.

Over the next three days, I explored the ship and enjoyed its amenities – sitting on the sundeck, reading in the library, doing aerobics in the health centre, swimming in the pool and drawing pen characters for my writing. In the course of my perambulations, I came across a newly – married young couple enjoying a delayed honeymoon. The girl constantly complained about being sea sick whenever I met her. I was puzzled because the boat had magnificent stabilisers. Once, she did so when Dr. Mwaniki was with me and he immediately put her right. "Madam," he said to her. "You better go and see the ship doctor for your urine to be checked. By the sound of it, you are most likely to be suffering from morning sickness." And he was right. Then there was this obese lady who walked round the circumference of the cruise ship three times a day.

"One round makes 3 kms," she explained. "I still don't seem to lose any weight. From tomorrow, I intend to walk carrying a fully loaded suit case in each hand!"

Finally, there was this egghead, a walking encyclopaedia on navigation, his head constantly buried in maps, compasses and telescopes. Every time I passed him, he would raise his head and reassure me. "Still on the right course, old boy."

We were due to dock in Mauritius the following morning. The night before, there was the traditional captain's dinner and dance. The men wore dinner jackets and women appeared in long dresses. Shashi was in his element and wore a white tuxedo. The large, golden cuff-links were tactically visible under his jacket sleeves. One wrist was adorned by a gold omega and the other by a platinum bracelet. There were gold strands in his bow tie and a diamond shone out of its clip. His sparse but recently dyed hair was fluttering in the cool sea breeze on the open deck. He was seated on the captain's table with Natasha. Dr. Mwaniki and I sat with lesser mortals.

After dinner, the band started playing. First, they played the modern tunes and then went on to the oldies. Partners danced close to each other, leaving not enough space for an envelope to pass between them. Dr. Mwaniki excused himself and went to the captain's table. He said something to Shashi and took Natasha on the dance floor. While they were dancing, Shashi moved over to our table. "Look for me when we are all back in Nairobi. I have great ideas about investment," he advised me. "Like the gardener's green fingers, I have the investor's gold fingers and everything I touch turns yellow." He lit his large Cuban cigar and went on. "Gold is the best commodity to buy in uncertain times. It's the investor's refuge in financial crisis". He bored me to death. I had taken an instant dislike to his size, shape, speech, smugness, and swagger. I felt envious of Dr. Mwaniki dancing with Natasha and wished we could change places.

Next morning, Dr. Mwaniki and I disembarked. Our conference hosts were waiting for us at the port. Dr. Mwaniki had a strange expression on his face. The writer's curiosity in me overpowered the surgeon's tact. "You seemed to have embarked on a terrific affair on the voyage," I said.

"Only one constraint prevented it," replied Mwaniki. "The fear of being charged with professional misconduct. As you know, a doctor is not allowed to have an improper relationship with his patient."

"I didn't think Natasha was ever your patient," I remarked.

"A pretty thing like that married to such a big bore and left alone for long periods while he is on business trips is bound to look for company," he replied. "As a result, she is in constant need of gynaecological services, mostly preventive but sometimes curative, if and when things accidentally spill over!"

35
An eye for an eye

Recent reports about husband battering that have appeared in the local press might give the impression that it is a new phenomenon in our country. It certainly is not because, as I read these reports, I recollected a case which came under my care a few years ago. Perhaps, at the time they occurred, these cases did not receive the level of publicity that they are attracting now.

That notwithstanding, the man in Nyeri whose wife slashed his face with a panga and the man in Matunga trading centre whose spouse splashed hot water on his genitalia, on learning that he had found a new lover, got off lightly compared to my patient. To sensationalize the episode, the Nyeri man's photograph was splashed in all the newspapers, showing his face embroidered with surgical sutures. For obvious reasons, the man from Matunga did not get his picture displayed in our daily newspapers.

In the case I dealt with, the wife was really *kali* and followed the notorious example of Lorina Bobbit who emasculated her errant husband in the USA, by targetting the exact organ which she reckoned was responsible for his misdemeanours. She obviously took the stand; an eye for an eye and tooth for a tooth!

An eye for an eye

Nderi's story began with a night call I received from Dr. Lily Ogutu. Night calls, I might add here, are the bane of a surgeon's life. In this connection, I remember a discussion I had with my mentor when, after my graduation as a doctor, I was deciding as to which specialty I should take as my final career path. "Take dermatology," he advised. 'You don't kill anybody, you don't cure any one and there are no night calls!'

Of course I did not take his advice because I was determined to be a surgeon. With many years of being tied to the phone every night and being rudely woken up often by its shrill ring, I have developed two good habits. One is that I have become a light sleeper, so light that I wake up when the phone vibrates which it usually does before it actually rings. Secondly, once I have responded to the night call and done whatever is required of me, I can go back to sleep instantly and be able to carry out my scheduled duties the next day without any feeling of fatigue.

Now, to revert to the telephone call I received from Dr. Ogutu, she said, "I would not have bothered you at this time of the night, sir," she said apologetically, "but I have a man here bleeding furiously from his right testis which is literally in shreds. It is very likely that to stop the haemorrhage, he might need an orchidectomy."

I could now understand why Dr. Ogutu was calling me in the dead of the night. She had, in a nutshell, given me two reasons for doing so. She wanted an experienced hand to stop the haemorrhage without in any way compromising the blood supply to the injured testis. If that was not at all possible and the testis had to be removed to stop the bleeding, it had better be done by a senior surgeon, because of its medico-legal implications.

I drove to the hospital and Dr. Ogutu met me. "The patient tells me that he was attacked by thugs on the way home." As we walked to the patient's cubicle, Dr. Ogutu gave me his history. "They wanted to rob him of his mobile and all his money, but he resisted. They, therefore, pinned him down to the ground and emptied his pockets. Apparently, one of the robbers was holding a knife, threatening to plunge it into his belly if he made a wrong move." I was listening to Nderi's bravado with great interest, remembering the conventional wisdom of not resisting under those circumstances. "Nderi tells me that, as a man, he could not take it lying down and continued hitting the robber's face with his fist. In a fit of rage, the guy decided to carry out his threat. Since Nderi was trying to free himself, flinging his arms and legs in the air, the knife went into his scrotum by mistake."

Dr. Ogutu was known for her descriptive excellence but tonight she was beating her own record. "The sight of blood frightened the thugs who, having cleared him, hijacked Nderi's car and fled."

We had now arrived at the couch on which the intrepid patient was lying. Nderi, a man in his thirties, was obviously agitated. Seeing a large wad of blood-soaked, sterile cotton wool on his scrotum, and some fresh red blood trickling down from the side of the dressing, I decided that discretion was the better part of valour and so I explained to him. "Dr. Ogutu has given me your full history and has also described her findings. I don't want to cause you pain and start more bleeding by taking the dressing down. So, if you don't mind, I will take you to the operating theatre and do the needful after you have been put under anaesthesia." So saying, I asked the Sister to give Nderi a consent form to sign. In view of the distinct possibility of an orchidectomy, his express permission to allow me to do so was both necessary and important. Nderi was in no condition to argue. All he could say while signing the form was. "Please try to save my testis."

An eye for an eye

"Of course I will do so but I must warn you that the testis, being a vital organ, needs a lot of blood. The artery and veins to the organ are, therefore, large and if the bleeding can't be controlled, the choice is reduced to either life or testis." I left Nderi to surmise which way the decision would go.

"Looks rather strange for a stab wound, inflicted by a knife," I remarked to Dr. Ogutu, who was assisting me, when I had exposed the testis and found it in shreds; exactly as she had described it on the phone. "Even if we stop the haemorrhage, this testis is unlikely to be functionally viable." As if to prove my point, the testicular fragments started looking dusky, suggestive of lack of oxygen derived from its own blood supply. "Let us try a few warm packs and see if we can revive it." Nothing worked and, eventually, I decided to tie the testicular vessels, stop the haemorrhage and remove the testis.

On my ward round next day, Nderi was eager to know of the outcome. "Did you manage to save it?" he asked. I told him the truth and he seemed devastated. To comfort him I added. "Nature has been very kind to us and essential organs like the eyes, ears, kidneys, lungs, testes and ovaries have been given to us in pairs. The solitary single organ can adequately fulfill the function of both in the event of the other one being lost."

On the way to the Sister's office, I told Sister Mbuthia, in charge of the male surgical ward, Nderi's story as narrated by Dr. Ogutu the previous evening. I thought the testicular segment of the story might amuse her. Her reaction surprised me. "That's his story and I suppose he will stick to it." As she saw me off at the door, we were met by Nderi's wife, to whom Sister Mbuthia introduced me. "This is Irene, our patient's wife." Irene was smartly dressed and put her hand out to shake mine.

"Sorry about your husband," I said knowing how she must feel about her husband losing one of his two testes. "But," I reassured her as I had done to her husband, "One testis works as well as two."

I saw the two exchange knowing glances and wondered if Sister Mbuthia knew more than I did or had been privy to a different story than what Dr.Ogutu had heard.

The mystery was resolved a couple of years ago. It was almost ten years since I had treated Nderi and it happened when a Mrs. Kuria arrived at the Accident and Emergency Department with acute appendicitis. Sister Mbuthia had, by then, been promoted to a supervisor in that department. I was doing my usual operating list when, between cases, she caught me on the phone. "I have a patient here sent by her GP with a letter. According to the letter, the doctor wants me to refer the patient to the surgeon on call. The patient, however, has expressed a desire to be admitted under your care. Is that alright?"

"Yes," I said. "Has the doctor on duty in the A&E examined her?"

"Yes," replied Sister Mbuthia. "Dr. Omwega has done so and confirmed the diagnosis." So saying, she handed the receiver to Dr. Omwega. "Yes she has appendicitis, alright. The white blood cells are pretty high and the neutrophils are ninety percent." He gave me the blood report pathognomonic of acute appendicitis.

"In that case, may I talk to Sister Mbuthia again?" I asked. He put her on the phone.

"It is likely that I will be in the theatre for most of the day. In view of what Dr. Omwega has told me, would it be possible to finish the formalities at your end and send Mrs. Kuria to the theatre, where I can examine her and proceed with appendicictomy, if I agree with the diagnosis." She agreed.

In the waiting room of the theatre I took the history from Mrs. Kuria, examined her and, having confirmed the diagnosis, removed a grossly inflammed appendix in the course of the day. At the end of my operating session, I went to A&E to thank Sister Mbuthia for arranging everything so that I could proceed with Mrs. Kuria's appendicitomy while I was still in the theatre. "It also prevented the patient from suffering unnecessary delay and pain." I added.

There was an amusing look on Sister Mbuthia's face. "Did you notice anything special about Mrs. Kuria?" she asked.

"In what way?" I asked. "I was focusing on her appendix, not on her."

"Her first name is Emily. Does that ring a bell?" Sister Mbuthia asked tantalizingly.

I scratched my head. "Is she the wife of the shredded testis?" I guessed wildly.

"Yes," replied the Sister. "You do have a good memory," she complimented me.

"It's not only the memory," I teased her, a liberty I could take because of my long professional association with her. "In spite of my advancing years, for your information, all my faculties are running full blast!"

"You are right," she replied, laughing uproariously. "She is the ex-wife of the 'shredded testis' and she has an interesting story to tell you."

I could not wait. As soon as Mrs. Emily Kuria was pain-free, I was by her bedside. She, too, wanted to get it off her chest. "Nderi was a husband only in name. He neither gave me any housekeeping money nor paid the rent or school fees. All he did was enjoy his beer and come home for meals, while I slogged with my job in the office and chores at home. I put up with it until he started sleeping around. I was afraid of what he would bring from these other women." There was an angry frown on her otherwise gentle face. "That night too he was drunk and, as he made his overtures in bed, I could see that he had already been elsewhere. When he persisted I really got annoyed, picked up the scissors lying on the bedside table and let him have it."

I recalled the state of Nderi's testis and the repeated stabs by an open scissors explained it.

"Why did you not come out in the open?" I asked.

"Suited us both at the time," replied Mrs. Kuria. "He was too embarrassed to own up and I was too scared. There was also the matter of the police, insurance and family reputation. He concocted a good story which Sister Mbuthia told me. When I heard it, I went along with it. But after that episode, we called it quits and I am happily remarried."

"What a terrible thing to do," I remarked casually.

"Not so terrible," retorted Emily. "I only destroyed one testis and left the other one to my successor!"

www.ingramcontent.com/pod-product-compliance
Lightning Source LLC
Chambersburg PA
CBHW051351290426
44108CB00015B/1970